KEYSTONE TOMBSTONES

BIOGRAPHIES OF FAMOUS PEOPLE BURIED IN PENNSYLVANIA

CIVIL WAR

JOE FARRELL AND JOE FARLEY
WITH LAWRENCE KNORR

SUNBURY
Mechanicsburg, PA USA

Published by Sunbury Press, Inc.
Mechanicsburg, Pennsylvania

SUNBURY
PRESS
www.sunburypress.com

For information about special discounts for bulk purchases, please contact Sunbury Press
Orders Dept. at (855) 338-8359 or orders@sunburypress.com.

To request one of our authors for speaking engagements or book signings, please contact
Sunbury Press Publicity Dept. at publicity@sunburypress.com.

SECOND SUNBURY PRESS EDITION: October 2020

Set in Adobe Garamond | Interior design by Crystal Devine | Cover by Lawrence Knorr |
Edited by the authors.

Publisher's Cataloging-in-Publication Data
Names: Farrell, Joe, author | Farley, Joe, author | Knorr, Lawrence, author.
Title: Keystone tombstones civil war : biographies of famous people buried in pennsylvania /
Joe Farrell, Joe Farley, and Lawrence Knorr.
Description: Second trade paperback edition. | Mechanicsburg, PA : Sunbury Press, 2020. |
Includes biographical references and index.
Summary: Biographies of participants in America's Civil War who are buried in Pennsylvania
are featured in this special volume.
Identifiers: ISBN 978-1-620064-48-1 (softcover).
Subjects: HISTORY / US History / Civil War | BIOGRAPHY & AUTOBIOGRAPHY / Rich
& Famous | HISTORY / US History / Mid-Atlantic.

Product of the United States of America
0 1 1 2 3 5 8 13 21 34 55

Continue the Enlightenment!

The historian of the future undertakes an onerous task, a high responsibility, a sacred trust. Above all things, justice and truth should dwell in his mind and heart. Then, dipping his pen as it were in the crimson tide, the sunshine of heaven lighting his page, giving honor to whom honor is due, doing even justice to the splendid valor alike of friend and foe, he may tell the world how rain descended in streams of fire, and the floods came in billows of rebellion, and the winds blew in blasts of fraternal execration, and beat upon the fabric of the Federal Union, and that it fell not, for, resting on the rights and liberties of the people, it was founded upon a rock.

—Winfield Scott Hancock

Contents

Acknowledgments

The success of *Keystone Tombstones Volumes One* & *Two* has led to this volume. We want to thank all of those who purchased our first two books and encouraged us to continue this series.

Our work has been well-received and supported by many in the media. We especially want to thank Brian Lockman, Francine Schertzer, Corinna Wilson, and Alanna Koll as well as the whole crew at the Pennsylvania Cable Network for their tremendous support and interest in *Keystone Tombstones*. We are also grateful to Mike Rozansky and Tirdad Derakhshani of the *Philadelphia Inquirer* and Brian O'Neill of the *Pittsburgh Post-Gazette* for bringing our book to the attention of readers at both ends of the state. We extend special thanks to Stacy Smith, Jill Neely, Kristine Sorenson, and John Burnett for having us on *Pittsburgh Today Live* not once but twice. We sincerely appreciate it.

We want to thank David Dunkle of the *Harrisburg Patriot-News* for being the first to write about *Keystone Tombstones*. Other reporters to whom we would like to extend our appreciation to James McClure of the *York Daily Record*, Jack Brubaker of the *Lancaster Intelligencer Journal*, Jim Dino from the *Hazleton Standard-Speaker*, and Peter Durantine of *The Burg*.

We are also grateful to Betsy Benson, Julie Talerico, and Kristofer Collins of *Pittsburgh Magazine* and Jen Merrill and Patti Boccassini of *Harrisburg Magazine* for their reports on our adventures.

In Central Pennsylvania, we would like to extend our thanks to Megan Lello and Scott Lamar at WITF and Chuck Rhodes at WTPA-TV for their interest and support of our project.

Several bookstores took an interest in *Volume One*, and we are grateful to Debbie Beamer at the Mechanicsburg Mystery Bookshop, Dani Weller at the Harrisburg Mid Town Scholar, and Ann Barnett at the State Museum Bookstore. In addition, we would like to thank Kristi Fisher and Donna Wench at the Barnes and Noble Bookstores in Camp Hill and Wilkes Barre, respectively.

We want to thank Bill Isler for his assistance and many contributions to *Volumes One* and *Two*. Thanks to Frank Rausch at Laurel Hill Cemetery for his assistance during our visits there and a big shout out to Howell K Rosenberg, who sits on the Board of Visitors of the Richards Civil War Era Center at Penn State University for his inspiration, his interest, his friendship and constant prodding to be better.

Once again, we thank Julie Dougherty for her interest and technical support as well as Lawrence and Tammi Knorr of Sunbury Press for their continued support.

Lastly, we thank Sharon Farley and Mary Wigdahl for their emotional support and their promotional efforts throughout all volumes. If it were not for them, we would probably be drinking in some bar on the Lincoln Highway. And, most notably, to Marc Farrell, who contributed much as our copy editor and researcher.

Introduction

Poor is the nation having no heroes;
shameful the one that having them, forgets.

The Civil War is the defining event of our nation's history. Before the Civil War, not much of what most Americans value about America was true. The Declaration of Independence declared "all men are created equal" as a self-evident truth. Yet, men, women, and children were bought and sold as property and denied "certain inalienable rights" such as liberty and the pursuit of happiness. The Civil War and the subsequent legislation were indeed "a new birth of freedom" for our struggling democracy.

Democracy was not a new idea. It goes back as far as ancient Greece. It just did not have much success as a form of government, other than in small organizations. Many of the great thinkers of the time agreed that while democracy on paper had many useful features, it would ultimately fail. Eventually, they reasoned, an issue would arise that would be so important to a minority that they would be unwilling to submit to majority rule—an issue so divisive that a significant portion of the members would withdraw their consent, rebel, and leave.

Slavery was that issue.

When South Carolina and ten other southern states declared their secession from the Federal Union, representative democracy was at stake. Could a state (or any portion thereof) declare that it was no longer a part of the Union, and thus not bound by the Union's laws and government?

It took a horrible, long, bloody war—resulting in 650,000 deaths (more than the American Revolution, World Wars I and II, the Korean War, and Vietnam combined)—to answer that question. Another estimated 60,000 men lost limbs in the war.

Pennsylvania played a vital role in the Civil War. Our population was second only to New York in 1860. Our industry and natural resources were important to the country's economic strength, and our railroad system and agricultural wealth were vital to the war effort.

A total of 427,286 Pennsylvanians served in the Union armed forces, including 8,600 African American volunteers. Over 300,000 soldiers passed through Harrisburg's "Camp Curtin," making it the Civil War's largest federal camp. Pennsylvania was the site of the bloodiest battle of the entire war. The Battle of Gettysburg became widely known as the "High Water Mark of the Confederacy." Many historians consider this battle to be a significant turning point in the war.

Joe Farley and I were hard at work on *Volume III* of *Keystone Tombstones* when our publisher, Lawrence Knorr, called me and said, "Stop what you are doing and consider this." He reminded me that July 1–3, 2013 would mark the 150th anniversary of the Battle of Gettysburg, and a special edition on the Civil War might be a good idea. When Joe and I expressed some doubt as to whether we had enough time, Lawrence offered to help write some chapters. You hold in your hands the results. We hope you are as happy with it as we are. We think Lawrence waited to tell us his idea until he knew we would need his help.

We are thrilled to be a part of the 150th-anniversary celebration of one of the most important events in our nation's history.

—Joe Farrell

I.

JAMES BUCHANAN

Pennsylvania's Only President

County: Lancaster • Town: Lancaster
Buried at Woodward Hill Cemetery
501 South Queen Street

James Buchanan was the fifteenth President of the United States. He was the only president never to marry and the only president from Pennsylvania. Perhaps he was the only president from Pennsylvania because he is regarded as one of the worst ever to hold the office. It could be that his performance in office has adversely affected the chances of other Pennsylvanians that have aspired to hold the highest office in the land.

We looked at fifteen different polls, including Schlesinger, *Chicago Tribune*, Siena College, C-Span, *Wall Street Journal*, and others. In each poll, he was ranked in the bottom quartile, and five times he was rated the worst president. The best he was rated was in a 1982 poll, where he was fourth from last (36th). In 2006 and 2009, a survey of presidential historians organized by the University of Louisville listed Buchanan's feeble actions to oppose efforts by Southern states to secede from the Union as the worst blunder by any president.

Buchanan was born on April 23, 1791, in Cove Gap, Pennsylvania. He attended Dickinson College in Carlisle, Pennsylvania. At one point, he was expelled from the school for behavior issues. Given a second chance, he graduated with honors in 1809. After graduation, he relocated to Lancaster, where he studied law. He was admitted to the Pennsylvania bar in 1812. Even though he was strongly opposed to the War of 1812, Buchanan volunteered to fight and served in defense of the city of Baltimore.

James Buchanan (1791–1868), 15th President of the United States.

His political career began in 1814 when he was elected to the Pennsylvania House of Representatives as a member of the Federalist Party. He served five terms in the United States House of Representatives from March 4, 1821, to March 4, 1831. He did not seek re-election in 1830 and, from 1832 to 1834, served as Ambassador to Russia.

In 1834, he won a special election to the United States Senate, was re-elected twice, and resigned in 1845. President Polk offered Buchanan a nomination to the U.S. Supreme Court after the death of Supreme Court Justice Henry Baldwin in 1844, but he declined the nomination.

Robert Cooper Grier then filled the seat. Buchanan then served as secretary of state under President Polk from 1845 to 1849. He received this appointment even though Polk's vice president, George Dallas, opposed his selection. While serving as secretary of state, he aided in the negotiations that resulted in the Oregon Treaty of 1846. This treaty established the 49th parallel as the northern boundary of the western United States. No secretary of state has ever become president since Buchanan.

When Franklin Pierce became president, Buchanan was appointed to serve as Minister to the United Kingdom. While serving in this capacity (1853-1856), he helped draft the Ostend Manifesto. This document described the rationale for the United States to purchase Cuba from Spain and implied that the U.S. would declare war if Spain refused. The rationale was that Cuba should be acquired as a slave state. Once published, the idea was denounced in both the Northern States and Europe. The Manifesto was a major blunder for the Pierce administration and greatly damaged efforts to annex Cuba.

Buchanan sought the Democratic presidential nomination in 1844, 1848, and 1852 but was unsuccessful each time. Finally, in 1856, he was nominated on the seventeenth ballot largely because he was in England during the Kansas-Nebraska debate and did not have to take a position on the expansion of slavery. He went on to defeat John Freemont, the first Republican Party candidate for president, in the election.

Buchanan took over the presidency well aware of the growing divisions in the country between the North and the South over slavery. His strategy to address the problem was to maintain a sectional balance in his appointments and to allow the Supreme Court to make the decision relative to the expansion or restriction of slavery in the territories.

Two days after Buchanan took office, the Supreme Court issued the Dred Scott decision. Chief Justice Taney wrote the decision and it held that Congress had no constitutional authority to restrict the spread of slavery in the territories. It was widely believed that Buchanan supported the decision. The Dred Scott decision was hailed in the South and denounced throughout the North. Abraham Lincoln called Buchanan an accomplice of slave power. There is little doubt that on a personal level,

Here lies Pennsylvania's only president.

Buchanan favored slaveholders' rights. He believed that the slaves were treated with kindness by their masters. He was a Northern man who favored the policies of the South. He once vetoed a bill passed by Congress to create more colleges, for he believed the "there were already too many educated people." He believed that the Southern States could not secede from the Union and did little to prevent it.

By and large, most of Buchanan's policies drove a wedge between Northern and Southern Democrats; he was weakening his party. As a result, in the 1858 elections, the Republicans took control of the House of Representatives. Once they had control of the House, the Republicans used their power to block anything Buchanan wanted to be done. This included the purchase of Cuba. His motivation in this pursuit remained the expansion of slavery. It's ironic to note that had Buchanan succeeded in that purchase; the Spanish-American War may have been avoided.

When Buchanan delivered his inaugural address, he said he would only serve one term. True to his word, he did not seek re-election in 1860. The Democratic Party was so divided by this time that when they held their convention, no candidate was able to secure the votes needed to become the presidential nominee. With the convention deadlocked, the southern wing walked out and nominated Vice President John C. Breckinridge for the presidency. The remainder of the party nominated Stephen Douglas as their candidate. When the Republicans met, they nominated Abraham Lincoln, who, with the Democrats split, was sure to be elected.

The commanding general of the army, Winfield Scott, warned Buchanan that Lincoln's election would result in the secession of several Southern states. He urged the president to send more federal troops and supplies to these areas to protect federal property. Buchanan ignored Scott and took no action, which allowed the Southern states to secede without having to deal with federal interference.

When he left office on March 4, 1861, he told President-elect Lincoln that he hoped the new president was as happy entering the executive mansion as he was to be leaving. He retired in great wealth to his home, Wheatland, in Lancaster, Pennsylvania. He died at his home on June 1, 1868, at the age of 77. He is buried in Woodward Hill Cemetery in Lancaster.

If You Go:

James Buchanan's home, Wheatland, is also in Lancaster. Visitors can tour the residence. We visited Wheatland but didn't have time to take the tour. The grounds and the exterior of the residence, however, are beautifully maintained, so if you are in the area, you may want to take advantage of the tour. While there are many signs around the area direct-ing people to Wheatland, that is not the case with the grave. We had to ask the staff of Wheatland for directions to the cemetery, and many people do since they had them ready in print to give us. The grave is the best maintained in an old decaying cemetery.

Across from Buchanan's grave, facing his gravestone just a few yards away is the grave of Lt. L.E. Bostwick, who was killed at the Battle of Antietam on September 17, 1862. The stone says that he was 25 years old and that Antietam was his 19th battle. We found it interesting that the tombstone of such a young man who had died in the Civil War was facing the grave of the President who did so little to prevent it.

Also buried within yards of Buchanan is Frederick Muhlenberg. Mr. Muhlenberg was a delegate from Pennsylvania to the Continental Congress, served in the Pennsylvania state legislature, and was head of the state's convention that ratified the U.S. Constitution in 1787. He became one of Pennsylvania's first congressmen and was the very first Speaker of the House of Representatives in U.S. history. His grave is badly deteriorated but marked with a plaque.

John Andrew Shulze, who served as Pennsylvania's governor from 1823 to 1829, is buried here as well.

Just across the road from President Buchanan lies Frederick Muhlenberg, America's first Speaker of the House of Representatives.

2.

SIMON CAMERON

Lincoln's First Secretary of War

County: Dauphin • Town: Harrisburg
Buried at Harrisburg Cemetery
521 North 13th Street

To some, Simon Cameron was a brilliant Pennsylvania politician who built a political machine to advance his friends and himself. Others view him as one of the most corrupt public servants in the history of the Commonwealth. One certain thing is that he was one of the most influential Pennsylvanians of his time. Indeed one could argue if not for a man like Simon Cameron, Abraham Lincoln may never have been elected president.

Cameron was born on March 8, 1799, in Maytown, Pennsylvania. Because his parents were poor, he received very little formal education. Cameron's parents both died by the time he was nine, leaving him an orphan. Even as a youth, he was driven and ambitious. He became an apprentice to a printer who was the editor of the *Northumberland Gazette* to ready himself to enter the field of journalism. By the time he was 21, his hard work had begun paying off as he found himself editor of the *Bucks County Messenger*.

Cameron then secured a position with the printing firm of Gales and Seaton. This firm happened to be the publishers of the Congressional debates. He made the most of this opportunity by making political friends in Washington and learning the art of politics. In 1824, he returned to Harrisburg, married Margaret Brua, and purchased a local newspaper. As the editor of his paper, he issued strong editorials addressing the issues of his day. His influence grew, and in 1825 he was made state printer for the

Simon Cameron

Commonwealth of Pennsylvania. Within a year, he was also appointed to the position of adjutant general as part of the governor's staff.

One thing we know for sure about Cameron is that the man could identify opportunities. He saw all the internal improvements going on in Pennsylvania and surrounding states. He jumped in, constructing both railroads and canals. To aid in financing these ventures, he founded a bank. This was in keeping with what he did his whole life: mixing private business with politics.

Cameron was a strong supporter of Democrats during the administrations of both Andrew Jackson and Martin Van Buren. During this time, he also helped elect James Buchanan to the United States Senate. President Van Buren rewarded Cameron in 1833 by appointing him commissioner in charge of settling Winnebago Indian claims. His term here was tainted by scandal and ultimately led to his dismissal. It seems that Cameron felt it would be a good idea to adjust the claims on notes paid through his bank. While his political career suffered damage, his ambitions remained, and he still was confident in the methods that he had chosen to employ.

In 1845, Cameron put together a coalition consisting of some Democrats, Whigs, and members of the Native American Party and succeeded in his quest to be elected to the United States Senate. He served one term.

When the Republican Party began to form, Cameron saw, yet again, opportunity. He built up a political machine that returned him to the Senate in 1858 as a Republican. After that election, he attempted to position himself to be the party's nominee for president in 1860.

The Republican Convention was held in Chicago, and Cameron arrived with little support outside Pennsylvania. However, the shrewd politician knew he had bargaining power. It was accepted that whoever the eventual nominee was, he was going to need Pennsylvania's support to secure the nomination and head the ticket. On the first ballot, William Seward received 173 and ½ votes. Lincoln was second with 102 votes, and the other candidates were far back. It would take 233 votes to secure the nomination.

Lincoln had chosen David Davis, who was a long-time friend, to represent him at the convention. He gave Davis the explicit instruction not to make deals that would bind him in any way. However, after the initial ballot, Davis was convinced that he needed Cameron's Pennsylvania votes to stop Seward. To secure Pennsylvania's support, Davis promised Cameron a cabinet position. Lincoln had received a mere four votes from Pennsylvania on the initial ballot, but that number increased to 44 on the second. Honest Abe had seized the momentum, and on the third ballot, he won the nomination.

Lincoln was not happy about the deal that had been made with Cameron. He made no effort to contact the Pennsylvanian. That did not deter Cameron. He made the trip to Springfield, Illinois, to meet with the president-elect. Cameron left this meeting with a letter from Lincoln that promised he would be named either the secretary of the treasury or the secretary of war. Later Lincoln, faced with opposition to the Cameron appointment, attempted to recall the letter. Not only did Cameron not respond to Lincoln's request, but he also persuaded elements of the Pennsylvania Legislature to pressure Lincoln on his behalf. Finally, Lincoln nominated Cameron to the position of secretary of war. He did so because he felt Cameron could do less damage there than in the Treasury Department.

Then came the Civil War, and the role of the War Department grew in terms of importance. It did not take long for rumors of corruption in the department to begin to grow. When the war began, Lincoln made clear to the members of his cabinet that the emancipation of the slaves, at this point, was not an option. Cameron and some Republican legislators were urging Lincoln to recruit Negro soldiers. Lincoln agreed to use Negroes as laborers in the army but not as soldiers. It was Lincoln's view that arming Negroes would lose the support of Southerners still loyal to the union.

Cameron went his own way on the issue. He released his annual report in 1861, and it publicly contradicted the president by taking the position that the Negroes should be freed and be made part of a Negro army. When word of this report reached Lincoln (Cameron had not run it past the president), he ordered it to be withdrawn and rewritten. It turned out to be too late as both versions found their way to the press. The publication of the two reports showed an administration at war against not only the rebels but against themselves.

During the holiday season between 1861 and 1862, things came to a head. Complaints about irregularities in the War Department had begun to flood Congress. On two occasions, Congress demanded that Cameron provide information on contracts awarded since he assumed office. He ignored both requests. In response, the House set up a committee to investigate the War Department. The investigation produced a 1,109-page report that was damning to the administration. Cameron and his "agents" were accused of ignoring the competitive bidding process. It claimed that the department had supplied the army by buying from favored suppliers who were often dishonest. The report alleged that the War Department purchased huge amounts of tainted pork, rotten blankets, knapsacks that couldn't hold up in foul weather, and hundreds of diseased and dying horses at inflated prices. The report also claimed that the department sold condemned Hall carbines cheaply, bought them back for $15.00 apiece, turned around and sold them again for $3.50, and then bought them back at the price of $22.00 apiece.

By early 1862, Lincoln concluded that Cameron had to go. The president made it easy for him. On January 11, 1862, the president wrote to Cameron, noting that he had requested a change in position. The president said he was pleased to inform Cameron that he was going to nominate him to be the minister to Russia. One wonders what Abe may have done had Siberia been an option.

Cameron served in Russia for a very short time before returning to Pennsylvania. He regained his Senate seat in 1867 and held it until 1877 when he was sure his son would replace him. Cameron then retired to

Final resting place of one of Pennsylvania's most controversial politicians.

his farm in the Maytown area, where he died on June 26, 1889. He was 90 years old. Perhaps he summed up his public career-best when he said, "An honest politician is one who, when he is bought, will stay bought." Simon Cameron is buried in the Harrisburg Cemetery.

If You Go:

Also buried in the Harrisburg Cemetery are John Geary (*see* Chapter 17) and Vance McCormick (*see Keystone Tombstones Volume 1*, Chapter 19). Also, the authors urge you to stop at the cemetery office where you can pick up a booklet that provides for a walking tour of the premises. It's a very old and interesting cemetery that includes a section where both Union and Confederate casualties of the Civil war were laid to rest. You are also very close to the State Capitol building, which is worth seeing and where tours are offered. If you choose to dine in Harrisburg, the city offers a restaurant row on 2nd Street that provides multiple options. The authors would point out that within about a half-mile of the cemetery, there is a small Italian place called the Subway Cafe. It is located on Herr Street, about a half a block below Cameron Street. The Subway offers fishbowls of beer and great pizza.

3.

ANDREW G. CURTIN

Pennsylvania's Civil War Governor

County: Centre • Town: Bellefonte
Buried at Union Cemetery
East Howard Street

The Commonwealth of Pennsylvania played a vital role in the Civil War. Everyone knows that the Confederate invasion of the North came to an end at Gettysburg. Far fewer know that the largest of the North's military camps was located just outside of Harrisburg. Harrisburg was the east-west junction location for the northern railroads, and as a result, the camp was a major military supply center. The camp was known as Camp Curtin, and it was named after Pennsylvania's governor at the time, Andrew Gregg Curtin.

Curtin was born on April 22, 1815, in Bellefonte, Pennsylvania. His father, Roland Curtin, was born in Ireland and became a successful iron manufacturer after arriving in America. His mother, Jane Gregg, was the daughter of a United States senator. Curtin decided to study law rather than join his father's iron manufacturing business. Curtin attended Dickinson College in Carlisle, Pennsylvania, where he studied under Judge John Reed, who was considered one of Pennsylvania's top attorneys. In 1837, Curtin was admitted to the bar in Centre County. During this period, one newspaper said of Curtin, "His great information, his vigorous mind, and his candor, recommended him to the courts, his winning style made him powerful with juries."

Curtin settled in his hometown of Bellefonte, where he made a fine living as a successful lawyer. In 1840, he became involved in his first political campaign by supporting William Henry Harrison for president.

Andrew Gregg Curtin

Curtin married Catherine Wilson in 1844, and the pairing produced seven children. In 1848, Curtin backed the successful presidential campaign of Zachary Taylor.

In 1854, Curtin considered a run for governor of Pennsylvania but decided against it. His decision not to run paved the way for the election of United States Senator James Pollock. As a result of being elected governor, Pollock was forced to resign from the U.S. Senate. Simon Cameron (*see* Chapter 2) ran for the vacant seat, and Curtin opposed him. Cameron was successful in winning the election, but it marked the first of many political battles between the two men.

In 1855, Governor Pollock appointed Curtin to the posts of secretary of the commonwealth and superintendent of public instruction. Curtin worked hard to improve the public school system in Pennsylvania. He was successful in increasing state funding for the schools, and he also established several state schools to train teachers. It was Curtin's view that education could set the United States ahead of the other nations in the world.

In 1860, Curtain and Cameron once again butted heads at the Republican convention. Cameron wanted the presidential nomination for himself, but Curtin threw his support to Abraham Lincoln. When it became clear to Cameron that he could not be nominated, he made a deal to support Lincoln (and influence other Pennsylvanians also to back Lincoln) in exchange for a cabinet position. As a result, Lincoln became President and Cameron became his first secretary of war.

Curtin became the Republican candidate for governor. He won the election and took office on January 15, 1861. As governor, he continued to support President Lincoln. He became a close friend of Lincoln's and made several trips to Washington to discuss the war effort with the president. He was instrumental in obtaining supplies and raising troops for the Union Army. He also made clear his belief that no state could secede from the union. Curtin believed that allowing a state to secede was admitting that our form of government was a failure.

Curtin continued to have problems with Simon Cameron. In the first months of the war, Curtin was successful in raising more troops than

Pennsylvania was required to muster, but Secretary of War Cameron refused to accept them. Moreover, Cameron insisted that the troops he did accept be transported on a railroad he owned rather than the one selected by Curtin. Curtin complained about Cameron's lack of action in mustering troops and obtaining supplies. Lincoln, who liked Curtin more than he did Cameron, found himself in the middle of the feud between the two Pennsylvanians. Cameron's poor—some would even say, scandalous—handling of the war effort resulted in Lincoln concluding that Cameron had to go. In January 1862, Lincoln "nominated" Cameron to be the minister to Russia.

In 1862, with the war going badly for the Union, Curtin organized the "Loyal War Governor's Conference." The conference met in September in Altoona, Pennsylvania. The conference endorsed the efforts of the Lincoln administration and showed that the northern states were united. A series of recommendations agreed to at the conference was presented to the president. Among the recommendations was that General George McClellan be replaced as commander of the Union forces. Six weeks later, Lincoln replaced McClellan.

The strain and responsibilities of office took a toll on Curtin's health. Some believe he suffered a breakdown toward the end of his first term as Pennsylvania's governor. Many did not believe he would run for reelection in 1863. However, he was once again selected to head the Republican ticket and ended up defeating his opponent by more than 15,000 votes.

Even though Cameron was no longer in charge of Lincoln's War Department, Curtin continued to have problems with the new secretary of war, Edwin M. Stanton. In many instances, Lincoln backed Curtin in his disputes with Stanton, which only created resentment on the part of the secretary. In one notable instance in 1864, Lincoln refused to overrule Stanton on an issue regarding the exchange of prisoners. Three different times Curtin made the trip to Washington and met with both Stanton and Lincoln, urging that the North adopt a process of exchanging prisoners with the South. Curtin understood the southern prisons were hellholes, and as a result, northern prisoners were ill-fed and subject to numerous diseases. In Curtin's view, it was a moral issue. Stanton's position was that he would be trading 30,000 well-fed men to the enemy where they could once take up arms against the North, and in return, he would be getting men unfit to fight. Lincoln backed Stanton, and only a partial exchange occurred.

Curtin is one of the most effective of the northern governors. He became known as "The Soldier's Friend." He pushed the War Department to supply the troops in the field adequately. He visited the army after the battles of Fredericksburg and Chancellorsville. He also established a system of state schools to care for war orphans. Also, after the Battle of Gettysburg, Curtin was the driving force behind the effort that led to the establishment of the Gettysburg National Cemetery.

After leaving the governor's office, Curtin continued to fight the growing political power of Simon Cameron. In 1869, Cameron defeated him in an election for a U.S. Senate seat. Curtin then served as Minister to Russia until 1872 (having been appointed to that position by President Ulysses S. Grant). Curtin switched parties and became a Democrat, finishing his political life by serving three terms in Congress during the 1880s. He died in Bellefonte on October 7, 1894. To honor his efforts during the Civil War, his body was escorted to his hometown of Bellefonte by military troops, where he was then laid to rest in Union Cemetery.

Grave of Andrew Curtin (Photo by Joe Farley)

If You Go:

There are several other graves in Union Cemetery worth checking out. Governor Curtin's nephew, John Irvin Curtin, is buried there. He was a Civil War brevet brigadier general who fought in several important battles, including South Mountain, Antietam, Cold Harbor, and Petersburg (where he was severely wounded). After he recovered, he took command of his brigade in 1864 and led it until the conclusion of the war.

Another grave of note is that of James Adams Beaver, who was also a Civil War brevet brigadier general. He lost his leg at the Battle of Ream's Station in 1864. He was later elected governor of Pennsylvania, serving from 1887 to 1891.

Yet another Civil War brevet brigadier general, William H. Blair, was laid to rest here. Blair fought in the Battle of Antietam and led Union activities around Suffolk, Virginia, in the spring of 1863.

Lastly, Union Cemetery is the final resting place for Evan Pugh. Pugh was the first president of Penn State University. Today, the highest honor the University can bestow on its faculty is the title Evan Pugh Professor.

If you are looking for a great place to stop for refreshments in Bellefonte, we recommend The Gamble Mill Restaurant and Microbrewery. The food, atmosphere, and service are all terrific. The restaurant is located at 160 Dunlap Street.

4.

JAY COOKE

Cooke's Books

County: Montgomery • Town: Elkins Park
Buried at St. Paul's Episcopal Church
Old York and Ashbourne Roads

Jay Cooke was the leading financier of the Union war effort during the Civil War. He was also a key investor in the postwar development of railroads in the northwestern United States.

Cooke was born in Sandusky, Ohio, on August 10, 1821. The family estate, a limestone dwelling overlooking Sandusky Bay and Lake Erie, was named "Ogontz" in honor of an Indian chief who once lived nearby. The area was a paradise of teeming deer, waterfowl, and fish. While growing up there, Jay developed his lifelong passion for hunting and fishing.

Jay's father, Eleutheros Cooke, a lawyer and Whig congressman, and his mother, Martha Caswell, were well-educated and highly active politically. Jay's early education was mainly from homeschooling. At age 14, he began work at a Sandusky dry goods store where he became the head clerk while the owner taught him business and financial procedures. At only 16, he moved to St. Louis and was employed with Seymour & Bool, where he earned an unheard-of sum of $600 a year. He lost that job due to the Panic of 1837 and returned to Ohio. In 1838, he moved to Philadelphia, Pennsylvania, where he accepted a position with a packet company. This company failed soon after that, and Cooke became a bookkeeper in a local hotel. Next, at age 18, he landed a clerk position with the banking firm E.W. Clark & Company, which, five years later, led to a full partnership. The company earned its investors a lot of money through its investments in railroads and loans to the federal government to fund the Mexican War.

Jay Cooke during the Civil War

The company collapsed during the Panic of 1857, but Cooke emerged from the economic hard times a very wealthy man.

On January 1, 1861, just months before the start of the Civil War, Cooke opened the private banking house of Jay Cooke & Company in Philadelphia. As the war began, the state of Pennsylvania borrowed $3 million from the firm to fund its war efforts. Cooke also worked with Treasury Secretary Salmon P. Chase to secure loans from the leading bankers in the north. Cooke and his brother, a newspaper editor, had helped Chase get his job by lobbying for him.

Cooke's firm was so successful in distributing Treasury notes that Chase engaged him as a special agent to sell the $500 million in bonds which the Treasury had previously tried and failed to sell. Promised a sales commission of 0.5 percent of the revenue from the first $10 million, and 0.375 percent of subsequent bonds, Cooke financed a nationwide sales campaign, appointing about 2,500 sub-agents who traveled through every northern and western state and territory, as well as the southern states as they came under the control of the Union Army. Meanwhile, Cooke secured the support of most northern newspapers, purchasing ads through advertising agencies, and often working directly with editors on lengthy articles about the virtues of buying government bonds. These efforts heralded a patriotism based on classical liberalist notions of self-interest. His editorials, articles, handbills, circulars, and signs most often appealed to Americans' desire to turn a profit, while simultaneously aiding the war effort. Cooke quickly sold the $500 million in bonds plus $11 million more. Congress immediately sanctioned the excess.

Although Cooke's bond campaigns were widely praised as a patriotic contribution to the Union cause, his vast personal financial gains did not go unnoticed. Notorious for stalling the deposit of bond proceeds into federal coffers, he was accused of corruption. On December 22, 1862, Massachusetts Representative Charles R. Train proposed a Congressional investigation of the Treasury—though the investigation never materialized.

In the early months of 1865, the government faced pressing financial needs. After the national banks saw disappointing bond sales, the government again turned to Cooke. He sent his agents into remote villages and hamlets, and even into isolated mining camps in the West, and persuaded rural newspapers to praise the bonds. Between February and July 1865, he disposed of $830 million in notes. This allowed the Union soldiers to be supplied and paid during the final months of the war. During this effort, Cooke pioneered the use of price stabilization, a practice whereby bankers stabilize the price of a new issue. It is still in use by investment bankers in IPOs and other security issuances.

During these years, Cooke built a multi-room limestone dwelling (dubbed "Cooke Castle"), constructed in 1864-65 and still standing, on the small island of Gibraltar in the Lake Erie harbor of Put-in-Bay, Ohio. The island, which has the highest land elevation in the Put-In-Bay area, was the lookout point for Commander Oliver Perry in the fight against the British during the War of 1812 (on September 10, 1813, Perry and his men defeated a fleet of British vessels during the famous Battle of Lake Erie).

Cooke also constructed a palatial residence in Cheltenham Township, Pennsylvania, dubbed Ogontz after his boyhood home in Sandusky. This influenced the naming of many area Philadelphia landmarks, including Ogontz Avenue. Two decades later, the estate and dwelling became the exclusive Ogontz School for Girls, and the surrounding area became the city of Ogontz, Pennsylvania.

By the end of the war, Cooke had three banking houses (each with a separate group of partners) in Philadelphia, New York, and Washington. In 1870, a similar bank was set up in London, and the next year all were brought together as a single partnership. Cooke expanded into many fields. He had been friendly to the National Banking Act of 1863 and obtained charters for national banks in Washington and New York; the national banks were the prime source of Cooke's strength.

To these banks and small investors at home and abroad, Cooke—now an investment banker—sold participation in state and railroad loans; the largest loans went to the great land-grant Northern Pacific Railroad, which was chartered to run from Duluth, Minnesota, to Tacoma, Washington. In this connection, Cooke introduced two new

Union bond advertisement

ideas into banking: the establishment of banking syndicates as underwriters to handle issues; and the active participation by bankers in the affairs of the companies they were helping finance. Thus, Cooke became the banker and fiscal agent of the Northern Pacific in 1869, and he made short-term loans to the railroad out of his own house's resources—what would prove to be a fatal step.

In 1870, Cooke was responsible for the proposal to refund the Civil War loans. Congress authorized the sale of $1.5 billion worth of lower rate Treasury securities in exchange for wartime issues. Meanwhile, Cooke's troubles with the Northern Pacific Railroad were mounting. In addition to making loans to the railroad, he underwrote mortgage bonds, which sold very slowly. The firm continued to make advances to the railroad out of the demand liabilities of its customers—a risky business. When the economy weakened in early 1873, investment markets dried up. Cooke's banks and his associated houses could not meet the demands of their depositors. On September 18, 1873, the New York office of Jay Cooke and Company shut its doors, as did the banks with which it was

Painting of Jay Cooke as an old man

associated. This started the Panic of 1873, which in turn resulted in the complete collapse of the Cooke financial empire and the end of Cooke's influence in the money markets. His fortune was wiped out.

Later, in the 1870s, he invested a small sum in a silver mine, which turned out to be a bonanza. Cooke was able to sell his holdings for $1 million, thus assuring a comfortable old age.

Cooke and his family spent every summer at Cooke Castle until his death. Today, Gibraltar Island and the Castle belong to Ohio State

Jay Cooke's crypt

University and is a lake laboratory for teaching, learning, and research. The Castle is a Federal Historic Site and is currently being refurbished.

A devout Episcopalian, Cooke regularly gave 10 percent of his income for religious and charitable purposes. He donated funds to the Philadelphia Divinity School and for the building of Episcopal churches, including St. Paul's Episcopal Church in Elkins Park, Pennsylvania (near his Philadelphia "Ogontz" residence) and another on South Bass Island (across the bay from his "Cooke Castle" summer home). After he had been forced to give up his Ogontz estate in bankruptcy, he later repurchased it and converted it into a school for girls.

Cooke died in the Ogontz (now Elkins Park) section of Cheltenham Township, Pennsylvania, on February 16, 1905. He is buried there at St. Paul's Episcopal, in a mausoleum that he designed.

Several geographic features are named in Cooke's honor, including:

- Jay Cooke State Park, a large state park located near Duluth, Minnesota.
- The village of Cooke City, Montana.
- Cooke Township in Cumberland County, Pennsylvania.
- Jay Cooke Elementary School in Philadelphia, Pennsylvania.

- Cooke Road in Cheltenham Township, Pennsylvania.
- Jay, Pitt, and Cooke Streets in the Lakeside neighborhood of Duluth, Minnesota.
- A statue of Jay Cooke by Henry Shrady is in Jay Cooke Plaza near the intersection of 9th Avenue East and Superior Street in Duluth, Minnesota.

If You Go:

Also buried at St. Paul's is Brigadier General Ario Pardee Jr. He commanded the 28th Pennsylvania Infantry at Antietam. He was brigadier commander at Gettysburg and on Sherman's March to the Sea. For his special gallantry at the Battle of Peach Tree Creek during the Atlanta Campaign, he was brevetted a brigadier general.

5.

CHARLES H. VAN WYCK

Traveled Anywhere,
Without Fear of Anyone

County: Pike • Town: Milford
Buried at Milford Cemetery
Route 209

Charles Henry Van Wyck was a Dutch American who devoted much of his life to public service. He represented the people of New York as a representative in Congress, the people of Nebraska as a senator in the United States Senate, and he served as an officer in the Union Army in the Civil War (at the end of which he was brevetted to brigadier general). What he is best known for, however, is surviving an assassination attempt motivated by his vociferous opposition to slavery on the same day as an alleged plot against Abraham Lincoln.

Van Wyck was born in Poughkeepsie, New York, on May 10, 1824. He graduated from Rutgers College in New Brunswick, New Jersey, in 1843. After college, he studied law. He was admitted to the bar in 1847, at which time he opened a law practice in Bloomingburg, New York. In 1850, he was elected district attorney and served in that capacity until 1856. In 1858, he ran as a Republican for a U.S. House seat and won. He won again in 1860. On March 7, 1860, Van Wyck took the floor in the House of Representatives and delivered a speech denouncing the Democratic party and its support of slavery. It was one of the most blistering denunciations of slavery ever uttered in the Capitol. He claimed slavery was a crime against the laws of God and nature and violated the instincts of common humanity. As he concluded, Van Wyck accused Southerners of cowardice and charged them with burning slaves at the

Charles Henry Van Wyck

stake. Reuben Davis, a congressman from Mississippi, called him a liar and scoundrel and asked if Van Wyck would "go outside of the District of Columbia and test the question of personal courage with any Southern man?" Duels were illegal in the District and thus the reference to "outside the District." Van Wyck responded, "I travel anywhere, and without fear of anyone."

The speech received widespread newspaper coverage, and for months afterward, Van Wyck received death threats (usually postmarked from south of the Mason-Dixon line).

On the night of February 22, 1861, Van Wyck was returning to his lodgings in the National Hotel after a visit with New York Senator Preston King. As he walked past the north wing of the Capitol, he was suddenly attacked by "a stout-built man," as reported by the *New York Tribune*. The man seized him from behind and tried to stab him in the chest. The blade cut through Van Wyck's topcoat and likely would have killed him, except that the blow was deflected by a notebook and double-folded copy of the congressional records that were in his breast pocket. As he fought for his life, a second attacker—also with a knife—suddenly appeared. Van Wyck caught the blade with his left hand, punched this second attacker with his right hand (knocking him down), then drew a revolver and shot the first assailant. As the wounded man fell to the ground, a third man sprang out of the shadows and knocked Van Wyck out with a blow to the head with a bludgeon of some kind. As he fell to the ground, Van Wyck's three attackers ran off.

After regaining consciousness, Van Wyck made it to the National Hotel. Bleeding and groggy, he was treated by doctors as he gave his statement to the police. No sign of his attackers was ever found, and no motive was given. Many, however, felt sure that it was retribution for his speech.

On that same night, President-elect Lincoln was en route to Washington for his inauguration. As he traveled from Harrisburg, Pennsylvania, through Baltimore, Allan Pinkerton—founder of the Pinkerton Detective Agency—became convinced that a plot to kill or kidnap Lincoln in Baltimore existed. Pinkerton was hired by the Philadelphia, Wilmington & Baltimore Railroad to protect railroad property along Lincoln's route. According to Pinkerton, his sources reported a plan to have several assassins (armed with knives) interspersed

Memorial to Van Wyck at Gettysburg

throughout the crowd that would gather to greet Lincoln at the station. When Lincoln emerged to change trains, at least one of the assassins would be close enough to attack.

To thwart this plan, Pinkerton had telegraph lines to Baltimore cut on the evening of February 22 to prevent communication between conspirators, and he had Lincoln arrive secretly in Baltimore in the middle of the night. For the rest of his presidency, the story of Lincoln sneaking like a coward through Baltimore was used repeatedly by his enemies.

Van Wyck recovered from his wounds and remarkably was not at all intimidated by this close call with death. Soon after the attack on Fort Sumter, Van Wyck wrote to the White House asking for a military commission. "Those who had talked should act," he wrote. "I desire to be called on at any time, no matter what the danger or risk." He was appointed colonel of the 56th New York Infantry, a regiment that he led valiantly until the end of the war. The 56th New York suffered heavy losses

Van Wyck's grave

at the Battle of Fair Oaks and participated in the Siege of Fort Wagner, South Carolina, in July 1863. Later that year, more heavy losses occurred at the Battle of Honey Hill, which was part of Sherman's famous March to the Sea. The regiment was mustered out in October 1865.

In 1866, Van Wyck again ran for Congress as a representative from New York, winning that election and serving until 1871. He moved to Nebraska in 1874 and engaged in agriculture on a farm in Otoe County. He was a delegate to that state's constitutional convention, after which he was elected three times to the Nebraska State Senate. In 1881, he was elected as a Republican to the United States Senate and served there until 1887. In 1892, he ran for governor of Nebraska as a populist but was defeated. He retired shortly after and settled in Washington, D.C. He died there on October 24, 1895, at the age of 71. He is buried in a rather prominent grave in Milford Cemetery, Milford, Pennsylvania.

If You Go:

Also buried in Milford Cemetery is Pennsylvania's 29th and 31st governor, Gifford Pinchot. He was a noted forestry conservationist and progressive leader but is also responsible for Pennsylvania's much-maligned liquor system. Pinchot is featured in *Keystone Tombstones Volume One* (Chapter 22).

Stroudsburg Cemetery, in Monroe County (35 miles south of Milford), is home to two noteworthy Civil War figures. John Summerfield Staples was the paid draftee replacement for President Abraham Lincoln. During the Civil War, it became customary to pay substitutes to serve in the army in another's place. Lincoln, hoping to set a good example, selected Staples and offered him a bounty of $500. He saw little action, primarily working as a clerk and prison guard. Also in Stroudsburg Cemetery is John Schoonover. He was wounded three times on the second day of the Battle of Gettysburg while defending against Confederate assaults in the Peach Orchard. He was the last remaining officer in his regiment and, despite his wounds, led his men to a retreat on Cemetery Ridge.

John Summerfield Staples

Also of interest 30 miles to the south of Stroudsburg, in Easton (Northampton County), Pennsylvania, is the grave of Union Brigadier General Charles Adam Heckman. Heckman served in the Mexican War before the Civil War and served as Colonel of the 9th New Jersey. He was captured at the Battle of Drewry's Bluff, Virginia, and held at the Confederate stockade at Charleston. He was prisoner-exchanged in September 1864. After the war, he was a dispatcher for the Pennsylvania Railroad. He is buried at the Easton Cemetery, 401 North 7th Street.

6.

PROSPECT HILL CEMETERY

William B. Franklin
Soldiers Circle
5 Unknown Confederate Soldiers
2 Medal of Honor recipients

County: York • Town: York
Buried at Prospect Hill Cemetery
700 North George Street

Prospect Hill Cemetery in York, Pennsylvania is a large, beautiful, well-run cemetery that contains the graves of many interesting people and has many stories to tell.

Among them is Major General William Buel Franklin. Franklin was born in York, Pennsylvania, in 1823 into a historically prominent family. His father, Walter Franklin, was Clerk of the U.S. House of Representatives, and his great-grandfather, Samuel Rhodes, was a Pennsylvania member of the First Continental Congress.

James Buchanan appointed Franklin to the United States Military Academy in June 1839; Franklin graduated first in his class in 1843. He was assigned to the engineers and served in the Rocky Mountain South Pass Expedition before serving in the Mexican War as a topographical engineer. He received a promotion to a first lieutenant at the Battle of Buena Vista.

When Franklin returned from Mexico, he served as a professor at West Point and then supervised the construction of several lighthouses in New Hampshire and Maine. In 1859, he was appointed to supervise the construction of the United States Capitol dome.

Major General William Buel Franklin

When the Civil War began, Franklin was promoted to colonel and three days later, on May 17, 1861, named to brigadier general of volunteers. He led a brigade at First Bull Run, and in June 1862, he was brevetted brigadier general in the regular army, followed quickly by a promotion to major general on July 4. Franklin had a close relationship with General George McClellan, and some say that it was likely due more to their friendship than to Franklin's skill as a commander that he rose so quickly through the ranks.

During the Northern Virginia Campaign, Franklin stayed with the main army and did not participate in it. The reasons are intricately linked to his loyalty to McClellan. McClellan and General-in-Chief Henry Halleck disagreed about strategy, and Franklin sided with McClellan despite receiving orders directly from Halleck to move in support of General John Pope at the Second Battle of Bull Run. He eventually did arrive, but too late to be of any assistance. General Pope brought charges against Franklin for his failure to obey orders, but nothing ever came of them since Pope was removed from command and reassigned. At Antietam, Franklin's corps was held in reserve and remained idle throughout the day.

At the Battle of Fredericksburg, Franklin commanded the so-called "Left Grand Division," which failed in its assaults against the Confederate right led by Stonewall Jackson. Army of the Potomac commander Maj. Gen. Ambrose Burnside blamed Franklin personally for this failure, although Franklin appears to have followed his orders strictly.

Political intrigue swept the Union Army after Fredericksburg. Franklin was alleged to be a principal instigator of a plot against Burnside's leadership. Burnside offered damaging testimony before a Congressional Committee on the Conduct of the War, which kept Franklin from field duty for months. Burnside demanded that Franklin be dismissed from the army, but President Lincoln refused to do so. In response, Burnside resigned his command. When General Joseph Hooker was given command of the Army of the Potomac in February 1863, Franklin refused to serve under him and resigned his command. During the Battle of Gettysburg, Franklin was home in York, developing plans to defend the area from an expected attack by Confederates.

Franklin's grave (photo by Joe Farley)

In August 1863, Franklin returned to duty and was assigned to corps command in the Department of the Gulf. He participated in the 1864 Red River Campaign, another Union disaster. He was wounded in the leg at the Battle of Mansfield, Louisiana, and captured by Confederate partisans while riding on a train in July 1864. He escaped the next day. The remainder of his army career was limited by the disability from his wound and the series of political and command misfortunes. He resigned from the army in March 1866 and became vice-president at Colt Firearms Manufacturing Company in Hartford, Connecticut. He remained there for 22 years until his retirement in 1888, after which he was named as the U.S. Commissioner-General for the Paris Exposition of 1889. He died in Hartford in 1903 at the age of 80.

Also in Prospect Hill Cemetery is Soldiers Circle, a federally owned site given to America after the Civil War as a final resting place for soldiers who died of their wounds after the Battle of Gettysburg. There are 161 known and two unknown graves in Soldiers Circle, all without headstones. The names are inscribed on two continuous circular curbs enclosing a central soldiers' monument, which consists of a 15-foot bronze figure of a soldier surrounded by four cannons. It was erected in 1874 to honor the Union troops, most of whom died in the hospital established in York to care for the wounded. Soldiers Circle is now a Civil War Landmark.

Near Soldiers Circle is the mass grave of five unknown Confederate soldiers who were also wounded at Gettysburg and sent to the hospital in York for treatment. Dr. Henry Palmer, the surgeon in charge of the York Hospital, had issues with the Confederates. In June 1863, as the Confederates approached York, he moved most of the convalescents to a temporary infirmary in Columbia, Pennsylvania, under the supervision of his assistant surgeon. Dr. Palmer stayed behind with a handful of men who were too gravely wounded to be safely removed. Confederate troops under the command of General Jubal Early captured him on June 28, when they occupied the hospital. Palmer managed to escape during the Battle of Gettysburg and returned to York to prepare the hospital for the trainloads of wounded men who would be arriving from Gettysburg. Taking exception to that entire experience, Dr. Palmer refused to allow

Soldiers Circle at Prospect Hill (photo by Joe Farley)

any wounded rebels to be taken to his facility and threatened to resign if forced to accept them. As a result, wounded Confederates were taken to the nearby Odd Fellows Hall. Five of them died in York and are buried in Prospect Hill. There is a stone marking their grave.

Prospect Hill Cemetery is also the final resting place for two Civil War Medal of Honor recipients: John Henry Denig, a United States Marine Corps sergeant who was awarded the Medal of Honor for his actions in Mobile Bay, Alabama, on August 5, 1864, while serving on the USS *Brooklyn*; and Charles Henry Ilgenfritz, for bravery in action at Fort Sedgwick, Virginia, on April 2, 1865.

If You Go:
York has a plethora of good eating and drinking establishments. The ones we visited were both on North George Street: The Left Bank Restaurant; and Maewyn's Irish Pub. We loved them both.

7.

THOMAS L. KANE

Liberty to the Downtrodden

County: McKean • Town: Kane
Buried at Kane Memorial Chapel
30 Chestnut Street

Thomas Leiper Kane was a Civil War Union brigadier general noted for being the commander of the Pennsylvania Bucktails, perhaps Pennsylvania's most famous Civil War unit. He received a brevet promotion to major general for gallantry at the Battle of Gettysburg.

Kane was born in Philadelphia on January 27, 1822, the son of a prominent Philadelphia judge. After completing college in Philadelphia in 1840, he studied in England for a time and then returned to the U.S. and studied law under his father's direction. He was admitted to the bar in 1846. It was also in that year that Kane became acquainted with the Mormon cause at a conference in Philadelphia. Kane was an abolitionist, as were most Mormons. He offered them his help in their conflicts with the U.S. government and their efforts to emigrate to western territories. He used his father's connections to help the Mormons in Washington, D.C., and influenced the government to enlist a battalion of 500 Mormon men to serve in the campaign against Mexico. While traveling on Mormon business in the summer of 1846, Kane became seriously ill with pulmonary tuberculosis in Fort Leavenworth, Kansas. The members of the church nursed him back to health. During his long convalescence, he decided to devote his life to helping the Mormons and other downtrodden people.

His most significant service was during what became known as the Utah War in the winter of 1857–58. President Buchanan—responding

Thomas L. Kane

to reports that the Mormons were in rebellion—ordered 2,500 U.S. troops to Utah to ensure the installation of Buchanan's appointment of Alfred Cumming (*see* Chapter 19, *"If You Go"* section) as territorial governor, replacing Brigham Young. The Mormons—fearing a forced removal from Utah—were prepared to fight. Kane acted as a mediator and helped arrange a solution that avoided violence.

When the Civil War broke out, Kane had spent two years exploring the Pennsylvania frontier in northwestern Pennsylvania. He immediately offered his services to the Union and was commissioned by Governor Curtin to recruit a regiment of riflemen from the highlands in western Pennsylvania. He recruited woodsmen and lumbermen who were experienced in the woods, could forage for themselves, and could shoot rifles. The latter marksman test for joining the unit was unique, as most volunteers did not have proficiency with a weapon.

This regiment adopted the deer tail as their symbol and became known as the Bucktails, eventually becoming one of the most distinguished units in the Union Army. After the men were trained and equipped, they built rafts so they could float down the west branch of the Susquehanna River to Harrisburg. They reported there, 315 strong, in May 1861 and were officially designated the 42nd Pennsylvania Volunteer Infantry (also referred to as the 13th Pennsylvania Reserves). Although elected colonel by his men, Kane—recognizing his lack of military skill—deferred to a more competent leader and instead became a lieutenant colonel. Veteran Charles J. Biddle was named as the colonel.

Kane was wounded at the Battle of Dranesville, Virginia, on December 20, 1861. It was a painful wound, inflicted by a rifle ball that struck him in the face, knocking out some teeth and crushing the roof of his mouth. For the rest of his life, he wore a full beard to cover the scar.

Soon Biddle resigned to take a seat in Congress, and Kane took over as colonel. He suffered additional wounds while his regiment was fighting Stonewall Jackson's forces in the Shenandoah Valley. At Harrisonburg, Virginia, he was struck by a bullet that split the bone below his knee and, while lying on the ground, he received a brutal crushing blow in the chest from a rifle butt, breaking several ribs. Kane was captured along with Captain Charles Taylor, who refused to leave Kane on the battlefield. He and Taylor were exchanged for Confederate prisoners and returned to duty. Kane's wound would repeatedly reopen for the next two years. Captain Taylor was later killed while fighting by his side at Gettysburg.

Kane participated in the Battle of Catlett's Station and the Second Battle of Bull Run, after which he was promoted to the rank of brigadier general. He led his troops in the Battles of South Mountain, Antietam, Fredericksburg, and Chancellorsville (where he distinguished himself

Gallant attack by 150 of the Pennsylvania Bucktails, led by Colonel Kane, upon a portion of General Stonewall Jackson's Confederate Army, strongly posted in the woods, near Harrisonburg, June 6th, 1862.

despite a Union defeat). After the latter battle, he developed pneumonia and was sent to a hospital in Baltimore, where he would remain until June 1863.

Upon hearing of Lee's invasion of the North, Kane rose from his sickbed to join his men. He traveled by railroad and buggy, at one point, avoiding capture by General J.E.B. Stuart's cavalry by disguising himself as a civilian. He arrived at Gettysburg on the morning of July 2, 1863, and resumed command of his brigade, occupying a position on Culp's Hill. On July 3, the Confederates attacked his position and were repulsed, although Kane fell ill during the fighting and sought assistance from Colonel George Cobham. Despite his brigade's victory, Kane was a broken man and never regained full health. The leg wound left him lame for life, the rifle ball through his cheek and mouth left him tormented by neuralgia, headaches, and poor eyesight, and his weakened lungs made him subject to recurrent respiratory illnesses. He resigned from the Army in November 1863. He bade a sad farewell to his beloved Bucktails and, at the age of 41, limped home to his wife and three children in Philadelphia. At the end of the war, he was breveted to major general.

Kane remained a friend and supporter of the Mormons. In 1872, he and his wife spent the winter in Utah as guests of Brigham Young. When Young died in 1877, Kane returned to Utah to express his sorrow. Kane died in Philadelphia on December 26, 1883, and at first, was buried in Laurel Hill Cemetery in the Kane vault that contains his brother's remains. A year later, the general's remains were moved to a memorial chapel erected in the town named for him. Today the chapel is administered by the Mormons and open to the public. A bronze statue of Thomas Kane is displayed in Utah's Capitol identifying him as a "Friend of the Mormons." Kane County, Utah, was named for him. In 2009, a biography written by Matthew Grow was published, entitled *Liberty to the Downtrodden: Thomas L. Kane, Romantic Reformer.*

If You Go:
The borough of Kane is in a very remote area in northwestern Pennsylvania. The Thomas L. Kane Memorial Chapel is a stone/gothic, revival-style chapel built in 1876–1878. It is listed on the National Register of Historic Places. Outside of the church stands a replica of the Kane statue that resides in the Utah state capitol.

8.

JOHN F. HARTRANFT

Old Johnny

County: Montgomery • Town: Norristown
Buried at Montgomery Cemetery
1 Hartranft Avenue

John Frederick Hartranft was a Union major general and recipient of the Congressional Medal of Honor. He also served as Pennsylvania's auditor general and then two terms as governor from 1873 to 1879.

Hartranft was born in Fagleysville, which is a village in New Hanover Township in Montgomery County, Pennsylvania, on December 16, 1830. He received a degree in civil engineering from Union College in Schenectady, New York, in 1853 and worked for two railroads in eastern Pennsylvania before returning to Norristown to work with his father's real estate and stagecoach businesses.

In the spring of 1861, his militia outfit became a 90-day volunteer regiment and was sent to Washington, D.C. On the eve of the First Battle of Bull Run, the regiment turned its back on the enemy and marched home just as the firing began. Their 90-day enlistment period was over, and despite pleas for them to stay from General Irvin McDowell, they left. Hartranft was humiliated by his men's decision, and he stayed to fight on July 21, 1861. This act earned him the Medal of Honor.

After Bull Run, he raised the 51st Pennsylvanian Infantry, a three-year regiment, and became its colonel. They first served on the North Carolina coast in the Burnside Expedition and then at the Battle of Roanoke Island and New Bern. In 1862 they fought in the Second Battle of Bull Run and at South Mountain. On September 17, 1862, at Antietam, Hartranft led the 51st in its famous charge across Burnside's

John Hartfranft

Bridge, suffering 120 casualties. They braved a storm of rifle and cannon fire to cross the bridge and threaten the Confederate right flank. They also participated in the Battle of Fredericksburg before being transferred to the Western Theater where Hartranft saw action at the battles of Vicksburg, Campbells Station, and Knoxville. He fought at the Wilderness and at Spotsylvania after which he was promoted to brigadier general. After continuing to lead his forces against Richmond and Petersburg, he helped repulse General Robert E. Lee's last offensive at the Battle of Fort Stedman on March 25, 1865. His role at Fort Stedman led to him being brevetted major general by U.S. Grant.

The end of the war did not end the violence and death in Hartranft's life. President Andrew Johnson appointed him the provost marshal during the trial of those accused in the Lincoln assassination. The accused were being held in the Arsenal Penitentiary in Washington, D.C., and he was responsible for the defense of the arsenal as well as the supervision of every aspect of the prisoners' daily lives. He made sure they were fed and cleaned and that no one would communicate with them unless authorized by Secretary of War Stanton.

He also saw to it that the inmates were never allowed to occupy adjacent cells to prevent tapping out messages through the walls. The guard detail was changed daily to make sure that no single guard would watch the same prisoner more than once. On July 7, 1865, General Hartranft completed his duties by carrying out the death sentences for four of the prisoners. Hartranft led Mary Surratt, Lewis Paine, David Herold, and George Atzerodt to the gallows in what is now called Fort Lesley McNair. They had received the news of their sentences only 24 hours earlier. One by one, the conspirators were assisted up the thirteen steps of the scaffold by the execution party and seated. All four sat quietly while Hartranft publicly read the orders of execution, a five-page hand-written document stating the charges against each of the four prisoners and the sentences of death that they received. Prayers followed, and then the prisoners were told to stand and were positioned on the traps that would be knocked out from under them. Their arms and legs were bound, nooses were fitted around the necks, and canvas hoods placed over their heads. From the scaffold Powell said, "Mrs. Surratt is innocent. She doesn't deserve to die with the rest of us." Surratt would be the first woman ever executed by the Federal government. The signal was given by Hartranft and the condemned fell. Surratt and Atzerodt appeared to die quickly. Herold and Powell struggled for nearly five minutes, strangling to death.

Shortly after, Hartranft decided to end his military career. "Old Johnny," as his troops called him, resigned from the army and decided to enter politics. He switched from the Democratic to the Republican party and gained the support of Republican state boss Simon Cameron (*see*

Destruction of the Union Depot by M.B. Leiser, shows burning of Union Depot, Pittsburgh, Pennsylvania, during Great railroad strike of 1877 from pgs. 624, 625 of Harper's Weekly, Journal of Civilization, Vol XXL, No. 1076, *New York, Saturday, August 11, 1877.*

Chapter 2), who recognized the voter appeal of his war record. He ran successfully for state auditor general in 1866 and again in 1869.

In 1872 he was Cameron's personal choice to succeed another Civil War hero, John Geary (*see* Chapter 17), as governor, and he won and served two terms until 1879. In contrast to Governor Geary, Hartranft had no objection to the expanding influence of the Pennsylvania Railroad and other industrial interests.

During his administration, the revision of the commonwealth's constitution was completed and ratified as the Constitution of 1873. He played an important role in celebrating our nation's centennial in 1876 that was centered in Philadelphia's Fairmount Park. At the Republican National Convention in June 1876, he was a contender for the presidential nomination that eventually went to Rutherford B. Hayes of Ohio. Hartranft's second term was marred by economic depression, unemployment, strikes, and civil unrest. He permitted the execution of twenty-one coal miners convicted of various crimes in the coal region in northeastern Pennsylvania. Called the Molly Maguires, these men were leaders of labor unrest in the coal region. Ten of them were hanged in one day in Pottsville and Mauch Chunk on June 21, 1877 (See *Keystone Tombstones Volume One*).

The "King of the Mollies," Jack Kehoe, was also executed on December 18, 1878, after another extremely controversial prosecution in which coal company employees conducted the investigation, arrested Kehoe, and then prosecuted him. Hartranft reportedly hesitated to implement the sentence explaining that he thought Kehoe should be punished but not hanged. Yet he waited until after the fall election and then signed a death warrant with one month left in his term.

In July 1877 a series of riots broke out triggered by wage cuts for railroad workers. The worst riots were in Pittsburgh and Hartranft sent state militia and National Guard troops to maintain order. When outraged protesters cornered troops in a Pennsylvania Railroad roundhouse the soldiers opened fire, killing twenty and wounding many more. In response, furious workers destroyed tracks, roundhouses, engines, and other railroad property. Protests spread to Altoona and Reading where National Guard troops killed another ten people. As the violence spread

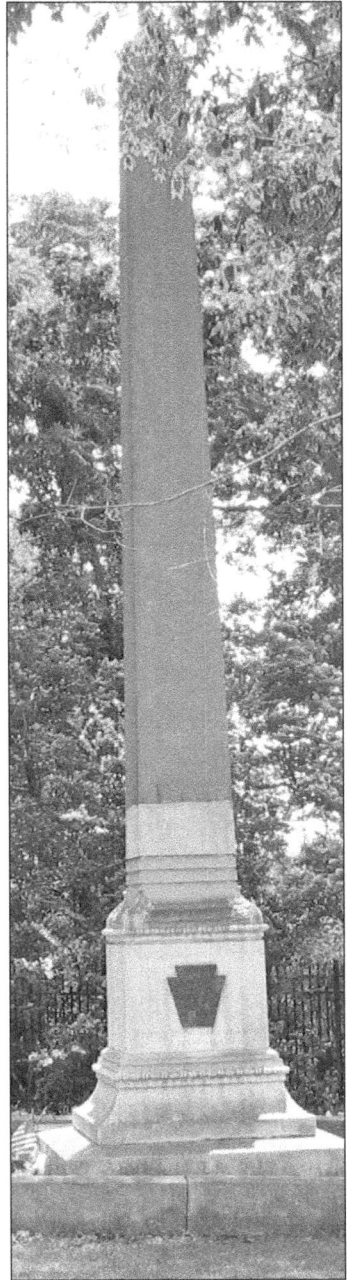

Hartranft's obelisk

49

to Philadelphia, Hartranft asked for (and received) federal troops from President Hayes, making him the first governor in U.S. history to request federal troops to put down a labor uprising.

In 1877, when 78-year-old Simon Cameron resigned his Senate seat, Hartranft appointed Donald Cameron—the senator's son—to replace him. After leaving office, Hartranft returned to his home in Montgomery County and accepted the position of postmaster. He later was appointed collector of the Philadelphia port.

John Hartranft died in Norristown on October 17, 1889. He is buried in a fine grave marked by a large obelisk in Montgomery Cemetery, near Norristown. The Pennsylvania National Guard provided the obelisk for his grave. Ten years after his death, a heroic bronze, mounted statue of him was dedicated on the grounds of the Pennsylvania State Capitol in Harrisburg.

Marble monuments at Petersburg and Vicksburg honor his Civil War service. Elementary schools in Norristown and Philadelphia are named after the governor, as is a residence hall at Penn State University. There are streets named after him in south Philadelphia and the Brookline section of Pittsburgh, and three avenues in Montgomery County are named in his honor. His Medal of Honor is commemorated by a stone bearing his name in Soldiers and Sailors Grove behind the State Capitol Building in Harrisburg.

If You Go:

There are a few interesting Civil War graves in Montgomery Cemetery. There are Generals Winfield Scott Hancock (*see* Chapter 14) and Samuel Kosciuszko Zook (*see* Chapter 20). Also buried there is General Matthew

General Winfield Scott Hancock

McClennan, who led his troops in battles in the Richmond Campaign and Edwin Schall, who served as lieutenant colonel of the 51st Pennsylvania and was killed at the Battle of Cold Harbor in June 1864.

Congressional Medal of Honor recipient Hillary Beyer is buried in a neighboring cemetery, and Brother Paul's is a great place to eat nearby.

9.

GENERAL CONTROVERSY

Alfred Sully
Joshua T. Owen
Francis Engle Patterson
Henry Morris Naglee

County: Philadelphia • Town: Philadelphia
Buried at Laurel Hill Cemetery
3822 Ridge Avenue

There are many Civil War generals buried in Philadelphia and many of them at the beautiful, historic Laurel Hill Cemetery. This chapter will feature four who generated some controversy then and now. All are buried in Laurel Hill Cemetery.

ALFRED SULLY

Alfred Sully was involved in controversy in both the Civil War and the Indian Wars. He was born on May 22, 1821, in Philadelphia, the son of a famous portrait painter, Thomas Sully. Thomas (who is also buried at Laurel Hill) is famous for his portraits of John Quincy Adams, Marquis de Lafayette, Thomas Jefferson, George Washington, and many other famous people of the early 1800s. Alfred, like his father, was also a noted watercolorist and oil painter. He graduated from West Point in 1841 and served in the Seminole Wars, the Mexican War, and on the American frontier in the West against the Cheyenne in the 1850s.

In February 1862, Sully was appointed colonel of the 1st Minnesota Volunteer Infantry and commanded them in the Peninsula Campaign and

Joshua T. Owen

Alfred Sully

Henry Morris Naglee

Francis Engle Patterson

the Seven Days Battles. After again commanding his regiment at the Battle of Antietam in September 1862, he was promoted to brigadier general.

He commanded a brigade in the II (Second) Corps of the Army of the Potomac at the Battle of Fredericksburg in December 1862. On May 1, 1863, just before the Battle of Chancellorsville, Sully was removed from his brigade by division commander Major General John Gibbon.

According to historian Stephen Sears in his book *Chancellorsville*, six companies of the 34th New York under Sully's command had stacked their arms and were refusing to serve any longer. The

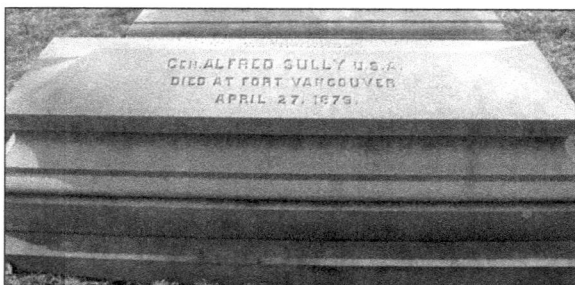

The grave of General Alfred Sully

dispute was about exactly when their two-year enlistment were up. John Gibbon had no patience or sympathy with such protests. He told Sully to deal with it, but Sully replied that he was unable to. Gibbon went to the 34th camp, accompanied by the 15th Massachusetts regiment with rifles in hand, and confronted the protestors. He called the protest a mutiny and said that unless they returned to duty, he would order the 15th Massachusetts to open fire "and kill every man it could." He then asked every man now ready to do his duty to step forward. By ones and twos, protestors stepped forward, then more followed, and finally, every man stood on the new line. That ended the mutiny of the 34th, whose members would serve faithfully until they were mustered out the next month.

Gibbon remembered trembling at the thought of what might have happened but still thought the action he took should have been taken by Sully earlier. He relieved Sully of his command on the spot. A court of inquiry would find Gibbon's action unjustified, but Sully never again served in the Army of the Potomac. He was transferred to the District of Dakota, where he was again involved in controversy at the Battle of Whitestone Hill against the Sioux in September 1863. Sully's troops killed, wounded, or captured 300 to 400 Sioux (including women and children) while losing 20 men and having 38 wounded. Whether this was a battle or a massacre is an ongoing debate.

Alfred Sully died in 1879 while in command of the U.S. Army Post at Fort Vancouver in the Washington Territory.

JOSHUA T. OWEN

Joshua Thomas Owen was born in Wales in 1822. At the age of nine, he emigrated to the United States and settled in Baltimore. He studied and practiced law, established the Chestnut Hill Academy for boys in Philadelphia, and served in the Pennsylvania legislature. He also served as a private in a local militia unit in Philadelphia.

When the war erupted, Owen was elected colonel of the 24th Pennsylvania Volunteer Infantry regiment. When the 24th enlistment expired after three months, he helped organize and was placed in command of the 69th Pennsylvania Volunteers. The 69th was a predominantly Irish regiment that was part of the Philadelphia Brigade. He saw action at Seven Pines and Glendale during the Seven Days Battles and then at Antietam. Owen was promoted to brigadier general for his service on June 30, 1862, at the Battle of Glendale.

At the Battle of Fredericksburg, he led his command in one of the futile Union assaults on Marye's Heights, where they suffered heavy losses. He led the brigade at Chancellorsville, where it took no active part. After Chancellorsville, Owen was arrested during the march into Pennsylvania and relieved of command for unclear reasons. His replacement, Brigadier General Alexander Webb, would be awarded the Medal of Honor commanding the brigade during Pickett's Charge at Gettysburg.

Owen was returned to command his brigade at the Wilderness, Spotsylvania, and Cold Harbor, where he was again arrested. Ironically, the arrest was made by General John Gibbon (who one year earlier had

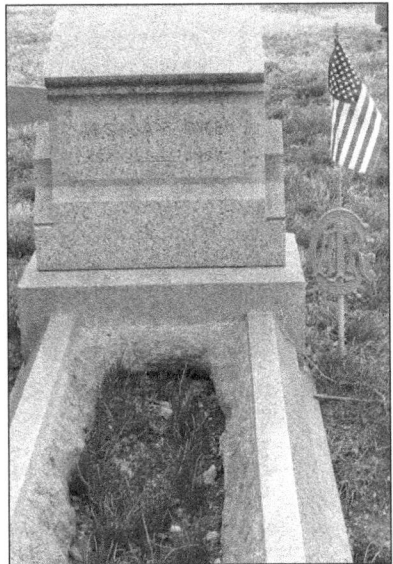

Owen's grave

relieved Alfred Sully of his command). Owen was charged with "disobedience of orders" in failing to support another brigade, the 164th New York. He was honorably mustered out of the service in July 1864.

After leaving the army, Owen returned to the practice of law and founded the *New York Daily Register*, a law journal that became the official publication of the New York court system. In 1866, he was elected recorder of deeds in Philadelphia, where he died on November 7, 1887.

FRANCIS E. PATTERSON

Francis Engle Patterson was born in Philadelphia on March 7, 1821, to Irish American army officer Robert Patterson and Sarah Engle. He came from a family with a military background. His father served as a general with distinction in the Mexican War. He also served briefly in the Civil War but received an honorable discharge in July 1861 after being widely criticized for his performance against Stonewall Jackson at the Battle of Hoke's Run. Francis's brother, Emmet Patterson, and his brother-in-law, John Joseph Abercrombie (*see* Chapter 21, "Gettysburg Generals"), were both generals in the Civil War.

Francis entered the army during the Mexican War and wound up a first lieutenant in the artillery. He transferred to the infantry, was promoted to captain, and resigned in 1857. He returned to service when the Civil War started and was commissioned a colonel in the Pennsylvania militia serving under his father. The militia unit's enlistment was for 90 days, after which Patterson was appointed as Brigadier General of Volunteers and given command of the 2nd New Jersey Brigade. He led his brigade in the Battles of Williamsburg and Fair Oaks.

Patterson's grave

In November of 1862, he led his unit in an unauthorized withdrawal near Catlett's Station, Virginia, due to unconfirmed reports about nearby Confederate forces. He was criticized by fellow general Daniel Sickles, who called for an inquiry on the matter. Before an investigation could be started, on November 22, Patterson was found dead in his tent near Occoquan, Virginia, either due to an accidental weapon discharge or suicide. His father and brother are buried next to him at Laurel Hill.

HENRY M. NAGLEE

Henry Morris Naglee was involved in controversy before and after his service in the Civil War. He was born in Philadelphia on January 15, 1815, and graduated from the United States Military Academy in 1835. He came to California in 1846 as a captain in the 1st New York Infantry Regiment and led troops in the last clash of the Mexican War in 1848, known as the Skirmish of Todos Santos. His men called him "Black Jack," and after the Skirmish, he and about 50 men pursued the enemy. During this pursuit, Naglee ordered the shooting of two men who they had captured, an act that was in direct violation of military orders. The military governor of Alta California ordered Naglee arrested, but he escaped punishment when President Polk granted him a pardon.

After his discharge from the army in 1849, Naglee became the first commanding officer of the 1st California Guards (which would become the California National Guard). He also entered a career in banking, real estate, and brandy making.

Naglee's grave (photo by Joe Farley)

In 1861, Naglee reentered the army as a lieutenant colonel and, in 1862, was made a brigadier general of volunteers. In May, he commanded a brigade in the Army of the Potomac during the Peninsula Campaign, where he was wounded at the Battle of Fair Oaks, Virginia.

He was again involved in controversy when—after returning to California—he was involved in two very public scandals. The first involved a San Francisco actress named Mary Schell, a young lady with whom Naglee corresponded during the war. When Naglee broke off their relationship to pursue Marie Antoinette Ringgold, the spurned actress tried to blackmail him by threatening to print some of his passionate love letters. Naglee refused to pay, and Miss Schell published a book entitled *The Love Life of Brigadier General Henry Naglee, Consisting of a Correspondence on Love, War, and Politics*. The book was quite popular and is still available.

Naglee married Miss Ringgold, who sadly died during the birth of their second daughter. He employed a nursemaid, Emily Hanks, in 1871 to take care of his children. When Hanks became pregnant, she insisted the general was the father. When Naglee refused to marry her, she filed a "breach of promise" suit. She won a settlement of $27,500 in a trial, but the award was overturned on appeal. The affair was headlined in local papers for three years.

Naglee died in San Francisco in 1886 at the age of 71. There is a memorial to him in St. James Park in San Jose, California.

If You Go:

There are so many Civil War officers buried at Laurel Hill that it seems the entire city must have gone to war. Below are four major generals and three brigadier generals who are also buried in historic Laurel Hill.

• **Charles Ferguson Smith:** served with great distinction in the Mexican War, first with Zachary Taylor and later with Winfield Scott. In the Civil War, he served under Ulysses S. Grant (one of his former students at West Point) in the Union capture of Forts Donelson and Henry. Smith personally led the charge that forced the surrender of Fort Donelson. Just before the Battle of Shiloh, he slipped while boarding a rowboat, scraping his shin. The wound got infected, ultimately resulting in his death on April 25, 1862.

• **Edgar M. Gregory:** a prominent pre-war businessman who participated in helping runaway slaves escape to Canada. As commander of the 91st Pennsylvania Volunteer Infantry, he was wounded at the Battle of Chancellorsville and missed Gettysburg while recuperating. He received a first brevet promotion for his gallant conduct at Poplar Spring Church and a second one for the Battle of Five Forks. After the war, he served in Texas as an assistant commissioner of the Freedman's Bureau. His grave was unmarked for over 100 years until a standard-issue government marker was placed there.

Smith's grave

• **Samuel Gibbs French:** A Confederate major general who was New Jersey-born and served with distinction in the Mexican War. He married a southern woman and moved to the South. He fought at Jackson, Atlanta, Nashville, and Mobile, Alabama. He wrote an autobiographical account of his war services entitled *Two Wars*, which is still available. He is buried in Pensacola, Florida, but a cenotaph stands for him in his family's plot at Laurel Hill. (*See* Chapter 33, "Rebels Among Us.")

• **Thomas Jefferson Cram:** a topographical engineer and 1826 graduate of West Point.

• **Caldwell Hall:** commanded the 14th

General French, CSA

New Jersey Volunteer Infantry and was severely wounded during the Battle of Monocacy, preventing him from ever returning to field service.

• **Joseph Roberts:** commanded the 3rd Pennsylvania Heavy Artillery regiment.

• **Charles Mallet Prevost:** served as a U.S. marshall in Wisconsin before the war. He commanded the 118th Pennsylvania Volunteer Infantry and was severely wounded at Shepherdstown, (West) Virginia. He returned for the Battle of Chancellorsville, where he led his men while his injured arm was strapped to his side. He later commanded Camp Butler Military Prison in Springfield, Missouri.

10.

GONE BUT NOT FORGOTTEN

U.S. Colored Infantry during the Civil War

The United States Colored Troops (USCT) were regiments of the United States Army during the Civil War that were composed of African American ("colored") soldiers. First recruited in 1863, by the end of the war, the men of the 175 regiments of the USCT constituted approximately one-tenth of the Union Army. This chapter features two cemeteries in Pennsylvania, where various members of the USCT are buried.

Zion Hill Cemetery

County: Lancaster • Town: Columbia
Address: 5th & Linden Streets

Joe Farrell and Joe Farley at Zion Hill Cemetery among the wooden crosses (photo by Lawrence Knorr)

Zion Hill Cemetery in Columbia, Pennsylvania, is the final resting place of many soldiers who fought with the USCT, including at least seven who fought with the famous 54th Massachusetts Company D regiment. This regiment was one of the first official African American units during the Civil War. Troops from Pennsylvania made up more than 20 percent of the unit. The story of the 54th Massachusetts was made famous by the Hollywood film *Glory*, starring Denzel Washington, Morgan Freeman, and Matthew Broderick. More than a dozen men from Columbia and Wrightsville volunteered for this new regiment of black soldiers serving under white officers. They were responding to recruitment efforts in the Keystone State by Frederick Douglass. They were all mustered in on March 19, 1863, and were all between 18 and 22 years old.

The men of the 54th Massachusetts buried at Zion Hill include:

- **William Edgerly:** killed on July 18, 1863, in the famous assault on Fort Wagner, South Carolina.
- **Henry Parker:** died of disease at Morris Island, South Carolina, on October 5, 1863. Morris Island was the scene of heavy fighting during the Union's campaign to capture Charleston.
- **George Prosser:** captured during the assault on Fort Wagner. He was prisoner-exchanged on March 4, 1865. After the war, he

returned to Columbia and became a minister in the AME Church. He died in 1904.

- **John Turner:** was wounded in July 1863 at St. Andrews Parish, South Carolina. He survived the war, but little else could be found out about him.

Graves of the men of the 54th Massachusetts (photo by Lawrence Knorr)

Three other veterans of the 54th Mass. are buried at Zion Hill, but their birth dates and dates of death are unknown: Pvt. John Anderson, Pvt. James Davis, and Warren Ryan.

There are at least a dozen other veterans of the USCT buried at Zion Hill. Among them is Robert Looney (or Loney), who was said to be a conductor on the Underground Railroad. Before he enlisted, Looney was a free black man who ferried fugitives across the Susquehanna River at night at various places south of Columbia. He was recruited by Captain Thaddeus Stevens Jr., the nephew of legendary Congressman Thaddeus Stevens.

Lincoln Colored Cemetery

County: Cumberland • Town: Mechanicsburg
Address: Winding Hill Road

There are black Civil War veterans buried in Mechanicsburg, Pennsylvania, in what is called the Lincoln Colored Cemetery. We were surprised to make this discovery as we have lived in Cumberland County for more than 30 years and were unaware that the cemetery even existed. If not for the Boy Scouts of America and Vietnam Veterans of Mechanicsburg,

Entrance to the Lincoln Colored Cemetery (photo by Lawrence Knorr)

the cemetery would likely have been forgotten. For a time, the Boy Scouts cared for the cemetery. That changed in 1998 when the Vietnam Veterans adopted the cemetery, taking on the responsibility of tending to the grounds. As a result of their efforts, a monument honoring the USCT was erected, tombstones were reset, and a flag pole flying American and a POW/MIA flags now stands in the cemetery. It is illuminated 24 hours a day, 365 days a year. Replacement of the flags and a memorial service is held there every Memorial Day at 2:00 P.M.

It is difficult to establish many of the facts of how this burial ground came to be and who is buried there. We visited the Cumberland County Historical Society in Carlisle to find out as much as we could. Documents there show that no organization or individual claims ownership of this plot of land. It was, however, an organized colored burial ground and had graves that date back as early as 1862. The Vietnam Veterans of Mechanicsburg name 12 USCT soldiers buried there, while the Cumberland County Veterans Affairs Office lists ten soldiers. Research done by Colonel Arthur Cunningham conflicts with both claims. Cunningham contributed this research to the website "Lest We Forget" (www.lwfaaf.net). He found two of the soldiers on the Vietnam Veterans' list as buried elsewhere in Pennsylvania (one in Cumberland County and another in Fulton County). This may explain the difference between the Vietnam Veterans' list and the list from the Veterans Affairs Office. The truth will probably never be known, but all agree that at least five veterans of the USCT are buried there:

Grave of William Pope (photo by Lawrence Knorr)

- **John W. Pinkney:** born in 1845 in Frederick, Maryland, and enlisted at 18 years of age. He served in Company D, 22nd Regiment USCT. On June 15, 1864, at Petersburg, Virginia, he lost the lower part of his left arm to a shell. Amputation was required, and his arm was removed below the shoulder. He died on December 4, 1882.

- **William Pope:** was born a slave in Page County, Virginia, in 1842. He enlisted in Chambersburg on February 19, 1864, and served in Company B, 32nd Regiment USCT. He died on July 1, 1902.

- **John Williams:** was born in Virginia in 1842. He enlisted in

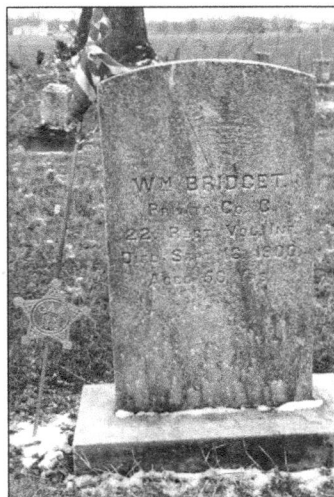

Grave of William Bridget (photo by Lawrence Knorr)

Harrisburg on October 13, 1864, and served in Company C, 41st Regiment USCT. He died September 30, 1885, while working in his stable.

- **Richard "David" Howard:** enlisted on June 14, 1864. No date or place of birth is known. He served in Company G, 45th Regiment USCT. He was discharged on November 4, 1865. He died on September 2, 1895.
- **William Bridget:** enlisted on December 30, 1863. He served in Company G, 22nd Regiment USCT. He was discharged on May 24, 1865, and died on September 16, 1900, at the age of 65.

The two USCT troops that appear to be buried elsewhere are:

- **John Berry Sergeant:** served with Company C, 5th Regiment Massachusetts Cavalry. He is buried in Carlisle, Pennsylvania.
- **James Spriggs:** served in Company C, 3rd Regiment USCT. He is buried in McConnellsburg, Pennsylvania.

Of the remaining five USCT members identified as possibly having their final resting place in the Lincoln Colored Cemetery, Ransom Babcock initially enlisted in Company B, 4th Regiment, New York Heavy Artillery, and was indeed a veteran of the Civil War, but may not be buried here. Enoch Cook, Reuben Jackson, and George Riley could be interred in the cemetery, but there is some doubt that they are Civil War veterans. Lastly, there is a Henry Butler who is also buried here, but the information on him supplied by the Veterans Affairs Office conflicts with Colonel Cunningham's research.

If You Go:

If you go to Mechanicsburg and visit the Lincoln Colored Cemetery, you might want to visit the historic Harrisburg Cemetery or the National Civil War Museum in Reservoir Park, Harrisburg.

If you go to Columbia, you might want to visit the grave of Medal of Honor recipient Charles D. Marquette (*see* Chapter 35). He was awarded the Medal of Honor for his action at Petersburg, Virginia, in 1865. He is buried in Fairview Cemetery in nearby Wrightsville. Also buried nearby in Columbia's Mt. Bethel Cemetery is Brigadier General Thomas Welsh.

Welsh fought at Antietam and South Mountain and died of malaria at the siege of Vicksburg.

If you get hungry or thirsty in your travels, as we often do, we recommend a visit to the John Wright Restaurant on North Front Street in Wrightsville. The food, spirits, and service were good, and it affords a view of the remains of the Columbia-Wrightsville Bridge, which was burned by Union militia to prevent Confederate troops from crossing the Susquehanna River on June 28, 1863, just before the Battle of Gettysburg.

Monument marking the entrance to the Lincoln Colored Cemetery

II.

ST. CLAIR AUGUSTINE MULHOLLAND

The Irish Commander

County: Philadelphia • Town: Philadelphia
Buried at Old Cathedral Cemetery
48th Street & Lancaster Avenue

St. Clair Augustine Mulholland was born on April 1, 1839, in Lisburn, County Antrim, Ireland. He and his parents came to the United States in 1846 and settled in New Jersey. Four years later, they moved to Philadelphia, where Mulholland remained for the rest of his life. In Philadelphia, he worked in a printing shop and later as a painter of window shades. However, even during these days before the Civil War, he demonstrated an interest in military life. He joined the Pennsylvania militia and developed into an expert drill instructor.

When the Civil War began, Mulholland tried to recruit men for a unit he wished to be made part of the Irish Brigade. While he was unsuccessful initially, he did manage to recruit two companies of men that would form the 116th Pennsylvania Volunteer Infantry and be attached to Meagher's Irish Brigade. Mulholland was initially made lieutenant of the 116th in June of 1862, and then lieutenant colonel on September 1, 1862.

Mulholland was wounded during the attack of the Irish Brigade up Marye's Heights at the Battle of Fredericksburg on December 13, 1862. Though the wound was severe enough to require Mulholland to use a cane to walk, he returned to the field in 1863. By all accounts, Mulholland was respected and admired by the men he commanded. He was also a personal favorite of Major General Winfield Scott Hancock (*see* Chapter 14), and the two developed a lifelong friendship.

St. Clair Augustine Mulholland

At the Battle of Chancellorsville on May 3–4, 1863, Mulholland and his men saved the guns of the 5th Maine Battery that had been abandoned to the Confederates. On the evening of May 4, General Hancock chose Mulholland to protect the army in a rear-guard action. Hancock fully expected that his friend and his men would be captured, and so he told Mulholland that he would try to work out a prisoner exchange for him should that occur. Mulholland and 400 men protected the retreat of

Marye's Heights at Fredericksburg

the Union Army. Also, he avoided capture and was able to return with his men. For those actions, Mulholland was awarded the Medal of Honor.

In early 1864 Mulholland returned to Philadelphia to recruit enough men to return the 116th to full strength. He was successful and was promoted to colonel. He was wounded again during the Battle of the Wilderness and a third time at Po River. After only ten days in the hospital, he resumed his command, only to be wounded again at the Battle of Totopotomoy Creek. After he recovered, Mulholland led his brigade in all the actions around Petersburg and again demonstrated his bravery by leading an assault on a fort on the Boydton Plank Road. He finally

Final resting place of St. Clair Augustin Mulholland, a true Civil War hero.

left the volunteer service on June 3, 1865. In 1866, upon the recommendation of General Hancock, President Johnson nominated Mulholland for the brevet grade of brigadier general of volunteers, and the Senate confirmed the appointment that year. In 1869, he was nominated for appointment to the brevet grade of major general, and the Senate also confirmed that nomination.

After the war, Mulholland was appointed Chief of Police in Philadelphia. President Grover Cleveland appointed him to the position of United States Pension Agent—a post he would continue to hold under Presidents McKinley and Teddy Roosevelt. He also lectured and wrote on the Civil War. He compiled a history of the 116th and another on the men who had been awarded the Medal of Honor. Mulholland died on February 17, 1910, in Philadelphia and was laid to rest in Old Cathedral Cemetery.

If You Go:
See the *"If You Go"* section in Chapter 22 (Dennis O'Kane).

12.

GENERAL JOHN FULTON REYNOLDS

A True American Hero

County: Lancaster • Town: Lancaster
Buried at Lancaster Cemetery
205 East Lemon Street

John Reynolds gave his life for his country during the Battle of Gettysburg. He was one of the Union Army's most respected senior commanders. He fought in the Battles of Second Bull Run, Fredericksburg, Chancellorsville, and Gettysburg. He was captured in June 1862 and held prisoner at the infamous Libby Prison in Richmond. Within two months, Reynolds was exchanged for Lloyd Tilghman, a Confederate general who was later killed at the Battle of Champion Hill. President Lincoln offered Reynolds command of the entire Army of the Potomac, but he turned it down because he thought he would not be given a free hand. It was Reynolds's opinion that previous commanders had become bogged down due to political influences.

John Reynolds was born in Lancaster, Pennsylvania, on September 20, 1820. He was one of nine children. Two of his brothers would also go on to have distinguished military careers. He was educated in local schools. The future President, Senator James Buchanan, nominated Reynolds to attend the United States Military Academy in 1837. He graduated in 1841, 26th in a class of 50.

Reynolds experienced his first real military action during the Mexican War. During the war, he served under General Zachary Taylor and performed quite well. He received two promotions during the conflict. Reynolds was made a captain as a result of his gallantry during

John Fulton Reynolds

the Battle of Monterrey. During the Battle of Buena Vista, his unit prevented the Mexican Army from outflanking the Americans. This earned him the rank of major. During this conflict, he befriended both Winfield Scott Hancock and Lewis A. Armistead. Hancock would be a fellow Union officer at Gettysburg, where he would be wounded. Armistead would fight on the Confederate side, and be killed on the third day of the battle at the high point of the Confederate advance during Pickett's Charge.

This monument marks the spot where Reynolds fell on the initial day of the Battle of Gettysburg.

After the Mexican War, Reynolds remained in the Army. He was stationed in Oregon, and he took part in the 1857 Utah War with the Mormons. Returning east, he became the Commandant of Cadets at West point from 1860-1861. Here he trained men, some of whom fought on the Union side, and some who rallied to the Confederacy during the Civil War.

Shortly after the War between the States began, Reynolds was promoted to the rank of brigadier general. Major General George McClellan took steps to see to it that Reynolds was assigned to the just-created Army of the Potomac. He was put in charge of a brigade of Pennsylvania volunteers.

The first major battle he fought in was the Battle of Beaver Creek Dam. The Confederates launched a major attack on June 26, 1862, but Reynolds held his position. The Confederates attacked the next day again. Reynolds had gone 48 hours without sleep. Believing he was safe, he found a place to get some rest. The Union's retreating troops left him behind, and he was captured. The Confederates who captured him brought him before their general, D. H. Hill. Hill and Reynolds were friends from before the war, and Hill told Reynolds not to feel bad, that this is what happened in wars. As detailed earlier, the Union quickly arranged a prisoner exchange that resulted in Reynolds's release.

Reynolds, upon his release, quickly distinguished himself on the field of battle. On the second day of the Second Battle of Bull Run, the Union Army was disorganized and in a mass retreat. Reynolds led his men in a risky counterattack. It proved a success, giving the Union Army time to regroup and retreat in an orderly fashion. Some believe

THE FALL OF REYNOLDS.

Monument honoring John Reynolds on the Gettysburg battlefield.

that without Reynolds, the Union troops may have been totally defeated that day.

The Battle of Chancellorsville took place in May of 1863 and resulted in a major Union defeat. Reynolds was highly upset with the Commander of the Army at the time, Major General Hooker. After being overrun by a Stonewall Jackson flank attack, Hooker called his generals together. Three of the five generals urged Hooker to stay on the offensive, but he decided to retreat. Reynolds said in a manner that he intended Hooker to hear, "What was the use of calling us together at this time of night when he intended to retreat anyhow?"

Reynolds's final appearance on the field of battle was at Gettysburg. Brigadier General John Buford, a Union Cavalry officer, arrived in the small Pennsylvania town first. He occupied the town and set up defensive lines outside of town on high ground that he believed ideal to repel attacks. When General Buford decided to try to hold the high ground on Day 1 of the Battle of Gettysburg, he did so partly because it was John Reynolds who was supposed to arrive with his infantry. He respected Reynolds and believed he would arrive in time to relieve his cavalry troops. Buford did hold the ground for Reynolds, who arrived as fighting was underway. After a conference with Buford, Reynolds led his soldiers to the front lines and was putting them in place when he was downed by a shot, from what most believe was a Confederate sniper. He died instantly, and his command was assumed by Major General Abner Doubleday, who would become famous for allegedly creating America's national pastime.

Reynolds was the first and highest-ranking general to die at Gettysburg. His men loved him, and historian Shelby Foote wrote

Base of monument marking the grave of General John Reynolds in Lancaster

that many considered him the best general in the army. His body was transported to Lancaster, where he was buried on July 4, 1863. He was only 42.

Reynolds was so important to the Union effort and so highly thought of that he is memorialized by three statues in Gettysburg National Park (McPherson Ridge, The National Cemetery, and the Pennsylvania Memorial). There is also a statue of Reynolds in front of the Philadelphia City Hall.

A monument marks the spot on the Gettysburg battlefield where Reynolds fell. His grave is in Lancaster Cemetery near the entrance and one of the best kept in the old cemetery.

If You Go:

There are several other Civil War veterans' graves in Lancaster Cemetery, including John Reynolds's older brother, Rear Admiral William Reynolds, who served as commander on the USS *New Hampshire* in the Union Navy's blockade of the Southern ports. Two brevet brigadier generals, Henry Hambright and Samuel Ross, are also buried there as well as Colonel David Miles, who was captured at the Battle of Chickamauga and confined to Libby Prison. He successfully escaped and returned to Union army, where he led a brigade in Sherman's March to the Sea. Also, President James Buchanan, who was instrumental in getting Reynolds accepted to West Point, is buried in Lancaster. The former president (*see* Chapter 1) is buried in Woodland Hill Cemetery. Visitors to Lancaster may also want to check out *Keystone Tombstones Volume 1*, Chapter 21, on Thomas Mifflin.

13.

GEORGE G. MEADE
The Old Snapping Turtle

County: Philadelphia • Town: Philadelphia
Buried at Laurel Hill Cemetery
3822 Ridge Avenue

George Gordon Meade was a career United States Army officer and is best known for being the victor of the Battle of Gettysburg in 1863. He was born on December 31, 1815, in Spain. His father was serving there as an agent for the United States Government. In 1828, his father died, and six months later, the family, facing financial difficulties, returned to the United States. Initially, George was educated at the Mount Hope Institution in Baltimore. In 1831, with financial considerations being a prime consideration, he entered the United States Military Academy at West Point. He graduated ranked nineteenth in his class of 56 cadets in 1835 and was transferred to Florida at the beginning of the Seminole Wars. He became ill with a fever in Florida and was reassigned to Massachusetts. He was very disillusioned with the military and resigned his commission in 1836. He went to work for a railroad company as an engineer to survey territory for new rail lines.

In 1840 he met Margaretta Sergeant, and soon she became his wife. She was the daughter of John Sergeant, who was Henry Clay's running mate in the 1832 presidential election. They had seven children together. With a family to support, Meade found it difficult to secure steady employment. Though he had never intended to make the army a career, he reapplied to the military in 1842 and was appointed a 2nd lieutenant in the Topographical Engineers. He was assigned to General Winfield Scott's army during the War with Mexico. He was brevetted to first lieutenant as a result of his conduct during the Battle of Monterrey.

George Gordon Meade

After the war in Mexico, Meade moved back to Philadelphia, where he worked on building lighthouses for the Delaware Bay. He was eventually promoted to captain, and for the next ten years, he spent time in surveying and design work for lighthouses on the east coast. He oversaw the construction of lighthouses at Barnegat, Atlantic City, and Cape May, New Jersey. Among his accomplishments during this period was the design of a hydraulic lamp that was approved by the Lighthouse Board for use in American lighthouses. He also participated in the survey of the Great Lakes and tributaries.

He was promoted from captain to brigadier general in August 1861, just a few months after the start of the Civil War. The sectional strife took a personal toll on the Meades as his wife's sister was married to Governor Wise of Virginia, who became a brigadier general in the Confederate Army. Nicknamed "The Old Snapping Turtle," Meade gained a reputation for being short-tempered and obstinate. In March 1862, he was severely wounded at the Battle of Glendale. A musket ball struck him above his hip, clipped his liver, and just missed his spine as it passed through his body. He recovered from his wounds in Philadelphia and led his brigade at the Battle of Second Bull Run and the Battles of South Mountain, Antietam, and Fredericksburg. Soon after Fredericksburg, Meade was assigned to command the Fifth Army Corps of the Army of the Potomac. His assignment as corps commander took him through the trial of the Battle of Chancellorsville in May 1863. Though the army had been soundly defeated there, Meade handled his corps with great skill and protected the important fords on the Rappahannock River.

Unhappy with the performance of the Army of the Potomac, President Lincoln changed command from McClellan to Burnside to Hooker, He offered the position to John Reynolds, but he refused. Next up was Meade, who assumed command just days before the monumental Battle of Gettysburg, which is considered the turning point of the war. In defending his decision to appoint Meade as commander of the Union forces, Lincoln said, "Meade will fight well on his own dunghill."

Meade was fortunate to have such competent and brave officers as Reynolds, Buford, Hancock, Vincent, Custer, and Chamberlain with him

General Meade's monument at Gettysburg

at Gettysburg. Meade decided to fight a defensive battle and did well in deploying his forces. His forces repelled attacks on his flanks and, on the final day of the battle, stood tall against an attack on the center of their lines. This disastrous attack became known as Pickett's Charge. Although Meade field-marshaled the Union victory at Gettysburg, he was criticized severely then and now for not pursuing the defeated Confederate forces after the battle. Meade infuriated Lincoln when he reported that the "invaders have been driven from our land." Reportedly, upon receiving the dispatch, Lincoln said angrily, "Doesn't he understand it's all our land?"

Lincoln was overwrought at the missed opportunity to perhaps end the war and ordered Meade to pursue and attack Lee's retreating army. It was too late, however, and Lee escaped to Virginia. In March, Lincoln put General Ulysses S. Grant in charge of all Union Armies.

When Grant was appointed, Meade offered his resignation. He wanted to allow Grant to appoint the general of his choosing for the position. Grant told Meade he had no intention of replacing him. While Meade stayed with the Army, he did not approve of Grant's tactics. Meade had become a cautious general while Grant was willing to attack and suffer losses, secure in the knowledge that he had replacements available, and the Confederates did not. By all accounts, Meade served Grant well during the remainder of the war. He received a promotion to major

Final resting place of George Meade "The Old Snapping Turtle" who commanded the victorious Union Army at Gettysburg

general at the war's end. He was outranked by only Grant, Halleck, and Sherman.

After the war, General Meade was a commissioner of Fairmont Park in Philadelphia from 1866 until his death. Before his death, he received an honorary doctorate in law from Harvard University. Also, his scientific achievements were recognized by several institutions, including the American Philosophical Society and the Academy of Natural Sciences of Philadelphia. He died on November 6, 1872, in the house where he lived at 1836 Delancey Place in Philadelphia, from complications of his old wounds combined with pneumonia. He was 56 years old. Many felt his victory at Gettysburg had stopped a rebel invasion of the city. After his death, his widow accepted the house as a gift from the city of Philadelphia. To this day, the house still has the word "Meade" over the door though now it has been converted into apartments. Meade is buried in a modest grave in Laurel Hill Cemetery in Philadelphia.

If You Go:

Laurel Hill is a large well-kept cemetery rich in history with many interesting graves. (See *Keystone Tombstones Volume 1*, Chapter 12, on Harry Kalas). Once again, due to the size of this cemetery, if you visit, we advise you to make an initial stop at the cemetery office to obtain directions to the sites you are there to see.

Among the graves at Laurel Hill are three officers who fought with Meade at Gettysburg. Oliver Blatchy Knowles entered the war as a private and ended it as Brevet Brigadier General after fighting in Antietam, Shenandoah, Gettysburg, Spotsylvania, Petersburg, and the last campaign of Appomattox. He died less than two years after the war of cholera at the age of 25. William Lovering Curry fought at Gettysburg and was stationed at the famed "Copse of Trees" during Pickett's Charge. He was wounded at the Battle of Spotsylvania and died a month later. Alexander Williams Biddle fought at the Battles of Fredericksburg, Chancellorsville, Gettysburg, and Bristoe Station as a major and then lieutenant colonel.

Ulric Dahlgren was a Civil War army officer killed in a raid on Richmond in 1864. Papers found on him indicated he had orders to

Tombstone of Ulric Dahlgren, who was killed in a raid on Richmond, while carrying orders to assassinate Confederate President Jefferson Davis.

assassinate Confederate President Jefferson Davis and his Cabinet. The papers were published and created an enormous controversy (the Dahlgren Affair) in the following months and may have contributed to John Wilkes Booth's decision to assassinate Abraham Lincoln a year later.

Frank Furness served as a Civil War officer and was awarded the Congressional Medal of Honor for his bravery at Trevailian Station, Virginia. However, he was better known as a major architect from 1870 to 1890. He designed over 400 buildings, including banks, churches, synagogues, rail stations, and numerous mansions. His first major work, Philadelphia's Academy of Fine Arts, is still standing. His grave, however, is very modest and simple.

There are five other Civil War Congressional Medal of Honor recipients at Laurel Hill: Henry Harrison Bingham, George J. Pitman, John Hamilton Storey, Pinkerton Vaughn, and Robert Telford Kelly.

I4.

WINFIELD S. HANCOCK
Hancock the Superb

County: Montgomery • Town: Norristown
Buried at Montgomery Cemetery
1 Hartranft Avenue

Winfield Scott Hancock was an American hero named after an American hero and given an appropriate and well-earned nickname, "Hancock the Superb." He was a career U.S. Army Officer, a hero in the Civil War, a commanding general at the Battle of Gettysburg, and the Democratic nominee for president in 1880.

Winfield Scott Hancock was born in Montgomery County, Pennsylvania, on Valentine's Day in 1824. He was named after General Winfield Scott, a hero in the War of 1812. Hancock was born with an identical twin brother named Hilary Booker Hancock. Hancock was educated at Norristown Academy at first but transferred to public schools in the late 1830s. In 1840, he was nominated to West Point by Congressman Joseph Fornance. He graduated in 1844, ranked eighteenth of twenty-five. He was commissioned a second lieutenant and assigned to the infantry.

When the Mexican War broke out in 1846, he was initially assigned to recruiting in Kentucky. He worked hard to get assigned to the front, but he was so successful as a recruiter, they were reluctant to let him go. He finally did get assigned to the front in July of 1847 in a regiment that made up part of the army led by General Winfield Scott. He was promoted to 1st lieutenant for "gallant and meritorious conduct" at the Battle of Churubusco, where he was wounded in the knee and developed a fever. The fever kept him from participating in the final breakthrough

Winfield Scott Hancock

at Mexico City much to his regret. He remained in Mexico until the peace treaty was signed in 1848.

After the Mexican War, he served in the West, in Florida, and elsewhere. It was while serving in St. Louis that he met Almira (Allie) Russell, whom he married in 1850. The couple had two children, Russell (1850–1884) and Ada (1857–1875). In 1855, he was promoted to captain, and in November 1858, he was stationed in southern California and joined by Almira and the children. There, Hancock became friends with several officers from the South and became especially close to Lewis Armistead of Virginia. At the outbreak of the Civil War, Armistead and other Southerners were leaving to join the Confederate Army, while Hancock was remaining in the U.S. Army.

On June 15, 1861, Hancock and Almira hosted a party for their friends who were scattered because of the war. The party has become a legend and is recounted in Michael Shaara's *The Killer Angels* and the movie *Gettysburg*. Armistead, who was widowed twice, had grown very close to the Hancocks and shed tears when it became time to end the party and depart. He gave some personal effects to Almira for safekeeping and promised he would not take arms against his friend, "Winnie." Almira said later that at the Battle of Gettysburg, Hancock's men killed three of the six Confederates who attended that party.

Hancock headed east to assume quartermaster duties for a rapidly growing army, but on September 23, 1861, he was promoted to brigadier general and given command of an infantry brigade in the Amy of the Potomac. He took part in the Peninsula Campaign, and at the Battle of Williamsburg on May 5, 1862, he handled his troop so well that General George McClellan reported: "Hancock was superb." The epithet seemed to stick to him afterward, and "Hancock the Superb" was born.

He played a significant role at the Battle of Antietam and shortly afterward was promoted to Major

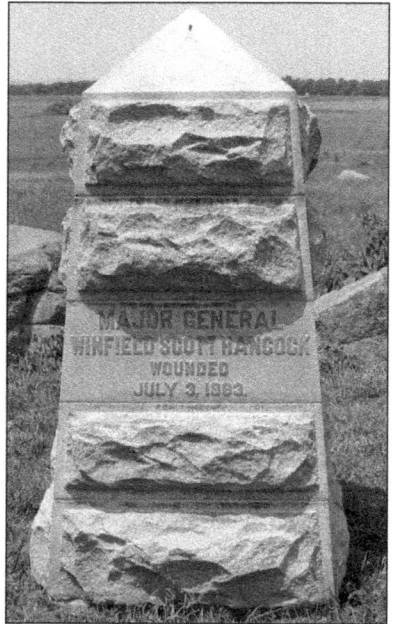

This monument marks the spot at Gettysburg where Hancock was wounded. The bullet that was removed from Hancock is preserved by the Montgomery County Historical Society.

General of Volunteers in November 1862. He led his division in the disastrous attack on Marye's Heights in the Battle of Fredericksburg the following month, where he was wounded in the abdomen. He was wounded again at the Battle of Chancellorsville, covering General Hooker's withdrawal. On that day, General Darius Couch asked to be transferred out of the Army of the Potomac in protest of the actions of General Hooker. As a result, Hancock assumed command of 11 Corps, which he would lead until shortly before the war's end (General Couch had a long distinguished military career and has the remains of a fortification built to defend Harrisburg named after him in Lemoyne, Pennsylvania.).

Hancock's most famous service was at the Battle of Gettysburg during July 1–3, 1863. On the first day, after his friend Maj. Gen. John Reynolds (*see* Chapter 12) was killed, Gen. George Meade (*see* Chapter 13), the new commander of the Army of the Potomac, sent Hancock ahead to take command and to decide whether to continue to fight there or to fall back. He decided to stay, rallied his troops, and held Cemetery Ridge until the arrival of the main body of the Federal Army. During the second day's battle, he commanded the left-center and, after General Sickles had been wounded, the whole left wing. On the third day, he commanded the left-center and thus bore the brunt of Pickett's Charge. Hancock was shot in the groin while rallying and commanding his troops on horseback. Although severely wounded, he refused to be evacuated to the rear until the battle was resolved. During the battle, his old friend General Lewis Armistead was mortally wounded. As he lay dying, he asked to see Hancock. When told that Hancock could not come to see him because he had been wounded himself, Armistead asked that Hancock be told that he was sorry. Armistead died two days later, while Hancock took six months to recover enough to return to command. There is a monument on the Gettysburg Battlefield commemorating their friendship and another marking the spot where Armistead fell. Hancock was considered by many to have made the most impact by a general at Gettysburg. His courage in the face of fire and leadership played a huge role in the Union victory.

This is the Friend to Friend monument in the Gettysburg National Cemetery. The monument portrays the final moments in the life of Confederate General Lewis Armistead who died at Gettysburg and was close friends with General Hancock.

This monument on the Gettysburg battlefield marks the spot where Confederate General Lewis Armistead fell mortally wounded.

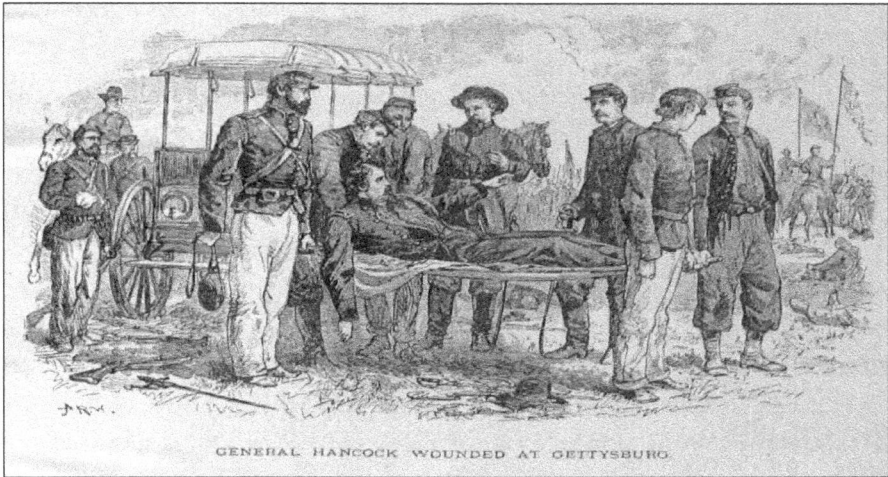

GENERAL HANCOCK WOUNDED AT GETTYSBURG

This drawing of a wounded Hancock at Gettysburg is in the office at the Montgomery Cemetery.

Hancock suffered from the effects of his Gettysburg wound for the rest of the war. After recuperating in Norristown, he returned in March to the front and led his old corps under General Ulysses S. Grant in the 1864 Overland Campaign but was never quite his old self. He performed well at the Battle of the Wilderness, which began in May, and continued to fight at Yellow Tavern, North Anna, Old Church, Cold Harbor, Trevilian Station, and finally, the siege of Petersburg. In June, his Gettysburg wound reopened, but he soon resumed command, sometimes traveling by ambulance. After his corps participated in the assaults at Deep Bottom, Hancock was promoted to brigadier general in the Regular Army, effective August 12, 1864.

In Grant's campaign against Lee, Hancock and his famed 11 Corps were repeatedly called upon to plunge into the very worst of the fighting, and the casualties were terrible. The losses and lingering effects of his Gettysburg wound caused Hancock to give up field command in November 1864. He left the 11 Corps after a year in which it had suffered over 40,000 casualties but had achieved significant military victories. He was again promoted in March 1865 to brevet major general in the Regular Army.

After the assassination of Abraham Lincoln in April, Hancock was placed in charge of Washington, D.C., and it was under his command that John Wilkes Booth's accomplices were tried and executed. Hancock was reluctant to execute some of the less-culpable conspirators, especially Mary Surratt. He hoped Surratt would receive a pardon from President Johnson. He was so hopeful that he posted messengers from the arsenal, where the hangings took place, to the White House, ready to relay the news of a pardon to him, but no pardon was forthcoming. Afterward, he wrote that "every soldier was bound to act as I did under similar circumstances."

Hancock remained in the postwar army, and in 1866 Grant had him promoted to major general in the Regular Army, and he served at that rank for the rest of his life. He served briefly in the West and then was named military governor of Louisiana during Reconstruction. His policies there angered Republicans and Grant but made him popular among Democrats. When Grant won the presidency in 1868, Hancock found himself transferred to the Department of Dakota, which covered Minnesota, Montana, and the Dakotas. It was during this tour that Hancock contributed to the creation of Yellowstone National Park and had a summit (Mt. Hancock) at the southern boundary named in his honor.

With the death of General George Meade in 1872, Hancock became the senior major general in the U.S. Army and was assigned to take Meade's place as commander of the Division of the Atlantic at Governor's Island in New York Harbor.

Hancock had been considered as a presidential nominee by the Democrats as early as 1864. In 1880, he was finally chosen at the convention in Cincinnati, along with William Hayden English of Indiana as his running mate. They ran against James Garfield and Chester Arthur in an election that was very close in the popular vote, but not so close in the electoral. Garfield won by less than 10,000 votes but won the electoral vote 214 to 155. Garfield was assassinated in September 1881.

Hancock finished his life as Commander of the Division of the Atlantic and died at Governor's Island from an infected carbuncle complicated by diabetes on February 9, 1886. After a funeral in New York City, General Hancock's remains were taken to his boyhood home of Norristown, Pennsylvania, and placed with his daughter Ada in a mausoleum that he had designed.

Winfield Scott Hancock is memorialized three times at Gettysburg: once in a statue on Cemetery Hill, once on a statue as part of the Pennsylvania Memorial, and as a sculpture on the New York State Monument. There are statues in Washington, D.C., at Pennsylvania Avenue and 7th Street N.W. and in Fairmont Park in Philadelphia and a bronze bust in Hancock Square, New York City. His portrait adorns U.S. currency on the $2 silver certificate series of 1886 and is quite valuable today.

Actor Brian Mallon portrayed Hancock in two films about the Civil War: *Gettysburg* (1993) and *Gods and Generals* (2003). He is portrayed very favorably in both films. There are numerous books about Hancock, the most notable is *Winfield Scott Hancock: A Soldier's Life,* written by David M. Jordan and published in 1998.

Here is the grave of one of the greatest Union Civil War generals.

If You Go:
There are a few other interesting graves in Montgomery Cemetery. The most notable is the grave of John Frederick Hartranft, who is the subject of chapter 8 in this volume. Hartranft was awarded the Congressional Medal of Honor for his actions at the first Battle of Manassas. He rose to the rank of brigadier general and, after the war, was appointed a special provost marshall during the trial of those accused in President Lincoln's assassination. He led the convicted parties to the gallows and read them their last rites before they were hanged.

Returning to civilian life, he served as auditor general of Pennsylvania in John White Geary's (see *Keystone Tombstones Volume One*, Chapter 9) administration before being elected governor in 1872. He was governor on the Day of the Rope, June 21, 1877, when ten Molly Maguires were hanged (see *Keystone Tombstones Volume One*, Chapter 13).

Also buried in Montgomery Cemetery with Hancock is Brigadier General Samuel Kosciuszko Zook who fought with him at Gettysburg and was fatally wounded on the second day, and Brigadier General Adam Jacoby Slemmer who ignored pressure by the Confederates to surrender his command at Fort Barrancas, Florida, in 1861, instead moving it to Fort Pickens, Santa Rosa Island. This move ensured Union control of the Gulf of Mexico throughout the war.

Nearby Montgomery Cemetery at Lower Providence Presbyterian Church Cemetery in Eagleville lies the body of Civil War Congressional Medal of Honor recipient Hillary Beyer. He was awarded his Medal of Honor for his bravery at the Battle of Antietam, Maryland, in September 1862.

We were hungry and thirsty after our visit to Norristown and found a great place just down the road from Lower Providence Presbyterian Church at 3300 Ridge Pike. It's called Brother Paul's and had a great menu and service. You can sit inside or outside and choose from many delicious sounding items on the menu. We both loved our sandwiches. There were many options for wetting your whistle too. While we were waiting for our food, we loved taking in the décor. There were many great photographs throughout the large bar and dining areas. We even got to meet one of the Pauls himself. The Pauls are brothers-in-law, so we found out. He seemed like a fine American, so we asked if he might have us back for a book signing some evening. It looks like a fun place to have a pint or two. We're hoping he says, "yes."

Here are the Joes at Brothers Pauls refreshing ourselves after visiting Montgomery Cemetery. We hope to get back to visit the brothers in the future.

15.

JOHN BURNS
The Hero of Gettysburg

County: Adams • Town: Gettysburg
Buried at Evergreen Cemetery
799 Baltimore Street

On July 1, 1863, soldiers of the 7th Wisconsin Infantry and the 24th Michigan Infantry were stunned to see an elderly man dressed in dark trousers and a blue swallowtail coat with brass buttons and a high black silk hat join them in McPherson's Woods to await an attack by Confederate troops. He fought beside these men of the famous Iron Brigade throughout the afternoon, in one case shooting a charging Confederate officer from his horse.

His name was John Burns. Burns was born on September 5, 1793, in Burlington, New Jersey. He was a veteran of the War of 1812, where he served as an enlisted man and fought in numerous battles. In 1846, when war broke out with Mexico, Burns was one of the first to volunteer. He also served with valor in that conflict. When the Civil War began, he was 67 years old, but he immediately volunteered to serve in the Union army. He was rejected due to his advanced age. Though rejected for combat duty, he was permitted to serve the army as a teamster. However, within a short time, he was sent home to Gettysburg. Little did he realize, at the time, that this would allow him to fight.

Confederates rode into Gettysburg on June 26. During General Jubal Early's brief occupation of Gettysburg, Burns was the local constable. The rebels had him jailed for his adamant resistance and assertion of civil authority. As Confederate troops were leaving for Harrisburg, he was released from jail, and he promptly arrested some of the Confederate

John Burns

stragglers. He held them in custody until the arrival of Federal cavalry under Brigadier General John Buford on June 30.

The next day, when major combat erupted, Burns calmly took up his flintlock musket and walked out to the scene of the fighting. On his way, he encountered a wounded Union soldier and asked if he could borrow his more modern rifle for the battle. The soldier agreed, and Burns moved on, putting cartridges in his pockets. He ran into Major Thomas Chamberlin of the 150th Pennsylvania Infantry and asked to be allowed to fight with the regiment. Chamberlin referred him to the regimental commander, Colonel Langhorne Wister, who agreed to let him fight. Burns was wounded three times, and when the Union forces fell back under Confederate pressure, the Union soldiers were forced to leave

This monument sits on the Gettysburg battlefield near where Burns took his spot beside Union troops.

him behind. Although wounded and exhausted, he was able to crawl away from his rifle and bury his ammunition so that when captured by Confederates, he could claim he was a noncombatant. He succeeded in convincing the Confederates of such, and their surgeons treated his wounds in the arm, leg, and breast. Had Burns not convinced his captors, he would have been subject to summary execution as a non-uniformed combatant.

After the battle, Burns became a national hero. Matthew Brady's photographer, Timothy O'Sullivan, snapped a picture of Burns recuperating from his wounds and took the story back home to Washington. The alleged inventor of baseball, Major Abner Doubleday, called Burns "the Hero of Gettysburg." When President Lincoln came to Gettysburg a few months later to dedicate the Soldiers National Cemetery, it was John Burns he wanted to meet. President Lincoln and Burns walked together from David Will's house to the Presbyterian Church on Baltimore Street. Lincoln extended his thanks to John Burns on their walk. His fame spread all across the nation, and in 1864, the famous poet Bret Harte published a poem about Burn's exploits called "John Burns of Gettysburg," and Congress passed a special act granting him a pension.

In the last few years of his life, Burns had dementia. He would often wander from his home. He somehow found his way to New York City, where on a winter's night in December 1871, he was discovered in a state of destitution. He was sent home to Gettysburg, where he died of pneumonia on February 4, 1872. He was 78 years old.

A monument depicting a defiant Burns carrying his rifle and with a clenched fist can be found on McPherson's Ridge near where Burns fought with the Iron Brigade. The monument was dedicated on July 1, 1903, the 40th anniversary of the battle. Burns is buried in historic Evergreen Cemetery in Gettysburg. His grave is one of only two there with permission to fly the American flag twenty-four hours a day. The other grave is Ginnie Wade (*see* Chapter 23). A full-length biography titled *John Burns: The Hero of Gettysburg* by Timothy H. Smith was published in 2000.

If You Go:
Gettysburg is a fantastic town steeped in history. There is so much to see
and do that we can only scratch the surface here. In the historic Evergreen
Cemetery are many interesting graves, including those of Ginnie Wade
(*see* Chapter 23) and Hall of Fame baseball player Eddie Plank. Nearby
Gettysburg National Cemetery is perhaps the most hallowed ground
in our country and a sight to behold. It is the site of Lincoln's famous
Gettysburg Address and the graves of 3512 Union soldiers, of which 979
are unknown.

Among those buried there are:
• **Amos Humiston** is the only individual enlisted man at Gettysburg
who has a monument on the battlefield. Humiston was killed on July 1,
1863, the first day of the battle. When his body was discovered later that
week, he was holding an ambrotype (an early kind of photograph) of
three small children. There was nothing else to identify him, and the few
soldiers from his unit, Company C, 154th New York Volunteer Infantry,
who survived had moved on before he was found. Efforts to discover his
identity using the picture started with a story in the *Philadelphia Inquirer*
with the headline, "Whose Father is He?" The story swept the North,
and his widow saw the photograph in a magazine and realized that her
devoted husband was dead. The family was living in Portville, New York,
and Amos had been dead for four months. The outpouring of sympathy
was so great that the proceeds from fundraising allowed for the creation
of an orphanage in Gettysburg for children of soldiers. Amos Humiston
is buried in the New York Section of the National Cemetery, and his
monument is on Stratton Street between York Street and the railroad,
beside the fire station. See more details in Chapter 16.
• **Cyrus James** is also buried in the New York plot. He is believed to
be the first soldier killed in this famous and monumental battle. Ewell's
forces, arriving from Cumberland County, killed him in a skirmish north
of town before the main engagement.

Amos Humiston is the only enlisted man to have his own monument on the Gettysburg battlefield.

The tombstone of Charles Collis a Medal of Honor recipient for his actions during the battle of Fredericksburg. The men who served under him erected this monument.

• **Charles Henry Tucky Collis** was awarded the Congressional Medal of Honor for his bravery at the Battle of Fredericksburg on December 13, 1862. He survived the war and has an impressive grave in the National Cemetery.

• **William E. Miller**, of Cumberland County, was awarded the Congressional Medal of Honor for his bravery on the third day of the Battle of Gettysburg. He is buried in the Officer's Section in the National Cemetery.

• **George Nixon** was wounded during the second day of the Battle of Gettysburg. That night, as he lay on the battlefield between Union and Confederate lines, he cried out in pain. Musician Richard Enderlin crawled out and dragged Private Nixon most of the way back to safety then dashed the rest of the way with Nixon in tow. For this act, Enderlin was promoted to sergeant and awarded the Medal of Honor. Nixon's wounds were mortal, and he died in a hospital seven days later. He was the great-grandfather of Richard Nixon, our 37th president. His grave is in the Ohio plot.

16.

AMOS HUMISTON

A Moving Story of a Father's Love

County: Adams • Town: Gettysburg
Buried at Gettysburg National Cemetery
97 Taneytown Road

The Gettysburg Battlefield is full of monuments. Hundreds of monuments commemorate the men who led the soldiers in this epic battle for the nation's soul. There are monuments to states, divisions, brigades, and companies. There are monuments to generals and officers and even civilians, but what about enlisted men? There is but one enlisted man who has his monument on the battlefield at Gettysburg, and that man is Amos Humiston.

Sergeant Amos Humiston of the 154th New York Volunteer Infantry was killed on the first day of fighting at Gettysburg. Months earlier, Humiston's wife had mailed him an ambrotype (an early type of photograph) in which the couple's three children were pictured: Frank (age 8), Alice (6), and Freddie (4). After Humiston was killed, his body was found by a local Gettysburg girl, the daughter of a tavern-keeper, in a secluded spot at York and Stratton Streets. Humiston was clutching the photograph, which, as it turned out, was the only thing found on his person that could be used to identify him.

The girl gave the picture to her father, Benjamin Schriver. It became a conversation piece at his tavern. A physician named Dr. John Francis Bourns was in Gettysburg from Philadelphia to care for the wounded and was touched by the story when he visited Schriver's Tavern. He was so moved by the story of the soldier found holding the picture that he convinced Schriver to give him the picture so that he could try to locate

Ambrotype of Amos Humiston—the only known picture of him.

the dead man's family. Dr. Bourns saw to it that the soldier's grave was well marked and returned to Philadelphia with a plan.

On October 19, 1863, the *Philadelphia Inquirer* published a story under the headline: "Whose Father Was He?" The article began by describing the final act: "How touching! How solemn! What pen can describe the emotions of this patriot-father as he gazed upon these children, so soon to be made orphans!" The column continued with a detailed description of each of the children's physical appearances, as shown in the picture, which was necessary because newspapers of the time could not print photographs. The article gave Dr. Bourns's address and a request for newspapers throughout the country to spread the story:

The Humiston children. This photo was used to help iden-tify their father, a Gettysburg casualty.

"It is earnestly desired that all the papers in the country will draw attention to the discovery of this picture and its attendant circumstances, so that, if possible, the family of the dead hero may come into possession of it. Of what inestimable value will it be to these children, proving, as it does, that the last thoughts of their dying father was for them, and them only."

On October 29, 1863, a reprint of the *Inquirer*'s article was published in the *American Presbyterian*, a church magazine. That is where Philinda Humiston of Portville, New York, a small town on the Allegheny River, saw the article and—having last received word from her husband weeks before Gettysburg—feared the worst. She contacted Dr. Bourns through a letter written by the town postmaster. Bourns sent a copy of the picture, and when it arrived, Philinda Humiston realized that her husband Amos was dead.

The *American Presbyterian* announced the news on Thursday, November 19, 1863, the same day that President Lincoln delivered the Gettysburg Address.

On January 2, 1864, Dr. Bourns paid a visit to the Humiston home, where he returned the bloodstained ambrotype to Philinda and gave her the profits from the sales of copies of it. He also raised with her the idea of a fundraising drive to establish an orphans' home in Gettysburg for the children of soldiers killed in the war.

Donations poured in from all over the nation, and the orphanage, called the Homestead Orphanage, became a reality in October 1866. With her children, Mrs. Humiston moved to the Homestead, where she was given the job of supervising the children's wardrobe. Three years later, Philinda, unhappy in Gettysburg, married Asa Barnes (a man she met as he passed through town) and moved with him to Massachusetts.

The Homestead Orphanage prospered for several years but met a tragic end, closing after 12 years. The woman who ran the orphanage, Rosa Carmichael, was accused of abusing the children and shackling some of them in the basement. She was convicted of aggravated assault on one of the children. Even Dr. Bourns himself was accused of embezzling large amounts of money from orphanage accounts.

Amos Humiston was born in Owego, New York, in Tioga County on April 26, 1830. After attending a local school, he became a harness maker and then a whaler based in New Bedford, Massachusetts. He responded to President Lincoln's call for 300,000 volunteers in July 1862, enlisting on July 26. He was assigned to the 154th New York and sent to Virginia. On January 25, 1863, he was promoted to sergeant. In March, he required hospitalization for chronic diarrhea or, as he called it, "the Virginia quick step." He recovered and went on to fight at the Wilderness, and later survived a terrible defeat at Chancellorsville on May 2, where the 154th lost 40 percent of its men. Humiston was wounded during the battle and wrote to his wife about missing home. She responded by sending him the ambrotype of their children.

On July 1, 1863, the 154th arrived at Gettysburg and soon were sent into battle. Most of the 154th were captured, but a few Union troops— including Humiston—made a mad dash for safety. He ran less than a quarter-mile before he met his fate.

Amos Humiston is buried in the New York Section of the Gettysburg National Cemetery. In 1999, a biography entitled *Gettysburg's Unknown Soldier: The Life, Death, and Celebrity of Amos Humiston* was published.

Near this spot on July 1, 1863 a Union soldier fell mortally wounded. When a local resident found the unidentified body, he also discovered a photograph of three children. News of this poignant find was soon widely covered by the press, and copies of the photograph were distributed and sold for charity. One of these reached Mrs. Phylinda Humiston of Portville, New York, who now realized that her husband, Sergeant Amos Humiston of Company C, 154th New York Volunteers, had been killed. The plight of the Humiston children--Frank, Frederick, and Alice--touched an outpouring of sympathy and donations from throughout the North, leading to the establishment of a Soldier's Orphan's Home in Gettysburg in 1866. Sergeant Humiston's body was removed from here to the Gettysburg National Cemetery.

Close-up of the monument to Humiston and his children in Gettysburg.

It was written by historian Mark Dunkelman, using Humiston's various war letters.

If You Go:

The monument to Amos Humiston is not in the National Cemetery but instead in the town itself (beside the Gettysburg fire station, on Stratton Street between York Street and the railroad).

See Chapter 15 (John L. Burns) and Chapter 23 (Ginnie Wade) for more information and suggestions if you visit Gettysburg.

17.

JOHN WHITE GEARY

An American Success Story
Few Have Heard

County: Dauphin • Town: Harrisburg
Buried at Harrisburg Cemetery
521 North 13th Street

John Geary has a county in Kansas named for him. Kansas also has a Geary State Park. There is a Geary Boulevard in San Francisco, California, named in his honor. There is a Geary Street in both New Cumberland (where he owned a home) and Harrisburg, Pennsylvania. Not to be left out, there is a Geary Street in South Philadelphia as well. There is a monument honoring Geary in Mount Pleasant, Pennsylvania. There is a dorm building at the Pennsylvania State University named Geary Hall. Finally, on August 11, 2007, a statue was unveiled on Culp's Hill, which is part of the Gettysburg Battlefield. It was erected to honor Geary. The subject of this chapter was a man who got around.

Geary was born on December 30, 1819, in what is today the greater Pittsburgh metropolitan area. His father, Richard Geary, was considered a well-educated man. Richard took on the task of educating his two sons. After being prepared by his father, Geary became a student of law and engineering at Jefferson College in Canonsburg, Pennsylvania. Before his graduation, his father passed away, and he was forced to leave school. He found work in Kentucky as a surveyor. While in Kentucky, he also tried his hand at land speculation. He was successful enough to earn the money he needed to return to college, and he graduated in 1841. Upon graduation, he worked at several professions, including mercantile trade and civil engineering. He also studied law and was admitted to the state bar.

John White Geary (by Mathew Brady)

In 1843, Geary married Margaret Ann Logan. In 1846, his first son, Edward, was born. During this time, Geary was employed by the Allegheny Portage Rail Railroad as an engineer. He was instrumental in creating the rail line that traversed the Allegheny Mountains. His ideas would later be used in the construction of the famed Horseshoe Curve.

Geary was already a high ranking officer in the Pennsylvania militia when the Mexican War began in 1846. He formed a company he called the "American Highlanders," all volunteers and all from Cambria County.

This unit was joined with a company from Pittsburgh, and Geary was elected second in command.

The combined unit sailed for Mexico but encountered delays due to both weather and disease. As they approached the Gulf of Mexico, a few cases of smallpox appeared, and the ship was sent to be quarantined. Finally, all signs of the disease disappeared, and on April 12, 1847, Geary and the rest of the company arrived in Vera Cruz. By this time, that city had already been taken by the Americans, so he had to wait for the Battle at Chapultepec to lead his men into an actual engagement with the enemy. He performed heroically and was wounded multiple times during the battle. Considering that he stood at six feet six inches tall and weighed 260 pounds, he must have made for an inviting target. At the war's conclusion, Geary had earned the rank of colonel and returned to the United States a hero of the Mexican War.

After the war, President Polk appointed Geary postmaster of San Francisco. Geary embarked for the west coast with his three-year-old son, his pregnant wife, and thousands of pieces of mail. He and his family arrived in 1849 at the height of the Gold Rush. He quickly dove into his duties, establishing post offices, mail routes, and appointing postmasters. His management skills earned him the admiration of the local citizens. Despite his success in this office, President Taylor, who succeeded Polk, replaced Geary as the postmaster.

It appears that the people of San Francisco did not agree with the new president. In 1850, Geary was easily elected the first mayor of the city. He remains the youngest mayor in San Francisco's history. By this time, due to his wife's failing health, Geary had sent her and his two sons back to Pennsylvania. He remained in California, where he governed capably. He worked hard to get the city's finances in order and was successful. At the same time, he added to his fortune by selling city lots he acquired at little cost to him. In 1852, he returned to Pennsylvania to be with his family and care for his wife. It was to no avail as she passed away in 1853. Geary would remarry in 1858.

At this point in his life, Geary was determined to devote himself to farming and his various business pursuits. This was not to be. His reputation as a war hero and capable administrator led to President Pierce offering him the governorship of the Kansas territory in 1856. At the time, "Bleeding Kansas," as it was called, was a battleground between pro and anti-slavery forces. Geary was not eager to accept the position but acquiesced when Pierce appealed to his patriotic spirit.

In this instance, Geary's initial reluctance may have been correct. His predecessor as governor remarked, "that to govern Kansas in 1855 and 1856, you might as well have attempted to govern the devil in hell." Bleak were the conditions Geary inherited when he arrived in Kansas on September 9, 1856. The Kansas territory was practically a war zone over the issue of slavery. The new governor pledged to be impartial and fair in dealing with the opposition factions in the territory. This policy resulted in the further alienation of both sides.

Geary's problems in Kansas were complicated by the fact that many of President Pierce's appointees in the territory were solidly pro-slavery. These officials resisted Geary's efforts to enforce the law, and bring peace to Kansas. Geary wrote to the president requesting the removal of multiple judges, and the replacement of the federal marshall, the secretary of state, and the attorney general. With a presidential campaign in progress, Pierce determined that the best course was to let his successor handle the problem. James Buchanan of Pennsylvania, who had no record on the issues in Kansas, won the election. Geary lacked confidence in the new president, and he tendered his resignation on March 4, 1857. It was the very day Buchanan was inaugurated. Later in recalling his Kansas experience, Geary wrote, "I have learned more about the depravity of my fellow man than I ever knew before."

After his time in Kansas, Geary returned to Pennsylvania, where he met Mary Church Henderson of Carlisle. Soon, the two were married. In a short time, they welcomed their first child, a girl, whom they named Mary.

Although Geary was a staunch Democrat, he was also firmly anti-slavery. As soon as Geary received word that rebel forces had fired on Fort Sumter, he began recruiting troops. He set up recruiting stations in Philadelphia and elsewhere. Based on his reputation, he had

Geary's monument stands where he fought, atop Culp's Hill on the Gettysburg Battlefield.

little trouble securing volunteers. Sixty-six companies from all over the Commonwealth requested to be put under his command. In the end, Geary formed a 15-company regiment. He and his men saw their first action in October 1861, near Harpers Ferry. In 1862, he led his men across the Potomac and captured the rebel town of Leesburg, Virginia. As a result, Geary was promoted to brigadier general.

Later that year, Geary faced rebel forces under the command of Stonewall Jackson during the Battle of Cedar Mountain. Geary was wounded in both the arm and the leg during the fighting. The wound to the arm was so severe that amputation was considered. While amputation was avoided, Geary was forced to return home to rest and recover.

When Geary returned to the army, he was put in command of the Second Division of the Twelfth Corps under General Slocum. Geary would remain in charge of this division until the war's end. Geary's men saw plenty of action performing heroically at both Chancellorsville and Gettysburg. It was at Gettysburg atop Culp's Hill that Geary and his men repulsed repeated Confederate assaults and succeeded in holding the union's right flank. The action on Culp's Hill cemented Geary's reputation as a Civil War hero. However, the man was not one to rest on his laurels.

In September of 1863, Geary's division was sent to Tennessee to join the forces of Generals Grant and Sherman. On October 27, 1863, Geary's forces were attacked by a superior force of Confederates. In an intense battle known as the Battle of Wauhatchie, the union forces turned back repeated Confederate assaults. During the fighting, Geary's son Eddie was mortally wounded. He died in his father's arms, but Geary and his men held their ground.

Geary's division went on to fight in the Battle of Lookout Mountain, the Atlanta campaign, and Sherman's March to the Sea. He led the Union forces into Savannah, where he was appointed military governor of the city. He ended his army career by serving on the military tribunal that tried Major Henry Wirtz, who had served as commandant of the Andersonville prisoner of war camp. Wirtz was found guilty of war crimes and was hanged in December of 1865.

Geary now returned to Pennsylvania. Though he had always been a Democrat, powerful elements of the Republican Party began looking at him as a potential candidate for governor. Supported by the former Secretary of War, Simon Cameron, Geary was selected to head the Republican ticket in Pennsylvania. He won the election by 17,000 votes and was inaugurated governor in Harrisburg on January 15, 1867.

Geary's grave in the Harrisburg Cemetery is the only one topped by a statue. The monument was erected by the Commonwealth of Pennsylvania.

Geary served two successful terms as governor. He championed education and was a big supporter of Penn State University. He also worked against the influence of the railroads, and for improvements in mine safety. His policies resulted in reduced public debt and an increase in revenues. He left the state in a far better condition than he had found it when he left the governor's office in 1873.

No sooner than Geary left office, rumors began to circulate that he was considering a run for president. That was not to be. Less than three weeks after leaving the office of governor, on February 8, 1873, Geary suffered a massive heart attack and died while preparing breakfast at his home. He was 54 years old.

Geary was given a state funeral that included speeches from the political leaders of the Commonwealth. A large procession followed the funeral to Harrisburg Cemetery where he was laid to rest. His grave is marked by a monument that is topped by a statue of the great man. It is the only statue in the cemetery and was erected by the Commonwealth of Pennsylvania.

If You Go:
See the *"If You Go"* section in Chapter 2 on Simon Cameron.

18.

STRONG VINCENT

Don't Give an Inch

County: Erie • Town: Erie
Buried at Erie Cemetery
2116 Chestnut Street

Strong Vincent was a hero at the Battle of Gettysburg, where he sealed with his life the spot entrusted to his keeping and on which so much depended. He was born in Waterford, Pennsylvania (near Erie), on June 17, 1837. He attended Trinity College in Hartford, Connecticut, and graduated from Harvard University in 1859. He was practicing law in Erie when the Civil War broke out. He immediately joined the Pennsylvania militia as a first lieutenant, and on September 14, 1861, he was commissioned lieutenant colonel of the 83rd Pennsylvania Infantry. He was promoted to colonel the following June.

Vincent looked like a soldier should look. He was athletic, barrel-chested, and disciplined. He married his wife, Elizabeth, the same day he enlisted. She was a skilled horsewoman and gave Vincent her riding crop to keep with him for luck. In one of his letters to her, he wrote: "If I fall, remember you have given your husband to the most righteous cause that ever widowed a woman."

In 1862, Vincent fought in the Peninsula Campaign and assumed command of the regiment when his regimental commander was killed on June 27 at the Battle of Gaines's Mill. He then developed a severe case of malaria and was hospitalized until the Battle of Fredericksburg in December of that year. It was around this time that Vincent was offered the position of Judge Advocate for the Army of the Potomac. This position would have assured his safety and his success in civilian

Strong Vincent

life after the war. He declined the position, saying he had joined the army to fight.

On May 20, 1863, Vincent assumed command of the 3rd Brigade, 1st Division, V (Fifth Army) Corps, replacing his brigade commander who was killed at the Battle of Chancellorsville. He turned 26 on the march to Gettysburg and had recently learned that his wife was pregnant with their first child.

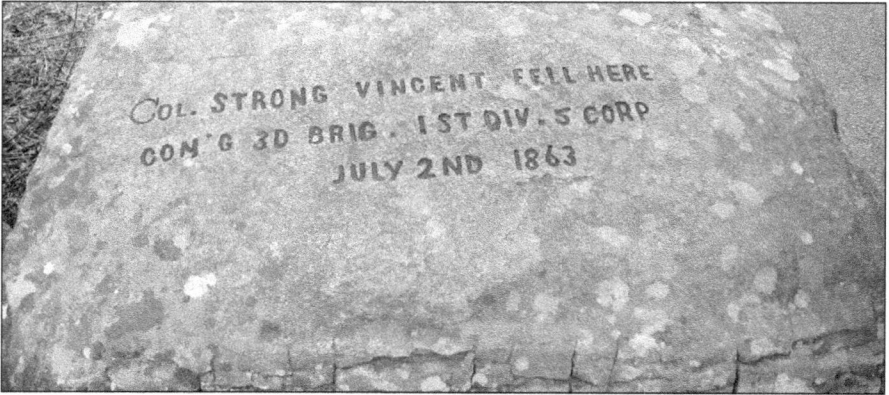

Stone marking where Vincent fell at Gettysburg (photo by Joe Farrell)

At the Battle of Gettysburg, Vincent and his brigade arrived on July 2, the second day of battle. Due to a move against orders, General Daniel Sickles had left a significant terrain feature, Little Round Top, undefended. General Gouverneur K. Warren, the chief engineer of the Army, saw the vital position uncovered and sent for help. He sent couriers scrambling for anyone to occupy and hold the position before the Confederates could. One of the couriers ran into Vincent's brigade and explained the situation. Vincent, without consulting his superior officers, rushed his troops to the hill. His regiments were the 16th Michigan, the 44th New York, the 83rd Pennsylvania, and the 20th Maine, and they were the extreme left flank of the Union line.

The now-famous Colonel Joshua Lawrence Chamberlain led the 20th Maine, and they were the end of the line on the left. Vincent impressed upon Chamberlain the importance of his position ("hold the ground at all hazards"), and then he went to attend to the brigade's right flank. They were attacked within minutes. As the fighting escalated, the 16th Michigan got into trouble and was starting to yield to enemy pressure. Vincent mounted a large boulder and, brandishing his wife's riding crop, cried out to his men, "Don't give an inch!" Moments later, a bullet tore through his thigh and groin and lodged somewhere inside his body. The line held, and Vincent was carried to the Bushman barn nearby. He lingered there for five days and died on July 7, 1863. General George

Stone marker on the Gettysburg battlefield (photo by Joe Farrell)

Meade recommended the promotion to brigadier general, which was approved on July 3, 1863, but it is doubtful that Vincent knew about the honor before he died.

Vincent's wife gave birth to a daughter two months later. Sadly, the baby girl, Blanche, lived only a year. She was buried next to her father in Erie Cemetery. In Gettysburg, there is a monument to Strong Vincent on the south slope of Little Round Top. There is also a carving in a rock marking the spot where he fell nearby. In his hometown of Erie, Strong Vincent High School is named in his honor, and there is a statue of Vincent at Erie's Blasco Library.

One can only speculate on what a future Strong Vincent may have had before him had he survived the war. He was a leader, a bright, educated, handsome, articulate man; and the best and brightest of that time. His country was struggling for its life, and he willingly gave his in that cause.

If You Go:

Also buried in Erie Cemetery is Civil War Medal of Honor recipient William Young (*see* Chapter 35), and two Civil War Union brevet brigadier generals: Hiram Loomis Brown, who commanded the 145th Pennsylvania Infantry and was wounded at the Battle of Gettysburg; and David Berkley McCreary, also of the 145th Pennsylvania, who was captured at the Battle of Chancellorsville and after the war served as Adjutant General of the Pennsylvania National Guard from 1867 to 1870.

19.

SAMUEL W. CRAWFORD

The Surgeon General

County: Philadelphia • Town: Philadelphia
Buried at Laurel Hill Cemetery
3822 Ridge Avenue

"I must sustain with honor my flag and the reputation of the name I bear." —*Samuel W. Crawford, delivering his lifelong motto while serving at Fort Sumter.*

Samuel Wylie Crawford was one of only two individuals who were present at Fort Sumter, the outbreak of the Civil War, and at Appomattox Court House for the surrender (the other was General Truman Seymour). Born in Fayetteville, Franklin County, Pennsylvania (just across South Mountain from Gettysburg) on November 8, 1829, Crawford pursued medical studies at the University of Pennsylvania, graduating in 1850. He subsequently joined the Army as a surgeon, serving as such until the outbreak of hostilities in Charleston Harbor in 1861. When the Confederates opened fire on Fort Sumter, commencing what would be a long and bloody war, Crawford commanded several of the cannon that returned fire. A month after this action, Crawford changed career paths, abandoning the surgeon role for a commission as a major in the 13th U.S. Infantry.

By April 25, 1862, Crawford was promoted to brigadier general of volunteers but had yet to see much action. On June 26, Crawford was assigned to Major General John Pope's newly constituted Union "Army of Virginia." The first action of the campaign was at Cedar Mountain on August 9, 1862. Crawford's brigade launched a surprise attack upon

Brigadier General Samuel Wylie Crawford

the Confederate left, routing a division that included the Stonewall Brigade. The Confederates counterattacked, however, and Crawford's brigade, which was unsupported by other units, was driven back with 50% casualties.

An interesting meeting occurred the day after Cedar Mountain. During a truce for burying the dead, Crawford met Rebel cavalry chief

J.E.B. Stuart, whom he had known in the Old Army, on the field. Stuart bet Crawford a hat that the Federals would claim Cedar Mountain had been a Union victory. In due time, under a flag of truce, a hat had arrived at the outpost for Stuart and with it a copy of a New York paper that proclaimed a triumph for Pope in that action. That hat shortly gained notoriety when it was captured in a Union cavalry raid that nearly netted Stuart himself at the start of the Second Bull Run Campaign.

The following month, on September 17, 1862, during what is known as the 'bloodiest single-day battle in American history,' Crawford was heavily engaged at the Battle of Antietam. When the commander of the XII Corps, Major General Joseph K. Mansfield, was killed early at Antietam, the next in line—General Alpheus S. Williams—was elevated and assumed temporary command of the corps. Since Williams was Crawford's superior, Crawford was elevated to Williams's former position. His opportunity was short, however, as Crawford was soon shot in the right thigh and bled profusely. He stayed on the field until he was weakened by the loss of blood and was carried off. Due to the nature of his wounds, he convalesced at his father's home for eight months.

In May of 1863, Crawford returned to the Army, following in the footsteps of Generals John F. Reynolds (*see* Chapter 12) and George G. Meade (*see* Chapter 13) as the commander of the Pennsylvania Reserves Division. In late June, in response to Lee's invasion of the North, the Pennsylvania Reserves were added to the Army of the Potomac. On July 2, 1863, the second day of the battle, Crawford and his division arrived at Gettysburg, under the command of Major General George Sykes. Crawford was ordered to assist the brigade of Colonel Strong Vincent (*see* Chapter 18) at Little Round Top but did not arrive in time to see any action.

Meanwhile, General James Longstreet's Confederates had swept through the Devil's Den, driving the Union defenders back to the west of Little Round Top, to an area that became known to the soldiers as "the Valley of Death." Crawford's division swept down the slope of Little Round Top along with the brigades of Colonels William McCandless and David J. Nevin. While McCandless's brigade led the charge, Crawford

Bronze statue of Crawford on the Gettysburg battlefield (photo by Tammi Knorr)

seized the colors of the First Pennsylvania Reserves from a surprised Corporal Bertless Slot. After a brief struggle and with Corporal Slot running alongside his horse grasping his pant leg, Crawford led his division in a charge that cleared the Valley of Death and, in his estimation, saved Little Round Top.

The following is Crawford's report of the action on July 2:

"The firing in front was heavy and incessant. The enemy,
concentrating his forces opposite the left of our line, was
throwing them in heavy masses upon our troops and was
steadily advancing. Our troops in front, after a determined
resistance, unable to withstand the force of the enemy, fell back,
and some finally gave way. The plain to my front was covered
with fugitives from all divisions, who rushed through my lines
and along the road to the rear. Fragments of regiments came
back in disorder, and without their arms, and for a moment,
all seemed lost. The enemy's skirmishers had reached the foot
of the rocky ridge; his columns were following rapidly . . . Not
a moment was to be lost. Uncovering our front, I ordered an
immediate advance. The command advanced gallantly with
loud cheers. Two well-directed volleys were delivered upon
the advancing masses of the enemy, when the whole column
charged at a run down the slope, driving the enemy back across
the space beyond and across the stone wall, for the possession
of which there was a short but determined struggle. The enemy
retired to the wheat-field and the woods."

Although this was a relatively minor engagement and casualties
were light, Crawford spent the remainder of his life basking in the glory
of Little Round Top. The next day, the final day of battle, Crawford
was again engaged in a heated struggle, this time with the troops from
Georgia and Texas:

"The line was then formed, and, under the immediate direction
of Colonel McCandless, dashed across the wheat-field and
into the upper end of the woods. The enemy's skirmishers
were driven back as he advanced, and the upper end of the
woods was now cleared. The command then changed front
to rear and charged through the entire length of woods. One

brigade of the enemy, commanded by Brigadier General Anderson and composed of Georgia troops, was encountered. It had taken position behind a stone wall running through the woods, and which they had made stronger by rails and logs. We fell upon their flank, completely routing them, taking over 200 prisoners, one stand of colors belonging to the Fifteenth Georgia, and many arms. The colors were taken by Sergt. John B. Thompson, Company G, First Rifles. Another brigade, under General Robertson, and composed of Texas troops, which lay concealed beyond the woods and near the foot of the ridge, ran, as reported by the prisoners, without firing a shot. The enemy's force at this point consisted of the division of Major-General Hood and was composed of three brigades, under the rebel Generals Anderson, Robertson, and Benning. They very greatly outnumbered us, but the rapidity of the movement and the gallant dash of my men completely surprised and routed them. They fell back nearly a mile to a second ridge and entrenched themselves. By this charge of McCandless' brigade and the Eleventh Regiment, Colonel Jackson, the whole of the ground lost the previous day, was retaken, together with all of our wounded, who, mingled with those of the rebels, were lying uncared for. The dead of both sides lay in lines in every direction, and the large number of our own men showed how fierce had been the struggle and how faithfully and how persistently they had contested for the field against the superior masses of the enemy. The result of this movement was the recovery of all the ground lost by our troops, one 12-pounder Napoleon gun, and three caissons, and upward of 7,000 stand of arms. Large piles of these arms were found on brush heaps, ready to be burned."

Though Crawford's men only attacked a small contingent of Longstreet's men on July 2, he later claimed that he had "completely surprised and routed" most of Hood's division. A few months after

Gettysburg, Crawford had the nerve to ask George Sykes to confirm claims which overstated Crawford's division's achievements to the detriment of Sykes's old Regular Division. Sykes refused Crawford's request, blisteringly.

Crawford remained in command of his division through the Overland Campaign (May/June 1864) and the Siege of Petersburg and was again wounded at the Weldon Railroad on August 18, 1864. Crawford was present for Robert E. Lee's surrender at Appomattox Court House in April 1865, making him one of the few soldiers to be present at both the beginning and the effective end of the Civil War.

After the war, Crawford was prominent in preserving the Gettysburg Battlefield and, at one point, attempted to raise money to cover the hill with a large memorial building and museum dedicated to his division. This plan was a failure, and Little Round Top remains close to its original condition, although sprinkled with smaller monuments. Crawford also spent considerable effort politicking to get the official records of the war changed to acknowledge his role as the savior of Little Round Top, but he

Crawford's grave (photo by Joe Farrell)

was also unsuccessful in that quest. Frank Wheaton commented wryly on Crawford's selfishness: "Crawford's innate modesty never prevented his appropriating his full share of all that was done by his division and by [Nevins's Sixth Corps brigade] that afternoon at Gettysburg." Crawford's attempts to garner acclaim, not due him, reached a pathetic state when, after the war, he offered former Confederate Maj. Gen. McLaws "a grade in the army" in exchange for a written acknowledgment that the Pennsylvania Reserves had driven back his forces on July 2nd. McLaws declined.

Crawford was a man very full of himself, never shy about taking full credit for his own and others' achievements on the battlefield. He was "a tall, chesty, glowering man, with heavy eyes, a big nose, and bushy whiskers," as one of his comrades remembered him, who "wore habitually a turn-out-the-guard expression." This description did not do justice to his spectacular sideburns, which reached to his shoulders. He was quite showy, mounted on a handsome "blood bay" horse given to him by Major General William S. Rosecrans. Joshua Chamberlain described him with a slightly acid tone as:

"a conscientious gentleman, having the entrée at all headquarters, somewhat lofty of manner, not of the iron fiber, nor spring of steel, but punctilious in a way, obeying orders in a certain literal fashion that saved him the censure of superiors—a pet of his State, and likewise, we thought, of Meade and Warren, judging from the attention they always gave him— possibly not quite fairly estimated by his colleagues as a military man . . ."

Crawford retired from the Army on February 19, 1873, and was given the rank of brigadier general, U.S. Army Retired. He was the author of *The Genesis of the Civil War*, published in 1887. On November 3, 1892, he died in Philadelphia and was buried there in Laurel Hill Cemetery.

If You Go:

Also buried in Laurel Hill Cemetery are four men who were brevet-ted brigadier generals in March or April 1865 for "meritorious service." They are:

• **Alexander Cummings:** nicknamed "Old Straw Hat." He served as commander of the 19th Pennsylvania Volunteer Cavalry, and as the Superintendent of Colored Troops in the Department of Arkansas after the Union opted to allow black troops into the army.

• **Robert Thompson:** commanded the 115th Pennsylvania Volunteer Infantry.

• **William Redwood Price:** served in a variety of administrative posts in Washington, D.C.

• **William Delaware Lewis, Jr.:** commanded the 110th Pennsylvania Volunteer Infantry.

20.

SAMUEL K. ZOOK

The Mennonite Master of Profanity

County: Montgomery • Town: Norristown
Buried at Montgomery Cemetery
1 Hartranft Avenue

From his obelisk monument at the Wheatfield on the Gettysburg Battlefield:

To the memory of
Samuel
Kosciusko Zook.
Brevet Major
General U.S. Vols.
Who fell mortally
wounded at or near
this spot. while
gallantly leading
his brigade in battle
July 2nd, 1863.
Erected by Gen. Zook
Post. No 11 G.A.R.
of Norristown, Pa.
July 25th, 1882.

General Samuel Kosciuszko Zook (born Samuel Kurtz Zook) (March 27, 1821–July 3, 1863) was born and raised in Tredyffrin Township, Chester County, Pennsylvania, not far from George Washington's

Samuel K. Zook

Valley Forge encampment. On his father's side, he was descended from Mennonites; specifically, the Anabaptist order started by Menno Simmons in Switzerland. As a boy, Zook played soldier on the earthworks where the Revolutionary War soldiers roamed. His grandfather Zook was a major during the American Revolution. As a young man, he decided to take Kosciuszko as his middle name, in honor of the Revolutionary

131

War general from Poland who assisted the Americans. Of course, all this martial activity among the Zooks is contrary to the pacifist practices of the Mennonites. The Zooks had not been pacifists for several generations.

In the years before the Civil War, Zook was a pioneer in the information technology of his day—the telegraph. As Kenneth Silverman writes in his book *Lightning Man: The Accursed Life of Samuel B. Morse*:

> "On the New Orleans route, O'Reilly intended to use what he advertised as 'A NEW AND IMPROVED TELEGRAPH (and NOT Morse's plan).' Not Morse's, or House's either. While publicly beating the drum for House's telegraph, he had always privately thought it 'not simple enough.' For his potentially lucrative line to New Orleans, he chose an instrument called the Columbian telegraph, designed by two young telegraphers in his Cincinnati office, Samuel K. Zook and E. F. Barnes. Admirers of the Columbian alleged that it differed from Morse's system in two ways. Its registers used permanent magnets instead of electromagnets; and it had a novel galvanometer-like relay that supposedly protected transmission during thunderstorms. . . ."

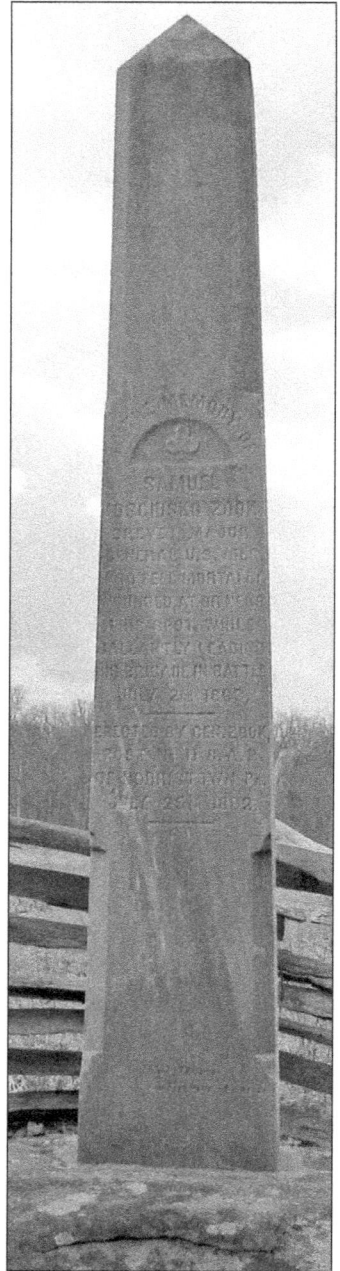

Zook's obelisk

Morse thought this was an infringement of his patent and the two sides battled for years in the marketplace. When the patent suit was heard in September 1848, the judge ruled for Morse. O'Reilly was not deterred and continued his battles for several more years before eventually relenting. Zook, meanwhile, moved to New York City and became the superintendent of the Washington and New York Telegraph Company. While in New York, he had risen to lieutenant colonel in the 6th New York Governor's Guard by the time of the Civil War.

During the summer of 1861, while with the 6th New York Militia, Zook served as the military governor of Annapolis. When this 90-day regiment was mustered out (thanks to connections made in Annapolis), he raised a new regiment—the 57th New York, to which he was the colonel.

Zook's first action was in 1862, serving in Major General Edwin V. Sumner's division of the Army of the Potomac, during the Seven Days Battles. While scouting enemy positions at the Battle of Gaines's Mill, Zook noticed a Confederate deception regarding troop numbers. Zook reported this discovery up to General George McClellan but was ignored, and an opportunity was lost.

Zook missed the Battle of Antietam while on medical leave but returned in time for Fredericksburg. There, he served in the division of Major General Winfield S. Hancock (*see* Chapter 14). Zook's brigade arrived early at the battle. Zook recognized the Union could gain a significant advantage if he could cross the Rappahannock River immediately. However, the new commander of the Army of the Potomac, Ambrose Burnside, preferred to wait until more troops arrived, and pontoon bridges could be put in place. Wrote Zook of this missed opportunity:

"If we had had the pontoons promised when we arrived here,
we could have the hills on the other side of the river without
cost over 50 men—now it will cost at least 10,000 if not more."

While he waited, Zook served as military governor of Falmouth, Virginia. During the ensuing battle, Zook's brigade led the first assault on Marye's Heights, achieving one of the farthest advances of the battle.

Zook had his horse shot out from under him as the Confederates repulsed the attack. Hancock was incredibly pleased with Zook's bravery on the field. In March 1863, Zook was promoted to brigadier general. Zook wrote about the Fredericksburg battle:

> "I walked over the field, close under the enemy's picket line, last night about 3 o'clock. The ground was strewn thickly with corpses of the heroes who perished there on Saturday. I never realized before what war was. I never before felt so horribly since I was born. To see men dashed to pieces by shot & torn into shreds by shells during the heat and crash of battle is bad enough, God knows, but to walk alone amongst slaughtered brave in the 'still small hours' of the night would make the bravest man living 'blue.' God grant, I may never have to repeat my last night's experience." —*Samuel K. Zook, letter to E. I. Wade, December 16, 1862*

Zook had a reputation for being a disciplinarian and a master of profanity, despite his Mennonite background. While on the road to Chancellorsville, he was one half of a famous battle of profanity with General Hancock. Wrote an enlisted man about the incident: "It was the greatest cursing match I ever listened to; Zook took advantage of Hancock, by waiting until the latter got out of breath, and then he opened his pipe organ, and the air was very blue."

Zook fought at Chancellorsville and then missed some time due to rheumatism. He returned to the field in time for Gettysburg, where he served under Brigadier General John C. Caldwell. On the second day, at the Wheatfield, while reinforcing Stony Hill, which was under attack by Longstreet, Zook was shot three times in the shoulder, chest, and abdomen. He was moved to the Hoke house on the Baltimore Pike, in the care of Dr. William Potter, a friend of the general. Wrote Potter about Zook's wounds: "fatally shot, a shell having torn open his left shoulder and chest, exposing the heart-beats to observation."

Zook's grave

Zook succumbed to his wounds the next day. He was posthumously awarded the rank of major general. Samuel K. Zook is buried near his good friend and cursing partner General Winfield S. Hancock, at Montgomery Cemetery, near Norristown, Pennsylvania.

If You Go:

See the *"If You Go"* sections of Chapter 14 (Winfield Hancock) and Chapter 8 (John Hartranft).

21.

GETTYSBURG GENERALS

This chapter will feature several generals who fought at the monumental Battle of Gettysburg: David Bell Birney; Alexander Hays; Thomas Rowley; David McMurtrie Gregg; and Alexander Schimmelfennig.

David Bell Birney

County: Philadelphia • Town: Philadelphia
Buried at Woodlands Cemetery
4000 Woodlands Cemetery

David Bell Birney was a controversial figure. He was the son of James B. Birney, a Kentuckian who had once owned slaves but later became one of the country's most vehement abolitionists. Birney's father had an international reputation; he ran twice for President (1840 and 1844) and published a weekly abolitionist publication while living in Cincinnati, Ohio.

When the Civil War broke out, Birney was practicing law in Philadelphia very successfully and had many influential clients and friends. The family had moved to Philadelphia because of numerous threats from pro-slavery mobs. Birney foresaw the coming of the war; in 1860, he began studying military science and

General Birney

got appointed as a lieutenant colonel of the Pennsylvania militia. When the war began, he was appointed to colonel in August 1861, and then to brigadier general in February 1862. These were purely political promotions, however, and they spawned a lot of envy and resentment. At the Battle of Seven Pines, Virginia, on May 31, 1862, he was removed from command and accused of disobeying an order from corps command. He was court-martialed but acquitted and restored to command.

Birney fought at the Second Battle of Bull Run, losing over 600 men in

Birney's grave

intense fighting. While fighting at Fredericksburg, he again encountered military discipline problems for balking at an order—yet once again, he was ultimately able to escape punishment. He went on to lead his brigades in extremely heavy fighting at Chancellorsville, suffering still more heavy casualties. After Chancellorsville, he was promoted to major general.

On the second day of the Battle of Gettysburg, Birney was part of General Daniel Sickles's insubordinate and foolish abandonment of their assigned defensive position on Cemetery Ridge and subsequent movement to Devil's Den, the Wheatfield, and the Peach Orchard. They were attacked and decimated by Confederate troops under the command of Generals Hood and McLaws. Birney himself received two minor wounds. The entire III (Third Army) Corps was finished as a fighting force.

He emerged months later as division commander in II (Second Army) Corps and served well in the Wilderness, Spotsylvania Court House (where he was again wounded), and Cold Harbor. In July 1864, General Grant gave Birney command of X (Tenth Army) Corps in the Army of the James. During the Siege of Petersburg, he fell ill with typhoid fever.

He returned to Philadelphia, where he died on October 18, 1864. He is buried in Woodlands Cemetery.

If You Go:

Woodlands Cemetery is itself a National Historic Landmark and has many interesting graves and noteworthy people buried there. There are several other Civil War generals buried there. Among them are:

• **Brevet Brigadier General Hartman Bache**, who was a great-grandson of Benjamin Franklin and brother-in-law of General George Meade.

• **Brevet Major General James Gwyn**, who distinguished himself in the Battle of Poplar Spring Church and the Battle of Five Forks.

• **Brevet Brigadier General Charles Herring**, who lost his right leg at the Battle of Dabney's Mills, Virginia, and gained distinction at the Battle of Hatcher's Run, Virginia.

• **Brevet Brigadier General James Lynch**, who was cited for his action at the Battle of Deep Bottom, Virginia.

• **Brevet Brigadier General John Abercrombie**, who was wounded at the Battle of Fair Oaks, Virginia, and was one of the oldest officers to serve on the battlefield.

• **Brevet Major General George Crosman**, who served as Chief Quartermaster of the Philadelphia Depot.

• **Brevet Major General John Ely,** who served as commander of the 23rd Pennsylvania Volunteer Infantry.

• **Brevet Brigadier General Clement Finley,** who served as Surgeon General of the Army when the war broke out (retiring in 1862).

• **Brevet Brigadier General John Quincy Lane,** who served as colonel and commander of the 97th Ohio Volunteer Infantry.

• **Brevet Brigadier General Richard Price,** who as commander of the 2nd Pennsylvania Volunteer Cavalry, gained distinction by capturing the colonel of the 6th Virginia Cavalry in September 1862.

Also buried at Woodlands Cemetery are two Civil War Medal of Honor recipients: Sylvester Bonnaffon, Jr., and Thomas Cripps. Bonnaffon was awarded the Medal of Honor for his service at the Battle of Boydton Plank

Road, Virginia, where he was severely wounded. Cripps was awarded the Medal of Honor for bravery during the Union naval assault on Mobile Bay, Alabama, on August 5, 1864.

There is also a large, prominent grave in Woodlands for Henry Boyd McKeen, who served as colonel of the 81st Pennsylvania Volunteer Infantry. He was wounded at Chancellorsville and led his regiment in the Wheatfield and Rose Woods on the second day at Gettysburg, as well as the battles of the Wilderness and Spotsylvania. He was killed at the Battle of Cold Harbor.

Woodlands is also the final resting place for Civil War figures Dr. Jacob Mendez Da Costa and Emily Bliss Souder. Dr. Da Costa was the first to identify what has become known as "post-traumatic stress disorder" while serving as an assistant surgeon in the Union Army. He called it "irritable heart" or "soldier's heart," and later, it became known as Da Costa syndrome. Souder was a volunteer nurse at the Battle of Gettysburg and author of *Leaves from the Battlefield of Gettysburg*, published in 1864.

Alexander Hays

County: Allegheny • Town: Pittsburgh (Lawrenceville)
Buried at Allegheny Cemetery
4734 Butler Street

Alexander Hays was born in Franklin, Pennsylvania, on July 8, 1819. He attended Allegheny College and then transferred to the United States Military Academy, where he became a close friend of Ulysses S. Grant. He served in the Mexican American War then returned to civilian life and was a civil engineer for the city of Pittsburgh when the Civil War broke out. He re-entered the service as colonel of the 63rd Pennsylvania Infantry. He led his troops in battles at Yorktown, Williamsburg, Seven Pines, Savage's Station, and Malvern Hill, after which he suffered blindness in his right eye and partial paralysis of his left arm.

He returned to duty in time for the Second Battle of Bull Run, where he led a charge and received a painful wound that shattered his leg and put him out of action for many months.

Hays was a fiery, emotional fighter and had an extraordinary intensity when he returned to command at Gettysburg. His division defended the right of the Union line on Cemetery Ridge. They held firm in the repulse of the Confederate attack on July 3, even counterattacking the left flank of the Confederate force. When the smoke cleared, Hays was unhurt but had had two horses shot from under him. In his exhilaration, he grabbed a Rebel battle flag and rode down his division's line dragging it in the dirt behind his horse. After the battle, Hays explained:

> "I was fighting for my native state, and before I went [in] I thought of those at home I so dearly love. If Gettysburg was lost all was lost for them, and I only interposed a life that would be otherwise worthless."

Hays went on to lead a division at the Battle of Morton's Ford, where there were stories of him being drunk during battle.

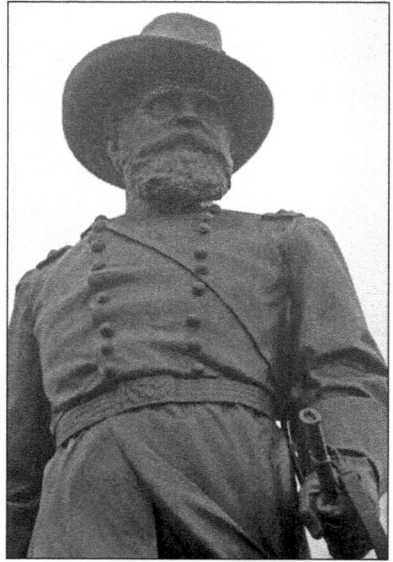

Bronze statue of General Hays at Gettysburg (Photo by Tammi Knorr)

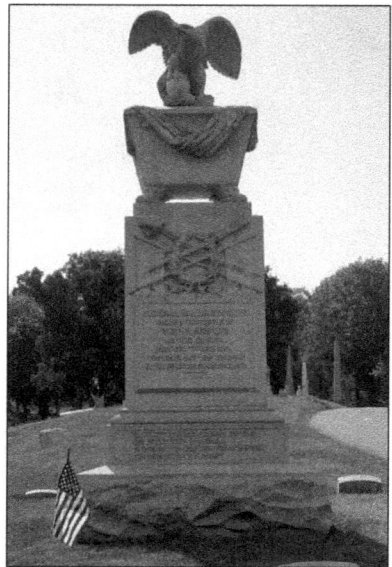

Grave of General Hays

On the first day of the Battle of the Wilderness, May 5, 1864 (during the earliest phase of the Overland Campaign), Hays was killed when a Confederate bullet struck him in the head.

Hays was buried in Allegheny Cemetery in Pittsburgh. Ulysses S. Grant visited Hays's grave during a campaign stop in his run for the presidency. Grant wept openly for his friend. A statue of General Hays stands on the Gettysburg Battlefield (at Cemetery Ridge), and a monument marks the spot where he was killed in the Wilderness.

If You Go:

Allegheny Cemetery is a large, historical treasure with many interesting graves. Thomas Rowley is buried there (see next page), as are Medal of Honor Recipients Archibald Rowand (*see* Chapter 35) and Major General Alfred Pearson (*see* Chapter 33).

Also of interest are the graves of Brigadier General Conrad Jackson, who was killed at the Battle of Fredericksburg, and Brigadier General James Scott Negley, who commanded Union forces at the Battle of Chattanooga and was relieved of his command after the defeat at Chickamauga.

Thomas Rowley

County: Allegheny • Town: Pittsburgh (Lawrenceville)
Buried at Allegheny Cemetery
4734 Butler Street

Thomas Algeo Rowley was born in Pittsburgh on October 5, 1808. He entered the United States military service in the Mexican War as a captain of a company of volunteers in 1847. He served with this company until July 1848, when he was honorably mustered out and returned to peaceful pursuits as a cabinet maker.

At the start of the Civil War, Rowley was a clerk of the courts for Allegheny County when commissioned a major in the 13th Pennsylvania Volunteers. After a few months, the army was reorganized, and he was promoted to colonel of the 102nd Pennsylvania Infantry. He led forces in the Peninsula Campaign at Yorktown, Williamsburg, Fair Oaks (where he was wounded), and Malvern Hill. He distinguished himself at the Battle of Fredericksburg and was promoted to brigadier general on November 29, 1862. He next commanded a brigade at the Battle of Chancellorsville.

General Rowley

The day before the Battle of Gettysburg, Rowley was given command of a division due to the death of General John Reynolds (*see* Chapter 12). What happened on July 1, 1863, the first day of the battle, is mired in controversy. The I (First) Army Corps line gave way under the Confederate onslaught led by General Harry Heth. The Union troops retreated through the streets of Gettysburg to the heights of Cemetery Hill. During this retreat, Rowley—who suffered from severe boils that made it difficult for him to remain on his mount—fell from his horse. Soon after that, he had a confrontation with Brigadier General Lysander Cutler, who concluded from

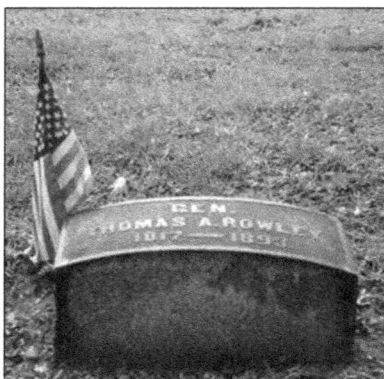

General Rowley's grave

Rowley's actions and demeanor that he was drunk. Rowley was placed under arrest for drunkenness and disobedience. A court-martial subsequently convicted him.

The testimony was conflicting. Rowley's inexperience, distracting, and painful physical ailment, and the blistering heat may have led to his strange behavior. His alleged drunkenness was never proven to the satisfaction of Secretary of War Edwin Stanton, who reinstated him. When assigned only a district command and not a field command, Rowley resigned in December 1864.

After the war, Rowley served as a U.S. marshal and practiced law. He died on May 14, 1892, and is buried in Allegheny Cemetery. A book entitled *Disgrace at Gettysburg: The Arrest and Court Martial of Brigadier General Thomas A. Rowley*, was written by John F. Krumwiede and published in 2006.

David McMurtrie Gregg

County: Berks • Town: Reading
Buried at Charles Evans Cemetery
1119 Centre Avenue

David McMurtrie Gregg was born in Huntingdon, Pennsylvania, on April 10, 1833. He was the first cousin of future Pennsylvania Governor Andrew Curtin (*see* Chapter 3). He graduated from the United States Military Academy in 1855. While a cadet, he came to know J.E.B. Stuart, who was a year ahead of him. His first assignment was in the New Mexico Territory as a company commander in the 1st U.S. Dragoons. When Fort Sumter was attacked, Gregg was called to Washington and assigned to the cavalry. In October 1861, he was stricken with a severe case of typhoid fever and was hospitalized in Washington. While there, he barely escaped death when the hospital caught fire. When he recovered, he became the colonel of the 8th Pennsylvania Cavalry. The 8th

Equestrian statue of General Gregg at Centre Avenue in Reading, Pennsylvania (photo by Lawrence Knorr)

Pennsylvania took part in the Peninsula Campaign, particularly in the Seven Days Battle, where they served as a screen between the Confederates and the retreating Union Army. He was at Antietam, but cavalry played a minor role.

While on furlough on October 6, 1862, Gregg married Ellen Sheaff at St. Thomas Church in Whitemarsh, Pennsylvania. After honeymooning in New York City, he was promoted to brigadier general and sent to participate in the Battle of Fredericksburg, where again, the cavalry was held in reserve and underutilized. At Chancellorsville, the Cavalry Corps (including Gregg's 3rd Division) were ineffective, and General Alfred Pleasonton was put in charge of the Cavalry Corps replacing General George Stoneman.

In early June, the Federal Cavalry was again reorganized, and Gregg was made commander of the 2nd Division. As the Confederate troops moved north into Pennsylvania, his division engaged them at Aldie (June 17), Middleburg (June 18-19), and Upperville (June 21). Gregg's division arrived in Gettysburg mid-day on July 2 and took up positions to protect the right flank of the Union Army. On July 3, Gregg's division, along with General Custer's brigade, met J.E.B. Stuart's cavalry in what is now called "East Cavalry Field." A lengthy mounted battle—including hand-to-hand combat—ensued. Stuart was blocked from achieving his goals.

Gregg led his cavalry division in almost two years of hard fighting after Gettysburg, including the Battle of Yellow Tavern, where J.E.B. Stuart—his friend from West Point—was killed, dealing the Confederacy a severe blow.

Gregg resigned his commission on January 25, 1865, for personal reasons. He missed the end of the war, and his real reasons for quitting are not known. In a biography of General John Buford, the writer (Edward Longacre) claims that Gregg feared a violent death and simply lost his nerve.

Final resting place of General Gregg

Gregg was reportedly bored with life as a farmer. He became active in state and local affairs and visited Gettysburg numerous times. In 1891, he was elected to a term as Auditor General of Pennsylvania.

Gregg died in Reading, Pennsylvania, on August 17, 1916, at the age of 83, the last of Pennsylvania's Civil War leaders. He is buried in historical Charles Evans Cemetery and memorialized with a life-sized bronze equestrian statue at North Fourth Street and Centre Avenue in Reading. Buried near Gregg in Charles Evans Cemetery is the prominent grave of Alexander Schimmelfennig (*see below*).

Alexander Schimmelfennig

County: Berks • Town: Reading
Buried at Charles Evans Cemetery
1119 Centre Avenue

Alexander Schimmelfennig was born in Germany in 1824. A graduate of the German military academy, he took part in the failed 1848 German Revolution. He was wounded twice in battle, captured, rescued, and eventually fled to Switzerland. For his involvement, he was tried in absentia and sentenced to death by the Prussian authorities.

In 1854 Schimmelfennig emigrated to the United States. At the start of the Civil War, he joined the Union Army and helped organize the 74th Pennsylvania Volunteer Infantry out of mostly German immigrants; he was commissioned its colonel in July 1861. In August 1862, he fought at the Second Battle of Bull Run and was promoted to brigadier general in

General Schimmelfenning

145

November. He commanded a division of mostly Germans at the Battle of Chancellorsville in May 1863. The Corps performance at Chancellorsville came under significant criticism in the press and by corps commander General Otis Howard, as they engaged in a mass retreat after being flanked by Stonewall Jackson.

At the subsequent Battle of Gettysburg, Schimmelfennig commanded the 1st Brigade in XI Corps. On the first day of the battle, his men were driven back in a retreat through town, and many were captured. During the retreat, Schimmelfennig briefly hid in a culvert on Baltimore Street. Then—stunned from having his horse shot from under him and cut off by the advancing Confederates—Schimmelfennig successfully avoided capture by hiding out in a shed on the Anna Garlach property for several days (until July 4).

After the battle, Schimmelfennig rejoined the corps, but his story was seized upon by the press and was promulgated as yet another example of German cowardice.

In the fall of 1863, he and his brigade were reassigned to the Carolinas

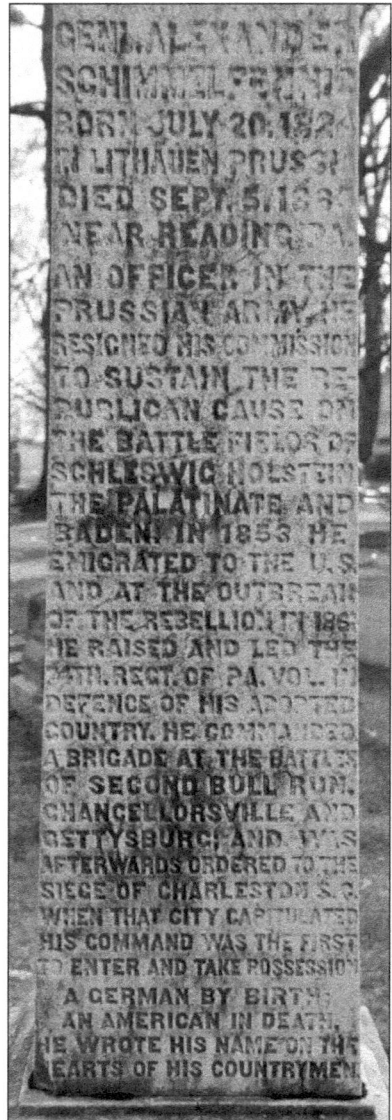

Detail of Schimmelfennig's grave (Photo by Lawrence Knorr)

and participated in the Carolinas Campaign. He was in command in Charleston, South Carolina, when the Confederates surrendered on February 18, 1865.

During his time of service in the swamps around Charleston, he contracted a form of tuberculosis that ultimately led to his death. He died on September 5, 1865, in Wernersville, Pennsylvania, having traveled there to visit a mineral springs sanatorium in the hopes of finding a cure for his disease.

If You Go:

Also, in historic Charles Evans Cemetery is the grave of Brigadier General William High Keim. Keim was a U.S. Congressman and Mayor of Reading before the war. He was commissioned general of the Pennsylvania militia and then brigadier general of volunteers. He participated in the Peninsula Campaign until he died of typhus in Harrisburg on May 18, 1862.

22.

DENNIS O'KANE
The Fighting Irishman

County: Philadelphia • Town: Philadelphia
Buried at Old Cathedral Cemetery
48th Street & Lancaster Avenue

He was born in Derry, Ireland, in 1818. He left Ireland and came to America with a wife and two daughters. After settling in Philadelphia, he and his wife had their third daughter. On July 3, 1863, he found himself on Cemetery Ridge in Gettysburg, commanding the 69th Pennsylvania Volunteers. His name was Dennis O'Kane.

The 69th Pennsylvania was part of the Philadelphia Brigade. It was made up mainly of Irish immigrants or the children of Irish immigrants. The 69th had been involved in numerous battles, including the Second Bull Run, South Mountain, Antietam, Fredericksburg, Chancellorsville, and Gettysburg.

O'Kane almost did not make it to Gettysburg. Nine months earlier, he had faced a court-martial. At the time, the 69th was at Harpers Ferry, and O'Kane's wife and eldest daughter had come to visit him. O'Kane rented a carriage and horses and proceeded to show his wife and daughter around the town. During the trip, O'Kane's commanding officer, Colonel Joshua Owen, showed up drunk and on horseback. He proceeded to guide his mount against the carriage horses. When he repeated the maneuver, O'Kane called out to him to stop it. At that point, Owen called O'Kane an Irish son of a bitch, and then he invited O'Kane's wife to spend the night with him in his tent. O'Kane immediately jumped from the carriage, grabbed Owen, and pulled him from his horse. Owen's head bounced as it hit the ground. This led to O'Kane's court-martial,

Dennis O'Kane

but he was acquitted. It also led to the dismissal of Owen and O'Kane's rise to command the 69th.

O'Kane was present on the third day of the Battle of Gettysburg when the Confederate cannons began the bombardment that would precede Pickett's Charge. During the shelling, O'Kane observed General Hancock calmly riding among the troops who had hit the ground for protection. Hancock, who had presided at O'Kane's court-martial, waved to O'Kane, and O'Kane responded with a salute.

Currier and Ives print of the highwater mark at Gettysburg

When the shelling ended and the smoke lifted, O'Kane could see the Confederates emerging from the woods on Seminary Ridge, making their way towards his troops. O'Kane reminded the men of the 69th that they were fighting today to protect their state. He ordered the 69th's colors uncased, and the green flag with a golden harp on one side and the Pennsylvania coat of arms on the other was soon in the air.

The Union artillery opened on the advancing Confederates, opening holes in their lines that other rebel soldiers rushed to fill as the charge continued. The soldiers of the 69th watched from behind a stone wall as the Confederates drew nearer. When a section of the Union line manned by the 71st Pennsylvania retreated, the 69th was unprotected on its right side. The Confederate General Lewis Armistead, with his hat resting on the tip of his sword, led his men toward that very spot. O'Kane then ordered his men to turn to the right and face the enemy. During the fighting that followed, O'Kane saw General Armistead collapse after being wounded. Shortly after that, O'Kane himself was seriously wounded and had to be removed from the field but not before knowing that his troops had played a crucial part in repulsing the Confederate attack.

O'Kane's grave

O'Kane died the next day, July 4, 1863. His funeral was held in Philadelphia at Saint James Church. His pallbearers were Union Army officers. After mass, his remains were transported to Cathedral Cemetery where he was laid to rest with full military honors.

If You Go:

Civil War Brigadier General Richard Dillon is also buried at Cathedral Cemetery. Dillon lost an arm at the Battle of Chancellorsville. He was brevetted brigadier general on March 13, 1865, for gallant and meritorious service during the war.

Cathedral Cemetery is also the final resting place for Civil War Medal of Honor recipient Edmund English. He received this honor for his actions during the Battle of the Wilderness. His citation reads that "during a rout and under orders to retreat, seized the colors, rallied the men, and drove the enemy back."

Also, Civil War Union Brevet Major General and Medal of Honor recipient St. Clair Augustine Mulholland was laid to rest at Cathedral Cemetery (*see* Chapter 11).

23.

GINNIE WADE
A Tragic Love Story

County: Adams • Town: Gettysburg
Buried at Evergreen Cemetery
799 Baltimore Street

On June 26, 1863, the Confederate troops first entered Gettysburg, and for a twenty-year-old local girl, it was a scary and frantic day. The Confederates had arrested her brother Samuel Wade for failing to obey orders to hand over the family horse to Confederate troops. Mary Virginia (Ginnie or Jennie) Wade was helping to care for Isaac Brinkerhoff, a six-year-old disabled neighborhood boy, when she heard of her brother's arrest and went to try to secure an arrest release from General Jubal Early.

Mary Wade was born on Baltimore Street in Gettysburg on May 21, 1843. When she grew older, she worked as a seamstress with her mother in their house on Breckenridge Street while her father was in a mental asylum. When Union troops arrived on July 1 and shooting began, Ginnie went to her sister's house on Baltimore Street to assist her sister Georgia McClellan with her newborn baby. She never expected that the McClellan house would be situated between Union and Confederate lines during the three-day battle.

As the fighting wore on, Union troops began asking the family for food and water. Surely Ginnie must have thought of her fiancé Johnston (Jack) Skelly, who was serving as a member of the 87th Pennsylvania Volunteer Infantry. She and Skelly and their friend Wesley Culp had been schoolmates who became close friends and often played together on nearby Culp's Hill. Wesley Culp had moved to Virginia and enlisted with the 2nd Virginia Infantry and was now engaged in a great battle on the

Mary Virginia "Ginnie" or "Jennie" Wade

farm where he was born and raised. Ginnie decided to do what she could for the Union troops and spent her time filling canteens and baking bread. What she didn't know was that her beloved Jack Skelly had been badly wounded and captured by the Confederates at the battle of Carter's Woods near Winchester, Virginia. Wesley Culp also fought in that battle against her friend, a brother William, and a cousin David Culp. Wesley Culp met up with the wounded Skelly after the battle, and Skelly gave him a message for Ginnie Wade should he make it back to Gettysburg someday. Culp did manage to slip away from the fighting to visit his two sisters on the Culp farm but discovered Ginnie had left her home to stay at her sister's and was in the crossfire between the lines. Shortly after, on July 2, Wesley Culp was killed within sight of the house where he had been born. He was never able to deliver his message to Ginnie Wade.

Ginnie had worked hard for two days, but on July 3, 1863, she awoke at 4:30 in the morning to prepare bread for the Union soldiers. Soon after, the house came under Confederate fire. Georgia McClellan later noted the last words Ginnie spoke to her. According to Georgia, Ginnie said, "If there is anyone in this house that is to be killed today, I hope it is me." According to Georgia, Ginnie didn't want any harm to come to her sister because she had a baby.

That day around 8:30 A.M., Ginnie was kneading dough for bread when a bullet came through a wooden door into the kitchen of the house and struck her in the back, killing her instantly. She had a picture of Jack Skelly in her apron pocket. She was buried in her sister's garden the following day, and her mother baked 15 loaves of bread with the dough Ginnie had kneaded.

She never got Jack Skelly's message, nor the news that he died nine days later on July 12 from his wounds. The two passed away without knowing the other's fate.

In January 1864, her body was relocated to the cemetery of the German Reformed Church on Stratton Street and, in November 1865, again relocated to the Evergreen Cemetery close to Jack Skelly.

Wesley Culp's commanding officer sent his orderly to Culp's sister's to notify them where to find his body. Some say he was never found, but his gun with his name carved in the stock was located. Others say that being a Confederate, he was secretly buried in Evergreen Cemetery. Some believe he was buried in the cellar of the Culp Farm House.

Ginnie Wade was the only civilian killed directly during the battle of Gettysburg. An elaborate monument marks her grave, including an American flag that flies around the clock. The only other site devoted to a woman that shares the distinction of the perpetual flag is that of the Betsy Ross House in Philadelphia.

In 1996, a book about Ginnie Wade was published. It was written by Cindy Small and called *The Jennie Wade Story*. You might notice the different spelling of Ms. Wade's name. Although Cindy Small used the "Jennie," and so does the Jennie Wade House in Gettysburg, the research we did says it is unlikely anyone ever called her Jennie. Her middle name was Virginia, and she was known as Ginnie. A newspaper account of her story shortly after the battle used the name "Jennie," and it spread all over the country.

If You Go:
Gettysburg is a history buff's paradise. The Evergreen Cemetery also contains many historic and interesting graves, including John Burns (*see* Chapter 15) and Major League Baseball Hall of Famer Eddie Plank (see *Keystone Tombstones Volume 2*, Chapter 17). Other graves of interest include James Gettys, the founder of Gettysburg, and a soldier in the Pennsylvania Militia during the Revolution. His wife, Mary Todd, was an ancestor of Mary Todd Lincoln.

The only civilian killed during the Battle of Gettysburg.

Elizabeth Thorn was the caretaker of Evergreen Cemetery during the Civil War. Her husband Peter enlisted in the 138th Pennsylvania and left her to care for the cemetery. She averaged five burials a month until the Battle of Gettysburg. At the time, she was six months pregnant, and her duties became overwhelming. A memorial at the gatehouse depicts a pregnant Elizabeth attending her duties.

Stephen Courson, a former Pittsburgh Steeler who played in two Super Bowl Championship games and authored *False Glory* in 1991, was also laid to rest here. The book tells of steroid use in the NFL.

Jennie Wade's fiancé who died fighting for the Union.

Also in Gettysburg is the famous Battlefield, the National Cemetery (we mention some interesting graves there in the chapter on John Burns), the Eisenhower Farm, and the Jennie Wade house, among other historical sites. The Jennie Wade House is the site of her tragic death on Baltimore Street. The House is marked by over 150 bullet holes and damage caused by an artillery shell.

The Gettysburg Hotel was established in 1797 and is located across the street from the historic Will's House, where President Lincoln stayed and finished the Gettysburg Address. It offers shelter at a reasonable price and contains McClelland's Tavern, a good place to obtain nourishment and replenish your fluids. The Dobbin House Tavern (est. 1776), which has a secret "underground railroad" slave hideout, is another place where the authors have taken some comfort. The Farnsworth House offers Ghost Tours and a bookstore with many publications of local interest. We also stopped for a pint at O'Rorkes Eatery and Spirits on Steinwehr Avenue.

24.

JOHN C. PEMBERTON

The Defender of Vicksburg

County: Philadelphia • Town: Philadelphia
Buried at Laurel Hill Cemetery
3822 Ridge Avenue

John Clifford Pemberton was best known as the Confederate major general who surrendered Vicksburg to Ulysses S. Grant in July of 1863, following a long siege. Pemberton was a career United States Army officer who fought in the Seminole Wars and with distinction during the Mexican War before joining the Southern cause during the Civil War.

Pemberton was born on August 10, 1814, in Philadelphia, Pennsylvania as the second child of John Pemberton (1783–1847) and Rebecca Clifford (1792–1869). As a student at the University of Pennsylvania, the young Pemberton decided he wished to have a career as an engineer. Believing the United States Military Academy the best way to gain this education, he applied to West Point, using his family's connection to President Andrew Jackson to secure an appointment. He was admitted to the Academy in 1833, where he was the roommate and close friend of George G. Meade (*see* Chapter 13). He graduated four years later, finishing ranked in the middle of his class.

Pemberton was commissioned a second lieutenant in the 4th U.S. Artillery Regiment on July 1, 1837. He served in the Seminole Wars in Florida and at various forts around the country before being stationed at the U.S. Army Cavalry School at Carlisle Barracks, Pennsylvania, in 1842 and 1843.

At the outbreak of the Mexican War, Pemberton was stationed at Fort Monroe in Virginia (from 1844 to 1845). Next, he was part of

Confederate General John C. Pemberton

the occupation of Texas (1845 to 1846), after which his 4th Artillery Regiment was sent into Mexico under Zachary Taylor. He fought at most of the major battles in that war and was appointed a brevet captain "for Gallant Conduct in the several Conflicts at Monterrey."

After the war with Mexico ended, Pemberton married a Virginian, Martha Thompson. Due to the lack of records to the contrary, many historians have come to believe Pemberton's marriage to this Norfolk native was the primary reason he later sided with the Confederacy. Pemberton again moved about the country for numerous assignments, including more action against the Seminoles (1856–1857); frontier duty at Fort Leavenworth, Kansas (1857–1858); and the Utah War (1858); returning to garrison duty at the Washington Arsenal in Washington, D.C., by 1861.

On April 24, 1861, just 12 days after the shots initiating the Civil War were fired at the Battle of Fort Sumter, Pemberton resigned from the United States Army. The resignation was not immediately accepted, however. First, Pemberton felt obligated to accept a meeting request he received from General Winfield Scott. Scott tried his best to persuade Pemberton to remain with the North. Scott felt he could convince Pemberton that he was making a wrong decision, a stance that received a significant boost when Pemberton received unexpected news regarding two of his younger brothers, Andrew and Clifford. He learned that on the very same day he resigned, Andrew and Clifford had joined the Union cavalry (the Philadelphia City Troop). Despite that development, despite his Northern birth, and despite Winfield Scott's best persuasive efforts, Pemberton stuck to his decision and joined the Confederate cause.

He was appointed a lieutenant colonel in the Confederate Army on March 28. He was made assistant adjutant general of the forces in and around the Southern capital of Richmond, Virginia, on April 29. He was promoted to colonel on May 8, and the next day was assigned to the Virginia Provisional Army Artillery, with the rank of lieutenant colonel. Pemberton was then appointed a major in the Confederate Army Artillery on June 15 and quickly promoted to brigadier general two days later. His first brigade command was in the Department of Norfolk, leading its 10th Brigade from June to November.

Pemberton was promoted to major general on January 14, 1862, and given command of the Confederate Department of South Carolina and Georgia, an assignment lasting from March 14 to August 29, with his headquarters in Charleston. Many South Carolinians feared that the Northern-born general was not dedicated to an all-out defense of the department. Pemberton added to their fears by publicly declaring that, if faced with a situation where he had to choose between abandoning an area, on the one hand, versus risk losing an outnumbered army on the other, he would choose to abandon the area. It was that public statement, combined with his generally abrasive personality and the distrust of his Northern birth, that led the governors of both South Carolina and Georgia to petition Confederate President Jefferson Davis seeking Pemberton's removal. Fortunately for Davis, it just so happened that he needed a commander for a new department in Mississippi. He also needed to find a command post for Gen. P.G.T. Beauregard. Davis decided to send Pemberton west and assigned the more popular Beauregard Pemberton's prior position in Charleston as commander of the Confederate Department of South Carolina and Georgia.

On October 10, 1862, Pemberton was promoted to the rank of lieutenant general and assigned to defend the fortress city of Vicksburg, Mississippi, as well as the Mississippi River (that command being known as the Department of Mississippi and East Louisiana). Davis gave him the following instructions regarding his new assignment: ". . . consider the successful defense of those States as the first and chief object of your command." Pemberton arrived at his new headquarters in Jackson, Mississippi, on October 14.

His forces consisted of fewer than 50,000 men under the command of Major Generals Earl Van Dorn and Sterling Price, with around 24,000 in the permanent garrisons at Vicksburg and Port Hudson, Louisiana. John D. Winters described the men under Pemberton as "a beaten and demoralized army, fresh from the defeat at Corinth, Mississippi." Pemberton faced his former Mexican War colleague, the aggressive Union commander Major General Ulysses S. Grant, and over 100,000 Union soldiers in the Vicksburg Campaign.

Pemberton immediately set to work solving supply problems and improving troop morale. For several months he enjoyed remarkable success, defeating attempts by Grant to take Vicksburg in the winter of 1862–63.

In the spring, however, Grant confused Pemberton with a series of diversions and crossed the Mississippi River below Vicksburg practically untouched. Grant was free to maneuver because Pemberton's responsibility to hold Vicksburg at all costs. Davis complicated matters by sending General Joseph E. Johnston to Mississippi to try to reverse declining

Confederate fortunes. Johnston ordered Pemberton to unite his forces and attack Grant, if practicable, even if that meant abandoning the defense of Vicksburg.

To make matters worse, Confederate General Joseph E. Johnston reassigned Pemberton's cavalry to the Army of Tennessee. Thus, in May of 1863, when Union General Ulysses S. Grant's campaign to take the city began in earnest, the Confederate defender was deprived of vital intelligence about his enemy's whereabouts. Poor communication and lack of coordination with Johnston—as well as the Pemberton's tactical errors—led to Confederate defeats at Champion Hill and Big Black River Bridge, and Pemberton was forced to back into the Vicksburg defenses. Two failed attempts to take the city by direct assault demonstrated the strength of the Vicksburg defenses and compelled Grant to lay siege to the city. Despite constant pleas to Johnston for aid, Pemberton was utterly isolated.

Caves at Vicksburg

Pemberton held firm for over six weeks, while soldiers and citizens were starved into submission. He was boxed in with lots of unusable munitions and little food. The poor diet was showing on the Confederate soldiers. By the end of June, half were out sick or hospitalized. Scurvy, malaria, dysentery, diarrhea, and other diseases cut their ranks. At least one city resident had to stay up at night to keep starving soldiers out of his vegetable garden. The constant shelling did not bother him as much as the loss of his food. As the siege wore on, fewer and fewer horses, mules, and dogs were seen wandering about Vicksburg. Shoe leather became a last resort of sustenance for many adults.

During the siege, Union gunboats lobbed over 22,000 shells into the town, and army artillery fire was even heavier. As the barrages continued, suitable housing in Vicksburg was reduced to a minimum. A ridge, located between the main town and the rebel defense line, provided a diverse citizenry with lodging for the duration. Over 500 caves were dug into the yellow clay hills of Vicksburg. Whether houses were structurally sound or not, it was deemed safer to occupy these dugouts. People did their best to make them comfortable, with rugs, furniture, and pictures. They tried to time their movements and foraging with the rhythm of the cannonade, sometimes unsuccessfully. Because of these dugouts or caves, the Union soldiers gave the town the nickname of "Prairie Dog Village." Despite the ferocity of the Union fire against the town, fewer than a dozen civilians were known to have been killed during the entire siege.

On the evening of July 2, 1863, Pemberton asked in writing his four division commanders if they believed their men could "make the marches and undergo the fatigues necessary to accomplish a successful evacuation" after 45 days of siege. With four votes of no, the next day, Pemberton asked the Federals for a truce to allow time for the discussion of terms of surrender, and at 10:00 a.m. on July 4, he surrendered the city and his army to Grant. The written terms (which in the first talks were simply unconditional surrender) were negotiated so that the Confederate soldiers would be paroled and: (1) be allowed to march out of their lines; (2) the officers permitted to take with them their side-arms and clothing; (3) the field, staff, and cavalry officers be permitted to take one horse each; and (4) the rank and file be allowed all of their clothing, but no other property.

Pemberton surrendered 2,166 officers and 27,230 men, 172 cannons, and almost 60,000 muskets and rifles to Grant. This, combined with the successful Siege of Port Hudson on July 9, gave the Union complete control over the Mississippi River, resulting in a significant strategic loss for the Confederacy, and cutting off Lt. Gen. Edmund Kirby Smith's command and the Trans-Mississippi Theater from the Confederacy for the rest of the war.

After his surrender, Pemberton was exchanged as a prisoner on October 13, 1863, and he returned to Richmond. There he spent some eight months without an assignment. At first, General Braxton Bragg thought he could use Pemberton, but after conferring with his ranking officers, he advised Davis that taking on the discredited lieutenant general "would not be advisable." Pemberton finally wrote Davis directly, asking he be returned to duty "in any capacity in which you think I may be useful." Davis replied that his confidence in him remained unshaken, saying, "I thought and still think that you did right to risk an army for the purpose of keeping command of even a section of the Mississippi River. Had you succeeded, none would have blamed; had you not made the attempt, few if any would have defended your course."

Pemberton resigned as a general officer on May 9, 1864, and Davis offered him a commission as a lieutenant colonel of artillery three days later, which he accepted, a testimonial of his loyalty to the South and the Confederate cause. He commanded the artillery of the defenses of Richmond until January 9, 1865. He was appointed inspector general of the artillery as of January 7 and held this position until he was captured in Salisbury, North Carolina, on April 12. Along with Pemberton and his 14 remaining guns, the Federals rounded up about 1,300 men and nearly 10,000 small arms. There is no record of his parole after his capture.

John Pemberton might have made a positive contribution to the Confederate war effort had his talents been effectively used. An able administrator, he was uncomfortable in combat. He had demonstrated his weaknesses in South Carolina, yet Davis had sent him to Mississippi anyway.

Grave of Confederate General Pemberton

After the war, Pemberton lived on his farm near Warrenton, Virginia, from 1866 to 1876, and then returned to Pennsylvania. He died in Lower Gwynedd Township, Montgomery County, Pennsylvania, five years later, on July 13, 1881. He was interred in the Laurel Hill Cemetery in Philadelphia. The families of General Meade, Thomas McKean (Signer of the Declaration of Independence), and Admiral John Dahlgren (whose brother also served as a Confederate General) made protests against his being buried there. It was decided that Pemberton would be interred elsewhere; however, he ended up in an obscure area of the cemetery. A ground-level plate notes he was a "Confederate General Staff Officer." A statue depicting Pemberton was erected in the Vicksburg National Military Park. His nephew, John Stith Pemberton, was also a Confederate soldier and was later credited with inventing Coca-Cola.

If You Go:
See the *"If You Go"* sections of Chapter 9 ("General Controversy"), Chapter 13 (George Meade), Chapter 19 (Samuel Crawford, and Chapter 28 (Oliver Knowles).

25.

HERMAN HAUPT

That Man Haupt...

County: Montgomery • Town: Bala Cynwyd
Buried at West Laurel Hill Cemetery
227 Belmont Avenue

"That man Haupt has built a bridge four hundred feet long and one hundred feet high, across Potomac Creek, on which loaded trains are passing every hour, and upon my word, gentlemen, there is nothing in it but cornstalks and beanpoles." —*Abraham Lincoln, discussing Haupt's timely repairs to the Potomac Creek Bridge after the Battle of Fredericksburg, May 28, 1862.*

Herman Haupt was born in Philadelphia, Pennsylvania, on March 26, 1817. He was the son of Jacob Haupt, a merchant by trade, and Anna Margaretta Wiall Haupt. His father died when Herman was only 12 years old, leaving widow Anna to support her three sons and two daughters.

A child engineering prodigy, he was appointed to the United States Military Academy at only 14 and graduated at the age of 18 with the 1835 class (ranked 35th out of 56). Upon graduation, he was commissioned a second lieutenant in the 3rd U.S. Infantry but resigned his commission a couple of months later to become a civil engineer. In 1838, he married Ann Cecelia Keller in Gettysburg, Pennsylvania, with whom he had seven sons and four daughters.

Before the Civil War, Haupt worked primarily in the railroad industry as an engineer designing bridges and tunnels. He patented a bridge construction technique known as the "Haupt Truss." For most of the 1840s,

Herman Haupt

he was a professor of mathematics and engineering at Pennsylvania (now Gettysburg) College, before returning to the railroad industry.

Early in 1862, the second year of the Civil War, Secretary of War Edwin M. Stanton appointed Haupt chief of all U.S. military railroads and transportation, with the rank of colonel, serving under General Irvin McDowell, who was responsible for the defense of Washington, D.C.

HAUPT TRUSS BRIDGE

C. 1854   PENNSYLVANIA RAILROAD

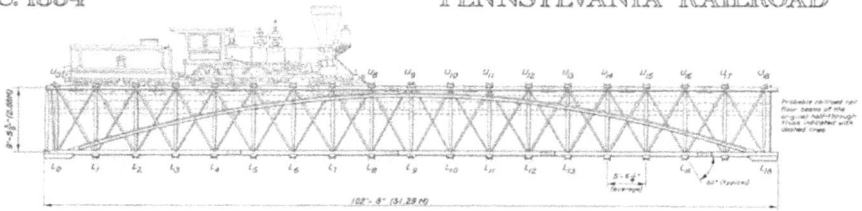

Haupt repaired damaged rail lines, built bridges, and improved telegraph communications.

On September 5, 1862, Haupt was promoted to brigadier general of volunteers. He refused the appointment but was willing to serve without rank or pay. He did not enjoy the protocols of military service and wanted the freedom to continue working in private business. The offer was officially rescinded one year later, in September of 1863, at which time he left the military.

However, during his year of service, he made an enormous impact on the Union war effort, being one of the few experts in the nation at that early time who understood the functioning of railroads and their value to the military. He assisted the Union Army of Virginia and the Army of the Potomac in the Northern Virginia and Maryland Campaigns. He was particularly effective in supporting the Gettysburg Campaign, conducted in an area he knew well from his youth. His hastily organized trains kept the Union Army well supplied, and he organized the returning trains to carry thousands of Union wounded to hospitals.

Haupt was known to show up at the war front or the White House at critical points in the war—like at George McClellan's headquarters just after the Second Battle of Bull Run, and at Joseph Hooker's headquarters before Lee invaded Maryland. Haupt also visited Fredericksburg shortly after the battle there in December 1862. According to Haupt biographer James A. Ward, "That evening Haupt and Congressman John Covode called on Lincoln in Washington to present firsthand reports of the

Excavating for "Y" at Devereux Station, Orange & Alexandria Railroad. The lo-comotive, General Haupt *is being used for work detail. Standing on the bank is USMRR Supt. for the O & A railroad, John Henry Devereux, who reported to General Haupt.*

battle. Haupt's account so upset the president that the three men walked at once to Halleck's house to confer on future action."

While on his way to Gettysburg, during a stop in Harrisburg, Haupt observed to a subordinate about the coming conflict: "We are in the most critical condition we have been in since the war commenced, and nothing but the interposition of Providence can save us. If the army is destroyed, no new force can be collected in time to make effectual resistance. Washington, Baltimore, Philadelphia, and New York will fall, and the enemy can then, as masters of the situation, dictate their own terms."

Haupt was extremely disappointed with General Meade's unwillingness to pursue Lee's army after Gettysburg. Said Haupt on July 5, 1863, to Meade, who was sure the Confederates' retreat would be slowed by

USMRR engine General Haupt

the lack of bridges: "Do not place confidence in that. I have men in my Construction Corps who could construct bridges in forty-eight hours sufficient to pass that army, if they have no other material than such as they could gather from old buildings or from the woods, and it is not safe to assume that the enemy cannot do what we can."

After this meeting, around midnight, Haupt jumped on a locomotive and rushed to Washington. Before breakfast, he showed up at President Lincoln's office. According to historian Fletcher Pratt:

"On July 6 came Haupt in person to the White House, direct from the front, and officers with eyewitness accounts of the battle, including General Daniel Sickles, who had had a leg shot off on the second day. Haupt was no more comforting than Meade's order; he had seen the General the day before to tell him that the new railhead and telegraph had been carried through Hanover Junction to Gettysburg (which surprised Meade very much), and to plead with him to follow the enemy hard. Meade replied that his men needed rest; Haupt told him they could not be as tired as the Confederates: 'You must pursue Lee and crush him. His ammunition and stores must be exhausted, and his supply trains can be easily cut off. He is in desperate straits, like a rat in a trap, and you can whip and capture him'."

Upon hearing this report, Lincoln asked of Stanton, "What shall we do with your man, Meade, Mr. Secretary?"

"Tell him," said Stanton to Haupt, "Lee is trapped and must be taken."

Then Stanton turned to Lincoln and added, "He can be removed as easily as he was appointed if he makes no proper effort to end this war now, while he has Lee in a trap."

Haupt then hastened back to Gettysburg by train, expecting the orders from Washington would be obeyed. He offered his help, but Meade did nothing, thereby allowing Lee to escape. This greatly disappointed Lincoln, Stanton, and Halleck, and frustrated Haupt. If Meade had acted, or if anyone had thought to place Haupt in command on Sunday, July 5, 1863, Lee would doubtless have been captured, and the war ended.

Said Robert Lincoln, the President's son, about one of his visits to the White House in mid-July 1863:

"Entering my father's room right after the battle of Gettysburg, I found him in tears with his head bowed upon his arms resting on the table at which he sat. 'Why, what is the matter, father?' I asked. For a brief interval, he remained silent, then raised his head, and the explanation of his grief was forthcoming. 'My boy,' he said, 'when I heard that the bridge at Williamsport had been swept away, I sent for General Haupt and asked him how soon he could replace the same. He replied, 'If I were uninterrupted, I could build a bridge with the material there within twenty-four hours, and Mr. President, General Lee has engineers as skillful as I am.' Upon hearing this, I at once wrote Meade to attack without delay, and if successful to destroy my letter, but in case of failure to preserve it for his vindication. I have just learned that at a council of war of Meade and his generals, it has been determined not to pursue Lee, and now the opportune chance of ending this bitter struggle is lost."

After his war service, Haupt returned to the railroad business. He and his wife purchased a small resort hotel at Mountain Lake in Giles County, Virginia. He invented a prize-winning drilling machine and was the first to prove the practicability of transporting oil in pipes. Haupt became wealthy from his investments in railroads, mining, and real estate. Still, he eventually lost most of his fortune due to political complications involving the completion of the Hoosac Tunnel in Massachusetts.

Herman Haupt died of a heart attack at age 88, on December 14, 1905, in Jersey City, New Jersey. He was stricken while traveling by train on a journey from New York to Philadelphia. He is buried in West Laurel Hill Cemetery in Bala Cynwyd, Pennsylvania. He outlived every one of his West Point classmates.

Haupt's grave

If You Go:

West Laurel Hill Cemetery is a large, beautiful cemetery filled with history and exciting stories. It is home to the graves of eight Civil War Medal of Honor recipients, including George Stockman, Elwood Williams, Wallace Johnson, Richard Binder, Jacob Orth, Joseph Corson, Charles Betts, and Moses Veale. Details of their service can be found in Chapter 35 (Medal of Honor Recipients).

Also buried at West Laurel Hill Cemetery is Francis Adams Donaldson, whose letters and correspondence during the war to his family were published in the book *Inside the Army of the Potomac: The Wartime Letters of Captain Francis Adams Donaldson*.

26.

GETTYSBURG
NATIONAL
CEMETERY

"Four score and seven years ago, our fathers brought forth on this continent a new nation, conceived in liberty, and dedicated to the proposition that all men are created equal.

Now we are engaged in a great civil war, testing whether that nation, or any nation so conceived and so dedicated, can long endure. We are met on a great battlefield of that war. We have come to dedicate a portion of that field, as a final resting place for those who here gave their lives that that nation might live. It is altogether fitting and proper that we should do this.

But, in a larger sense, we cannot dedicate—we cannot consecrate—we cannot hallow—this ground. The brave men, living and dead—who struggled here, have consecrated it far above our poor power to add or detract. The world will little note, nor long remember what we say here, but it can never forget what they did here. It is for us the living, rather, to be dedicated here to the unfinished work which they who fought here have thus far so nobly advanced. It is rather for us to be here dedicated to the great task remaining before us—that from these honored dead we take increased devotion to that cause for which they gave the last full measure of devotion—that we here highly resolve that these dead shall not have died in vain—that this nation, under God, shall have a new birth of freedom—and that government of the people, by the people, for the people, shall not perish from the earth."

Bronze bust of Lincoln at the Gettysburg National Cemetery near the site of the Gettysburg Address (photo by Tammi Knorr)

President Abraham Lincoln's now immortal words were spoken at Gettysburg, Pennsylvania, on November 19, 1863, as part of the consecration of the new Soldiers' National Cemetery (now most often commonly referred to as the "Gettysburg National Cemetery," located a mile or so south of Gettysburg's town square with an east or "front" entrance off of Baltimore Pike and a west entrance off of Taneytown Road). Oddly

Rows at the Gettysburg National Cemetery (photo by Tammi Knorr)

enough, Lincoln was not even the featured speaker that day. One of the great orators of the time, Edward Everett from Massachusetts, mesmerized the crowd for two hours before Lincoln took the podium and, in a somber delivery, spoke for approximately two minutes.

Said Everett in a letter to Lincoln written shortly afterward, "I should be glad if I could flatter myself that I came as near to the central idea of the occasion, in two hours, as you did in two minutes." Lincoln replied he was glad to know the speech was not a "total failure."

Pennsylvania Governor Andrew Curtin, who sat on the speakers' platform that day, was pleased with the speech. He said of Lincoln, "He pronounced that speech in a voice that all the multitude heard. The crowd was hushed into silence because the President stood before them . . . It was so impressive! It was the common remark of everybody. Such a speech, as they said it was!"

In contrast, eyewitness Sarah A. Cooke Myers recalled in a 1931 interview, "I was close to the President and heard all the Address, but it seemed short. Then there was an impressive silence like our Menallen Friends Meeting. There was no applause when he stopped speaking." Historian Shelby Foote, in his book *The Civil War, A Narrative. Vol. 2: Fredericksburg to Meridian*, described the applause as delayed, scattered, and "barely polite."

Large statue of General John Reynolds at the entrance to Gettysburg National Cemetery (photo by Tammi Knorr)

One of the many rows of unknown graves (photo by Tammi Knorr)

Likely, the crowd probably was not expecting such a short speech from the president, especially after Everett's long one. The fact that the photographers in attendance were unable to get a good picture of Lincoln that day further confirms the brevity of the remarks and the likely lack of preparedness among those gathered. Of course, none of this detracts from the importance of the moment, especially when looking back many years later. What more could or should someone say on such an occasion? Since then, many have said that Lincoln's speech was one for the ages.

Lands, in general, can be sanctified in several different ways. One way is for something of momentous significance in human history to have transpired at a place. Without a doubt, the Gettysburg National Cemetery is the epitome of that type of sacred space. The final resting place of those buried here—in the very soil on which the three-day, turning-point-of-the-war battle occurred—makes these graves a collection of "Keystone Tombstones" unlike any other. Moreover, given the extreme significance of both the Battle of Gettysburg and the Civil War, this multi-thousand-acre site has served and will continue to serve as arguably the most important and enduring forum through which generations of Americans have held on to and grappled with their collective memories of the events that took place here over 150 years ago. There are few cemeteries on American soil as hallowed as this one.

Today, Gettysburg National Cemetery remains an incredibly special place. As you enter the cemetery's front gate, you behold a well-landscaped park. A statue of Major General John Fulton Reynolds greets you. Reynolds was the highest-ranking soldier killed at Gettysburg. While he is not buried here, the life-sized bronze statue of him standing near the entrance beckons you in to walk among his fallen comrades. Gettysburg buffs will note this is not the first—nor the last—large statue of Reynolds one encounters in Gettysburg. (*See* Chapter 12 herein for a more detailed discussion of Maj. Gen. Reynolds.)

There is an excellent display of Lincoln's Gettysburg Address at the far end of the cemetery, near a pavilion about 50 yards east of the Taneytown Road gate. However, neither the display nor the pavilion is the exact spot from which Lincoln made his Address. The Soldiers National Monument, a large monument in the center of the park, is close to the actual location. However, some have said it was just over the fence in neighboring Evergreen Cemetery.

There are 3,564 Union soldiers buried in Gettysburg National Cemetery. Of those, 979 (more than one-fourth) are unknown. New York (867) and Pennsylvania (534) claim over half of the known fallen. The rest are from 16 other states. There are no Confederates buried within the confines of the National Cemetery (but some may be forever resting within just a stone's throw—see the *"If You Go"* section below). Regarding the thousands of Confederates who fell and were interred on the battlefield, the National Park Service web site (http://www.nps.gov/gett/faqs.htm) states:

> The southern dead were removed to cemeteries in North and South Carolina, Georgia, and Virginia between 1871 and 1873. Most of the Confederate dead were interred at Hollywood Cemetery in Richmond, Virginia, in a special section set aside specifically for the casualties of Gettysburg.

If You Go:

Adjacent to the National Cemetery is a 29.12-acre, private, historic, rural cemetery called Evergreen. Founded nine years before the Battle of Gettysburg, Evergreen Cemetery became the eponym for Cemetery Hill, a landform most noted as the keystone of the Union position during the epic battle. While visiting Evergreen, be on the lookout for the less-than-a-handful of Confederate soldiers that may or may not have their final resting places here. Also, consider paying homage to David Wills and Henry Louis Baugher, both of whom are buried at Evergreen and had important connections to the creation and dedication of the National Cemetery.

Wills, acting on behalf of Governor Curtin, was responsible for coordinating the creation of the cemetery. He was a prominent attorney in the area and was the one who sent an invitation to President Lincoln to make "a few appropriate remarks" at the dedication. Lincoln stayed at Wills's house on the square in downtown Gettysburg. A visit to the David Wills House, now a museum, is highly recommended. After visiting the Wills House, we also recommend a stop at The Pub and Restaurant on the square for some refreshments and nourishment.

Baugher attended the Lutheran Theological Seminary in Gettysburg and became a minister. By 1863, he was the second president of Pennsylvania (now Gettysburg) College. He spoke immediately after Lincoln's Gettysburg Address and gave the formal benediction for the National Cemetery.

Wills' grave at Evergreen (photo by Tammi Knorr)

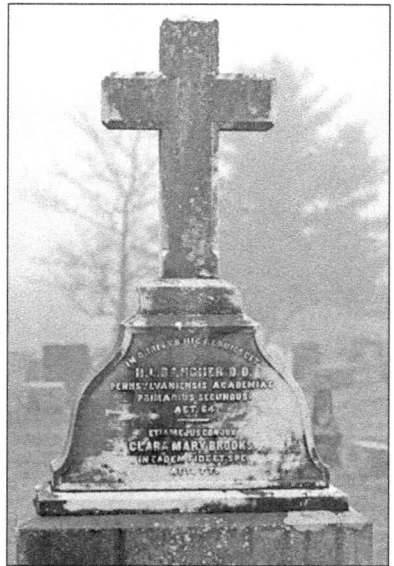

Baugher's grave at Evergreen (photo by Tammi Knorr)

27.

ULRIC DAHLGREN

The Dahlgren Affair

County: Philadelphia • Town: Philadelphia
Buried at Laurel Hill Cemetery
3822 Ridge Avenue

Ulric Dahlgren was born on April 3, 1842, in Bucks County, Pennsylvania. His father was Rear-Admiral John Adolf Dahlgren. Dahlgren's father influenced much of his short life. After completing school in 1858, he decided to go into civil engineering as he had already received training in this field from his father. In 1860, obeying the wishes of his father, he began work in a Philadelphia law office. After President Lincoln took office, Dahlgren was determined to serve his country and was assigned to a naval expedition that was to aid in defense of Alexandria, Virginia. In 1862, he joined a light artillery company in Philadelphia. In that same year, Dahlgren, who was only 20 years old, was put in charge of a battery of navy howitzers at Harpers Ferry.

Dahlgren quickly earned the reputation of being an effective and heroic officer. At Fredericksburg on November 9, 1862, he led 60 men into the city while facing an enemy force that numbered between 500 and 600. He held the city for three hours and captured 31 Confederate soldiers. He also participated in the battles of Chancellorsville (April 30—May 6, 1863) and Beverly Ford (June 9, 1863). On July 4, while in charge of 100 men, Dahlgren attacked Confederate cavalry and captured Greencastle, Pennsylvania. On July 6, in another attack, Dahlgren was wounded, and his foot was amputated. Shortly after that, he was promoted to the rank of colonel.

Dahlgren returned to active duty on February 18, 1864, serving under General Hugh Judson Kilpatrick. On February 28, Kilpatrick led

Ulric Dahltren

3,600 Union cavalry troopers south toward Richmond, with a plan to raid the city and free Union prisoners being held there. The next day, on February 29, Kilpatrick sent Dahlgren at the head of 460 men off to the west. The plan called for Dahlgren to attack Richmond from the south while Kilpatrick led an attack from the north.

The plan was doomed to failure from the outset. Dahlgren found that the James River had swelled due to winter rains, and he was unable to cross. He continued toward Richmond, but he was on the wrong side of the river. Next, he ran into Confederates and was forced to turn north. Kilpatrick reached Richmond but was turned back. Meanwhile, in a cold hard rain, Dahlgren and about 100 of his men were separated from the rest of his command. On the night of March 2, Dahlgren and his men were ambushed by rebel troops, and he was killed.

A young boy searched Dahlgren's body and found two documents that historians would call the "Dahlgren Papers." The papers indicated that Dahlgren had been ordered to destroy the city of Richmond and to kill Confederate President Jefferson Davis and his cabinet members. The Dahlgren Papers were published in the Richmond newspapers, and there were those in the South who wanted to put Dahlgren's captured men on trial, convict them, and then execute them. Robert E. Lee's opposition may have saved the prisoners. However, Lee did have photographs of the Dahlgren Papers taken. He sent the photographs to General George Meade, along with a letter asking whether the United States government had approved these orders. Meade responded that the government had issued no such order. Privately, however, Meade had his doubts. He confided to his wife that "I regret to say that Kilpatrick's reputation, and collateral evidence in my possession, rather go against this theory."

Northern newspapers and Dahlgren's father claimed that the papers were forgeries. Whatever the real story is, the Dahlgren Papers provided the southern leaders with a reason to approve plans for Southern

The death of Ulric Dahlgren

Tombstone of Ulric Dahlgren, who was killed in a raid on Richmond, while carrying orders to assassinate Confederate President Jefferson Davis.

sympathizers in the North to join in the rebellion. They even encouraged a plan to bomb the White House. John Wilkes Booth was reportedly part of that plan, and some believe that when it failed, he may have decided to take matters into his own hands.

Seven months after Lee surrendered at Appomattox, Secretary of War Edwin Stanton took custody of the Dahlgren Papers. One historian later conducted an extensive search for the papers and finally concluded that Stanton had destroyed them.

Dahlgren was initially buried in Richmond, but after the war, his remains were sent north. His body lay in state in Washington's City Hall and Independence Hall in Philadelphia. General George Meade attended the funeral, and Dahlgren was buried with distinguished honors in Laurel Hill Cemetery in Philadelphia.

If You Go:

See the *"If You Go"* sections of Chapters 9 ("General Controversy"), 13 (George Meade), 19 (Samuel Crawford), and 28 (Oliver Knowles).

28.

OLIVER B. KNOWLES

An Unknown Hero

County: Philadelphia • Town: Philadelphia
Buried at Laurel Hill Cemetery
3822 Ridge Avenue

It is incredible how difficult it is to find information about Oliver Blatchy Knowles considering what he did in his short life. He entered the Civil War as a private at the age of 19 and ended the war four years later, a brevet brigadier general at the age of 23.

Knowles was born on January 3, 1842, in Philadelphia. His father, Levi Knowles, was a prominent flour merchant who was heavily involved in civic and charitable organizations in Philadelphia. Oliver quit high school after two years and joined his father's business. He was tall (6'2"), and through his love of horses, he developed into an excellent horseman. When the war broke out, 19-year-old Knowles was recruited by William Henry Boyd of Philadelphia. Boyd was raising a company of cavalry, which would become part of the First New York Cavalry (also called the "Lincoln Cavalry"). Boyd was a captain, and young Oliver Knowles became his orderly as he quickly established a reputation for dedication to his duty and for following orders. Their colonel was a man named Carl Schurz, a former German Revolutionary of 1848 and confidant of President Lincoln.

The Lincoln Cavalry saw its first combat at Pohick Church, Virginia, on July 22, 1861. It was a skirmish with Confederate cavalry, the first cavalry-against-cavalry action in the war. In the four years that followed, Knowles and the men of the Lincoln Cavalry never forgot the lesson of that first encounter: in a cavalry fight, the advantage is with the party that

Lee surrenders to Grant at Appamattox Court House, after which Knowles was promoted

moves first. Knowles performed so well that in September 1861, he was promoted to corporal.

In January 1862, he was promoted again to sergeant, and after the Peninsula Campaign, he received a commission as a second lieutenant. The Lincoln Cavalry saw action at Antietam and then spent much of the early part of 1863 pursuing the troops known as Mosby's Raiders, a cavalry battalion commanded by John "Gray Ghost" Mosby. Mosby's Raiders were known for their quick raids and disappearances.

In April 1863, Knowles was made a first lieutenant and took a furlough. He rejoined the regiment in Harrisburg just in time to participate in the Battle of Gettysburg.

In August 1863, after much of the First New Yorkers' enlistments expired, the 21st Pennsylvania Cavalry was formed and mustered in with Boyd as its colonel and Knowles as a major. The regiment was dismounted and served as infantry during the Overland Campaign in the spring of 1864. In June, at the Battle of Cold Harbor, Boyd was severely wounded, and Knowles took command of the regiment. He led the 21st in action during the siege of Petersburg. In October, the regiment was mounted

The grave of General Knowles

and acting as cavalry again, and Knowles was promoted to colonel. He was 22 years old.

Knowles led the unit in various actions around Petersburg and then was sent to participate in the Appomattox Campaign. They saw action at Dinwiddie Court House, Five Forks, Sayler's Creek, and Appomattox Court House, where Lee would surrender on April 9, 1865. In June, Knowles received a brevet to brigadier general of volunteers for gallant and meritorious service. He left the army in July and returned home to Philadelphia.

Oliver Knowles moved to Milwaukee, Wisconsin, where he was in the grain trade. He was stricken with cholera and died on December 6, 1866, less than a month before his 25th birthday. His remains were returned to Philadelphia and buried in Laurel Hill Cemetery. His gravestone reads:

He was:
Gentle, yet courageous
Firm, but magnanimous
Beloved by all

His name is on the 21st Pennsylvania Cavalry Regiment monument on the Gettysburg Battlefield.

If You Go:
There are numerous Civil War generals buried in Laurel Hill Cemetery. The following six were all at the Battle of Gettysburg:
• **Louis Francine:** fatally wounded in the Peach Orchard on July 2, 1863. The 7th New Jersey Infantry Monument on the Gettysburg battlefield stands on the spot where Francine was wounded.
• **Benezet Foust:** led the 88th Pennsylvania Infantry and was wounded on the first day of the battle.
• **William Painter:** was with Major General John Reynolds when Reynolds was killed on Day 1 (*see* Chapter 12).
• **John Hoffman:** led the 56th Pennsylvania Infantry, which was the first Union infantry regiment to participate in the battle.

• **Langhorne Wister:** assumed command of his brigade on Day 1, when the previous commander, Edmund Dana, was struck down.

• **George Alexander Hamilton Blake:** was a cavalry officer who served with distinction during the Gettysburg Campaign.

A stone's throw from Laurel Hill is St. James-the-Less Episcopal Churchyard, which contains the graves of several Civil War generals and heroes. Among them is Robert Morris, Jr., the great-grandson of Revolutionary War patriot and Declaration of Independence signer Robert Morris. Morris, Jr. was captured by Confederate forces at the Battle of Brandy Station in Virginia and died while imprisoned at the infamous Libby Prison in Richmond.

Also at St. James-the-Less Episcopal Churchyard are the graves of John Grubb Parke, a major general who led his troops in the assault and capture of Vicksburg and fought in the Battles of Knoxville, Petersburg, and Fort Stedman, Virginia; Benjamin Chew Tilghman, who commanded the 26th Pennsylvania Volunteer Infantry and later the 3rd United States Colored Troops; James Barnet Fry, who served as Provost Marshal General of the Union Army; and Medal-of-Honor recipient Anthony Taylor (*see* Chapter 35) who was awarded the Medal of Honor for his actions at the Battle of Chickamauga.

Libby Prison in Richmond, Virginia

29.

HENRY C. PLEASANTS

The Saddest Affair

County: Schuylkill • Town: Pottsville
Buried at Charles Baber Cemetery
1400 West Market Street

Henry Clay Pleasants was a coal mining engineer and a brigadier general in the Union Army during the American Civil War. He is best known for constructing an underground tunnel filled with explosives beneath the Confederate lines during the Siege of Petersburg, Virginia, to break the defense. Following the explosion, the Battle of the Crater ensued on July 30, 1864.

Pleasants was born in Buenos Aires, Argentina, on February 16, 1833, the son of a Philadelphia merchant and his Spanish wife. His father smuggled arms and ammunition to South American insurgents fighting against a dictator. After his father died in 1846, 13-year-old Henry was sent to live with his father's brother, a physician living in Philadelphia.

After overcoming a variety of educational difficulties, Pleasants graduated from Central High School with a B.A. in 1851 and then went to work as an engineer for the Pennsylvania Railroad. During these years, he showed a propensity for tunneling and deep mining. In 1857, he moved to Pottsville, Pennsylvania, to become a civil engineer in the mining industry. He married in 1860, but his wife died during pregnancy.

When the war erupted, Pleasants enlisted as a second lieutenant in the Tower Guard, a local Schuylkill County unit that became part of the 6th Pennsylvania Volunteers. After an uneventful three months, the unit was mustered out. Pleasants then enlisted as a captain in the 48th

Henrty C. Pleasants

Pennsylvania Volunteers, a regiment that was comprised of men from Schuylkill County.

After service on the North Carolina coast, the 48th Pennsylvania was assigned to the IX (Ninth Army) Corps for the remainder of its service. Pleasants saw action at Second Bull Run, Chantilly, South Mountain, and Antietam, after which he was promoted to lieutenant colonel. He was wounded in the leg at Fredericksburg but was able to rejoin his unit for their journey to Kentucky. In July 1863, Pleasants was promoted to provost marshal general of XXIII Army Corps and participated in the Knoxville campaign.

Upon his unit's return to Virginia, Pleasants led throughout General Grant's Overland Campaign during the battles of The Wilderness, Spotsylvania, North Anna River, Cold Harbor, and Petersburg.

Many of the 48th were coal miners. During the Siege of Petersburg, Pleasants said he heard his men suggest running a shaft under the Confederate lines and then blowing it up. He took the idea to his superiors, including elaborate drawings he had made. While the plan was approved, Pleasants struggled with a lack of supplies and a lack of interest from the leadership (until, that is, other attacks on Petersburg failed). The plan called for the mine to be detonated between 3:30 and 3:45 a.m. on the morning of July 30, 1864. Pleasants lit the fuse accordingly, but as with the rest of the mine's provisions, they had been given poor-quality fuse, which his men had had to splice themselves. After more and more time passed and no explosion occurred (the impending dawn creating a threat to the men at the staging points, who were in view of the

Sketch of the explosion

Confederate lines), two volunteers from the 48th Regiment (Lt. Jacob Douty and Sgt. Harry Reese) crawled into the tunnel. After discovering the fuse had burned out at a splice, they spliced on a length of new fuse and relit it. Finally, at 4:44 A.M., the charges exploded in a massive shower of earth, men, and guns. A crater (still visible today) was created, 170 feet long, 100-120 feet wide, and at least 30 feet deep. The explosion killed nearly 300 Confederate soldiers. However, the Union troops under Ambrose Burnside failed to take advantage of the explosion and suffered considerable casualties. The Confederates counterattacked and soon recovered their original position. General Grant considered the assault "the saddest affair I have witnessed in the war."

After Petersburg, Pleasants remained in command of the 48th until late 1864, but his health was failing. On August 1, 1864, Pleasants was rewarded for his ingenuity and efforts in the tunnel operation; he was promoted to command the 2nd Brigade, 2nd Division, IX Corps, under Brigadier General Robert Potter, the Division Commander, and Major General Ambrose Burnside, the Corps Commander.

The crater at Petersburg

Subsequently, on March 13, 1865, the Secretary of War Edwin M. Stanton promoted Colonel Pleasants to brevet brigadier general for his "distinguished services during the war, and particularly for the construction and explosion of the mine before Petersburg." Major General Meade issued a special order thanking Colonel Pleasants and his regiment for this, one of the most extraordinary feats of engineering performed during the war.

After mustering out honorably from the army in 1865 for health reasons, Pleasants returned to Pottsville and resumed his role as a mining engineer for the Philadelphia and Reading

Grave of Pleasants

Coal and Iron Company, rising to the positions of Chief Engineer and then Superintendent.

Unfortunately, wartime exposure had affected his health. In 1877, he took a one-year leave of absence to Europe to seek a cure. After a long and lingering disease, Henry Pleasants died on March 26, 1880, at the early age of 47. Showing the respect Pleasants had earned, more than 1,000 people attended his funeral. He is buried in the Charles Baber Cemetery in Pottsville, Pennsylvania. Pleasants's tombstone in Pottsville fails to mention his military service, a likely intentional omission on his part.

If You Go:

Also in Pottsville are the graves of:

• **James Nagle:** an officer in the United States Army in both the Mexican War and the Civil War, he is best known for his actions at the 1862 Battle of Antietam, where his brigade played a critical role in securing Burnside's Bridge—a key crossing over the contested Antietam Creek.

He commanded a brigade of emergency militia during the Gettysburg Campaign. He is buried in Presbyterian Cemetery in Pottsville (Howard St. at 12th St.).

• **Jacob Frick:** A Medal of Honor Recipient who is also buried in Pottsville's Presbyterian Cemetery. Colonel Frick was awarded the Medal of Honor for his actions at Fredericksburg and Chancellorsville (*see* Chapter 35); and

• **Nicholas Biddle:** buried at Bethel African Methodist Episcopal (A.M.E.) Church Cemetery in Pottsville (816 Laurel Blvd.). Biddle is credited by many as being the first person to shed blood in the Civil War. Born a slave in Delaware around 1796, he escaped to freedom by way of the Underground Railroad. Biddle had an interest in becoming a military man, but because he was black, he could not be mustered in as a soldier. Not to be deterred, however, around 1840, he became the orderly (an attendant to an officer) of Captain James Wren, the commanding officer of the Washington Artillery, and eventually became so associated with the company and so highly regarded by Wren and the members of the Washington Artillery that he was considered one of their own and even permitted to wear the company's uniform. Responding to President Lincoln's call for 75,000 volunteers to be sent to protect the nation's capital less than a week after the first shots were fired at Fort Sumter, the Washington Artillery made their way from Pottsville to Baltimore, where they were to board trains for the final leg of their journey to Washington, D.C. On April 18, 1861, while marching through Baltimore to the train station, a large group of Confederate sympathizers quickly gathered around the troops. It was the sight of the then-65-year-old Biddle in uniform that especially infuriated the mob in

Nicholas Biddle

Baltimore. Racial epithets were hurled in Biddle's direction, soon to be followed by bricks—one of which struck Biddle in the head, causing a wound so deep that a portion of his skull bone was exposed. Biddle survived, and the next day attended remarks given by President Lincoln in Washington, D.C. Biddle caught the eye of Lincoln, who spotted Biddle in the crowd and was particularly struck by his appearance (his head being wrapped with blood-soaked bandages). The president urged him to seek medical attention, but Biddle refused, preferring instead to remain with his company. His advancing age and head wound essentially brought an end to Biddle's service. He returned to Pottsville, where he would live out the rest of his life. Biddle died at his home there on August 2, 1876, at the age of 80.

30.

GALUSHA PENNYPACKER

The Youngest General

County: Philadelphia • Town: Philadelphia
Buried at Philadelphia National Cemetery
Haines Street & Limekiln Pike

Galusha Pennypacker was wounded seven times during the Civil War and became a brigadier general at the age of 20, making him the youngest person in United States military history ever to hold that rank. This record stands to this day.

Pennypacker was born on June 1, 1844, in Valley Forge, Pennsylvania, into a family with a history and tradition of military service. His father served in the Mexican War, and his grandfather served in the Revolutionary War. Galusha and George Armstrong Custer were fifth cousins and two of the youngest generals in the Civil War. Pennypacker was also a cousin to General Benjamin Prentiss. Shortly after the Mexican War, his father, Joseph, went to California in the Gold Rush and never returned. His mother died when he was three years old, and as a result, Pennypacker was raised primarily by his grandmother.

At the age of 16, he enlisted in the 9th Pennsylvania Infantry Regiment from West Chester, Pennsylvania. When the war broke out in 1861, he was working as a printer's assistant at the *Chester County Times* newspaper and had been offered an appointment to West Point. He probably would have entered West Point in 1862, but events intervened. In April 1861, after Fort Sumter surrendered to the Confederates, President Lincoln called for volunteers, and the 9th Pennsylvania answered the call as a body. In Harrisburg, they were designated as Company A of the 9th Regiment. Pennypacker turned down the post of a first lieutenant,

Galusha Pennypacker

believing he was too young for the responsibility. He was assigned to be regimental quartermaster, and he excelled at it. The 9th, however, was a three-month regiment and served in the Shenandoah Valley, suppressing secessionist activity. It was disbanded in July 1861, and Pennypacker set out to recruit a new regiment, the 97th, which served for the duration.

In August 1861, Pennypacker entered "for the war" as captain of Company A, 97th Pennsylvania Volunteers. He was promoted to major in October. The 97th Regiment joined the X (Tenth Army) Corps in the Department of the South, and during 1862 and 1863, participated in all the engagements and sieges in which that corps took part. These included: the capture of Fort Pulaski (Georgia), the taking of Fernandina and Jacksonville (Florida), and actions against James Island, Charleston, and Forts Wagner and Gregg (South Carolina).

In April 1864, the regiment and the Tenth Corps were ordered to Virginia and became part of the Army of the James. Pennypacker was promoted to lieutenant colonel and was engaged in the Bermuda Hundred Campaign under Major General Benjamin Butler. During that campaign, Pennypacker was severely wounded in the right arm, left leg, and right side at the Battle of Ware Bottom Church. He was hospitalized for three months and was promoted to colonel. He returned to duty in August and, during the Siege of Petersburg, led his brigade and was again wounded at the Battle of Chaffin's Farm and New Market Heights.

On January 15, 1865, Pennypacker was severely wounded yet again at the Second Battle of Fort Fisher, North Carolina. Fort Fisher, which guarded the harbor of Wilmington, was the last coastal stronghold of the Confederacy and a haven for ships running the Union blockade. It was referred to as the Gibraltar of the South and was an important objective for General Alfred Terry. During the successful assault on Fort Fisher, the 97th's color bearer went down. Pennypacker personally picked up the banner and carried it onto a rebel parapet, where he planted it in the sand. He was almost immediately after that felled by a Confederate bullet. The wound was considered fatal, and General Terry, calling him the "real hero of Fort Fisher," promised him a promotion to brigadier general.

Galusha Pennypacker did receive a brevet promotion to brigadier general dated January 15, 1865. He miraculously survived his wounds after ten months in the hospital, and on February 18, 1865, he received a full promotion to brigadier general of volunteers at the age of 20. To this day, he is the youngest officer to hold the rank of general in the history of the U.S. Army. Later he was awarded the Medal of Honor for his actions at Fort Fisher. His Medal of Honor citation reads: "Gallantly led the charge over a traverse and planted the colors of one of his regiments thereon, was severely wounded."

Pennypacker's grave (photo by Joe Farrell)

Pennypacker stayed in the army after the war, serving out West until he retired in July 1883. He settled down in a house on South 10th Street in Philadelphia. In 1911, on the 50th anniversary of the war, Pennypacker was interviewed by Phillip Dillon of the *New York World.* When asked if he had seen the man who shot him at Fort Fisher, Pennypacker responded that he had indeed and proceeded to tell how after the Confederates surrendered, a Union soldier asked the assailant to turn over his blanket so they could use it to carry Pennypacker from the battlefield. According to Pennypacker, the man refused, saying, "I won't give up my blanket; I'm a prisoner and entitled to my blanket." Hearing this remark sent Pennypacker's men into a rage. Immediately they began beating the Confederate. As Pennypacker recounted, "my men, with clubbed muskets, dashed out his brains," killing him instantly. "I closed my eyes, and they carried me away in that blanket, but the horror of it has never gone out of my mind to this day," he told Dillon.

Pennypacker died in Philadelphia on October 1, 1916, and is buried in Philadelphia National Cemetery. There is a large, prominent (and somewhat bizarre) statue honoring him at 19th Street and Benjamin Franklin Parkway on the north side of Logan Square. His name is also inscribed on the Smith Memorial Arch in Philadelphia's Fairmount Park.

If You Go:

About eight miles south of Philadelphia National Cemetery, in Philadelphia's downtown historic district, is the famous Christ Church Burial Ground (430 Arch Street, Philadelphia). There are two prominent Civil War generals buried there:

• **George Archibald McCall:** commander of the Pennsylvania Reserve Corps. In June 1862, he commanded his corps in the victory at Dranesville, Virginia, and the Battle of Mechanicsville, Virginia. Later that month, McCall was wounded and captured at Frayser's Farm, Virginia, and imprisoned at the infamous Libby Prison. He became ill from his wounds and confinement, and subsequently was prisoner-exchanged for a Confederate general, Simon Buckner, who would become governor of Kentucky in 1887. Pennypacker's poor health forced him to resign from the army in March 1863.

• **Major General George Cadwalader:** a hero in the Mexican War, he commanded the Department of Philadelphia during the Civil War. In that capacity, he oversaw the movement of thousands of Union troops and wounded men through the city of Philadelphia.

While in Philadelphia, you might find yourself craving an Irish pub. There are many to choose from, but we had a terrific experience at two that were only blocks

George Cadwalader

apart in the shadow of City Hall. McGillin's Olde Ale House at 1310 Drury Street (an alley connecting 13th & South Juniper Streets, between Chestnut & Sansom Streets, in Center City) threw open its doors the year Lincoln was elected president, making it the oldest continuously operating tavern in Philadelphia. As we partook of our cold, delicious brew served by friendly, enthusiastic staff surrounded by impressive historical artifacts, we wondered how many of the men we are writing about had been there quenching their thirst and discussing the issues of the day. We also wondered how McGillin's survived Prohibition, but that is for another book.

We also had a great time at nearby Fadó Irish Pub & Restaurant, situated at 1500 Locust Street. Fadó offers beautiful, modern decor with friendly, prompt service and a fantastic menu, which includes many Irish favorites. So many good places . . . so little time.

31.

ALFRED L. PEARSON

The Attorney General

County: Allegheny • Town: Pittsburgh
Buried at Allegheny Cemetery
4734 Butler Street

Alfred L. Pearson was born on December 28, 1838, in Pittsburgh. He studied law at Meadville College and Jefferson College. On January 14, 1862, he was admitted to the Allegheny County bar. He worked as an attorney for a short time before deciding to join the Union Army.

Pearson began his army career by enlisting in the 155th Pennsylvania Infantry on April 2, 1862, and was commissioned a captain in Company A. In the years that followed, he took part in all the regiment's operations and received a series of promotions. He was initially promoted to major, then to lieutenant colonel, and to colonel on August 31, 1863. In December of 1864, President Lincoln nominated Pearson for appointment to the brevet grade of brigadier general of volunteers, and in February 1865, the U.S. Senate confirmed the appointment.

In the final weeks of the war, Pearson's forces were involved in the Battle of Lewis's Farm in Virginia. During the battle, a Union brigade retreated in the face of Confederate fire. Pearson led his regiment in a counterattack and was successful in regaining the lost ground. It was for his performance during this battle that Pearson was eventually awarded the Medal of Honor on September 17, 1897. General Meade also complimented him for his actions. Pearson's troops fired the final shots at Appomattox Courthouse. He was mustered out of the army on June 2, 1865, and President Johnson nominated him for appointment to the

Alfred L. Pearson

brevet grade of major general of volunteers. The Senate confirmed the appointment on March 12, 1866.

Pearson returned to Pittsburgh and began a law practice. In 1868, he was elected to the office of District Attorney for Allegheny County. He served in that position until health problems forced him to retire. He was appointed a major general in the Pennsylvania National Guard in 1870. In 1877, during the Great Railroad Strike, his troops opened fire and killed dozens of rioters. As a result, he was arrested for murder, but the grand jury refused to indict him.

Pearson remained active in veterans' affairs and served for years as the manager of the National Soldiers Home. He also helped organize two veterans' groups: The Grand Army of the Republic and the Union Veteran Legion. Pearson was also a member of the Military Order of the Loyal Legion and the Medal of Honor Legion. He was 64 years old when he died on January 6, 1903, and was laid to rest at Allegheny Cemetery in Pittsburgh.

Pearson's grave

If You Go:

Allegheny Cemetery is enormous, and you could spend days there if you wanted to visit all the famous sites. For our purposes, we will mention a few graves that are Civil War-related:

• **Conrad Feger Jackson:** A Civil War Union Brigadier General, he saw action at Bull Run, South Mountain, and Antietam. During the Battle of Fredericksburg, he was mortally wounded. General Meade described him as an officer of merit and reputation, who owed his position to his gallantry and good conduct in previous actions.

• **James Scott Negley:** A Civil War Union Major General, he commanded the Union forces during the Battle of Chattanooga. After the defeat at Chickamauga, he was relieved of command. He then served on administrative boards until he resigned in January of 1865. After the war, he was elected to Congress, where he served from 1869 to 1875.

• **David Henry Williams:** A Civil War Union Brigadier General, he commanded the 31st Pennsylvania at Seven Pines, Malvern Hill, and during the Maryland Campaign. He also fought at Antietam and Fredericksburg. After the war, he worked in Pittsburgh as an engineer and a newspaper writer. He died in 1891.

Another site worth visiting at Allegheny Cemetery is the Arsenal Monument. The monument was built in 1928 to honor 43 young women who are buried in the cemetery. These women were some of the 78 workers killed by an explosion at the nearby Allegheny Arsenal. The explosion occurred on September 17, 1862, and was the worst industrial accident associated with the Civil War.

Not far from Allegheny Cemetery is a great restaurant called Piccolo Forno. It is located at 3801 Butler Street. The eatery offers great service and terrific Italian food that is very reasonably priced. It is worth checking out.

32.

LAFAYETTE C. BAKER

What Did He Know, and
When Did He Know It?

County: Montgomery • Town: Huntingdon Valley
Buried at Forest Hills Memorial Park
101 Byberry Road

Lafayette Curry Baker was a Union investigator and spy, serving under Presidents Abraham Lincoln and Andrew Johnson. Baker was born in Stafford, Genesee County, New York, on October 13, 1826. Though he later claimed to be a descendant of one of Ethan Allen's Green Mountain Boys, who had named him after the Marquise de Lafayette of American Revolution fame, no such lineage existed.

In 1839, his father, a poor farmer, moved the family to Michigan, where Baker spent the rest of his childhood. By 1848, Baker was a mechanic in Philadelphia and then New York. In 1853, he moved to Gold Rush-era California, pursuing the same occupation. By 1856, he had made a name for himself with the Vigilance Committee in San Francisco. During this period, he was involved in several lynchings, acting as a bouncer at a local saloon and informant to the local constabulary.

At the outbreak of the Civil War, Baker convinced General Winfield Scott he could spy on the Confederate military in Virginia. Scott agreed to the proposal, and Baker's life as a spy began. His initial plan was to pose as a photographer under the alias Samuel Munson, who would photograph the leaders of the Confederate Army. However, on July 11, 1861, Baker was arrested by the Union Army at Alexandria, Virginia, as a Confederate spy. He was in danger of being executed until General Scott intervened on his behalf.

Lafayette Curry Baker

Baker eventually reached the Confederacy, but a Confederate patrol quickly arrested him. According to Baker, he was interviewed by President Jefferson Davis, Vice President Alexander Stephens, and General Pierre T. Beauregard, the latter granting his release after he provided details about Union positions. Baker then began carrying a photograph of Beauregard with him, which he used to help him enter Confederate Army military camps. In Fredericksburg, Baker was once again arrested as a Union

Army spy. Convinced that he was about to be executed, Baker managed to use a small knife that he had hidden in his shoe to free two loose bars in his cell, slipped through the opening, and made his escape. He then returned to Washington.

At least, that was the story Baker later wrote.

The truth was much less spectacular. Baker was, indeed, captured and taken before Jefferson Davis. However, Davis did not give him a pass as a photographer. He did at least take a few minutes to listen to Baker's inept

General Winfield Scott

lies and then . . . promptly declared him a spy and ordered that he be held for trial. Baker did manage to escape from the Richmond jail, after which he wandered for weeks through Virginia, living in shacks and the woods, and stealing food where he could find it as he desperately tried to get to the Union lines. He was picked up in Fredericksburg as a vagrant and later held as a spy, but he again escaped, this time with the help of a local prostitute with whom he had been staying. Finally, he managed to return to General Scott's headquarters. The tales of Baker photographing Confederate officers were nonsense. He had lost his camera before being picked up by the first Confederate patrol. The information regarding Confederate forces he later relayed to Scott had been obtained by Baker from a Union officer he had met in the Richmond prison. All the information was outdated by the time Baker passed it on to Scott.

Baker took advantage of Scott's old age and lack of knowledge about espionage. Scott was so impressed he not only granted a commission to the conniving Baker, but he retold Baker's saga to several members of Lincoln's cabinet. Secretary of War Edwin M. Stanton was most interested in the tale and quickly recruited Baker to be the replacement for Allan Pinkerton, head of the Union Intelligence Service. Baker was given the job as head of the National Detective Police (NDP), an undercover, anti-subversive, spy organization.

Baker had some minor successes that did not amount to much. He was suspected of corruption. He would intimidate people who were themselves making profits from illegal business activities. He would arrest and jail those who refused to share their illegal gains with him. Baker was eventually caught tapping telegraph lines between Nashville and the office of Edwin M. Stanton. For this, he was demoted and sent to New York, where he was assigned to Assistant Secretary of War, Charles Dana.

Upon Abraham Lincoln's assassination on April 14, 1865, Baker was summoned by Stanton to Washington by telegraph: "Come here immediately and see if you can find the murderer of the President." Baker arrived on April 16 and sent out his agents to pick up what information they could about the people involved in the assassination. Within two days, Baker had arrested Mary Surratt, Lewis Powell (aka "Paine"), George Atzerodt, and Edman Spangler. He also had the names of the fellow conspirators: John Wilkes Booth and David Herold.

After the assassination, Stanton had taken over the government, declaring martial law. He issued a $100,000 reward for the capture of John Wilkes Booth, dead or alive. Much later, Baker admitted, before Lincoln had been shot, neither he nor Stanton had any knowledge regarding any supposed conspiracy. Yet within two days, Baker was able to round up all the conspirators? Somehow, Baker knew precisely where to find George Atzerodt (who failed to kill Vice President Andrew Johnson), Lewis Powell/Paine (who was targeting Seward), and Edward Spangler, the carpenter at Ford's Theater who had made a portable barrier for Booth so that he could successfully bar the inside of the door to Lincoln's box. Baker also knew that Spangler had drilled a hole in the door leading to Lincoln's box for Booth to spy on the President. Lastly, Baker somehow quickly deduced the exact escape route taken by John Wilkes Booth and David Herold.

When Baker's agents discovered Booth had crossed the Potomac near Mathias Point on April 22, he sent Lieutenant Edward P. Doherty and 25 men from the 16th New York Cavalry to capture them. On April

26, Doherty and his men caught up with John Wilkes Booth and David Herold on a farm owned by Richard Garrett. Doherty ordered the men to surrender. Herold came out of the barn, but Booth refused and so the barn was set on fire. While this was happening, one of the soldiers, Sergeant Boston Corbett, found a large crack in the barn and was able to shoot Booth in the back. His body was dragged from the barn, and, after being searched, the soldiers recovered his leather-bound diary. The bullet had punctured his spinal cord, and he died in great agony two hours later.

Secretary of War Edwin Stanton

Booth's diary was handed to Baker, who later passed it on to Stanton. Baker was rewarded for his success by a promotion to brigadier general and receipt of a substantial portion of the $100,000 reward.

In January 1867, Baker published his book *History of the Secret Service,* where he described his role in the capture of the conspirators. He also revealed that a diary had been taken from John Wilkes Booth when he had been shot. This information about Booth's diary resulted in Baker being called before a Congressional committee investigating the assassination. Stanton and the War Department were forced to hand over Booth's diary. When shown the diary by the committee, Baker claimed that someone had "cut out eighteen leaves." When called before the committee, Stanton denied being the person responsible for removing the pages. Speculation grew that the missing pages included the names of people who had been involved in the conspiracy.

Baker maintained his power for some time under Stanton's rule, even after President Johnson fired Stanton (who refused to leave his headquarters). In this incredible political battle for power, Stanton refused to leave his headquarters and threatened Johnson. Johnson was incensed at this

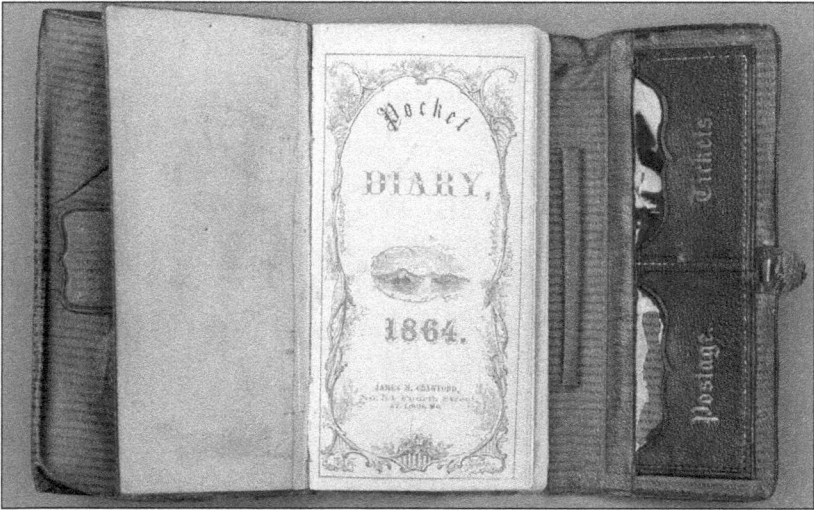

The diary of John Wilkes Booth

insubordination. Baker intervened, blackmailing Johnson with the release of scandalous information unless Johnson made peace with Stanton.

President Johnson replied by accusing Baker of spying on the White House. He fired Baker. Subsequently, both Stanton and Baker worked hard to have Johnson impeached. Baker testified at the impeachment hearings in 1868, but the scandalous documents he claimed to have could not be produced. As a result, the impeachment failed.

After his appearance before the Congressional committee, Baker became convinced someone in the government intended to murder him. He was found dead at his home in Philadelphia on July 3, 1868. Officially, Lafayette Baker died of meningitis. Some have suggested, however, that the War Department silenced him.

In recent years, using an atomic absorption spectrophotometer to analyze several hairs from Baker's head, Ray A. Neff, a professor at Indiana State University, determined Baker was killed by arsenic poisoning rather than meningitis. Baker had been unwittingly consuming the poison for months, mixed into imported beer provided by his wife's brother, Wally Pollack. *The Lincoln Conspiracy*, by Balsiger and Sellier, cites a diary Baker's wife kept, which chronicled several dates Pollack brought Baker beer; they correspond to the gradually elevated levels of toxin in the Baker hair samples Neff studied. Wally worked for the War Department, though whether he acted on orders or alone has yet to be determined. Nevertheless, Neff's studies, along with the information chronicled in Baker's diary, serve to bolster a persuasive and provocative alternate history of the Lincoln assassination, one distinct from the chronology most promulgated by mainstream U.S. historians. Baker had also left cryptic notes that pointed to a high-level conspiracy to murder Lincoln—one going far beyond that involving John Wilkes Booth.

Some years later, President Lincoln's only surviving son, Robert, was visited by a family friend in his home. Robert was in the process of burning papers in the fireplace. The friend tried to prevent the destruction of these historical documents, written in President Lincoln's hand. Robert Lincoln was firm and continued tossing sheaves of paper into the fire, saying, "I must—some of these letters prove that there was a traitor in my father's cabinet."

Initially buried in the Mutual Family Cemetery, Baker's remains (and all others in this cemetery) were moved en masse to Forest Hills Memorial Park in Huntingdon Valley, Pennsylvania. All the graves from the Mutual Family Cemetery are unmarked, but according to local cemetery historians, the locations of these re-internments are "behind the Hanover-Kensington M.E. Church Memorial."

Behind this marker are the Mutual Family Cemetery graves at Forest Hills Memorial Park

If You Go:

About 15 miles southwest of Forest Hills Memorial Park is St. James-the-Less Episcopal Churchyard, located at West Clearfield Street & Hunting Park Avenue, in the Allegheny West section of North Philadelphia. Brigadier General William Reading Montgomery is buried there. See also, the *"If You Go"* section of Chapter 28 (Oliver Knowles).

Also nearby is St. Dominic Church Cemetery, located at 8504 Frankford Avenue in Torresdale, Pennsylvania (about 11 miles east of St. James-the-Less Episcopal Churchyard). The remains of Major General Thomas Kilby Smith are buried there.

33.

REBELS AMONG US

Scattered across the Keystone State, you will find the occasional pocket of rebel graves. While John Clifford Pemberton's status as a general makes him arguably the most prominent Confederate soldier buried in Pennsylvania (*see* Chapter 17), there are many more of lesser renown. Below are some of the sites:

—•—

HELLAM TOWNSHIP, York County

One grave that recently received a lot of attention is the Unknown CSA marker along the Susquehanna River in Hellam Township, York County. The site is 1.2 miles north of the Accomac Inn. According to contemporary accounts, the soldier was a Confederate cavalryman whose body washed up along the western riverbank in June 1863. It was surmised he was a rebel scout drowned while trying to ford the river near York Haven. The body was found and buried by locals. In 1972, Hurricane Agnes supposedly washed away some of the bones. A more recent marker was lost in 2011 when tropical storm Lee pounded the county. In early 2013, there was an effort to restore the marker. Over

Temporary marker of Unknown CSA along the Susquehanna River in Hellam Township, York County (photo by Joe Farley)

100 people were present at the site for its rededication, including several people in period dress, according to the *York Daily Record*.

PROSPECT HILL CEMETERY, York County

Many of the wounded soldiers from Gettysburg were transferred via train to York County. Some of those were Confederates who were not welcome to convalesce with the Union casualties. Instead, they were moved to Washington Hall, the meeting place of the local Odd Fellows Lodge on South George Street. Dr. Henry Nes, a known Southern sympathizer, was believed to be one of the physicians who cared for them. Five of the soldiers did not survive. They were taken by wagon to scenic Prospect Hill Cemetery, where they were interred. The grave is part of the Civil War walking tour of Prospect Hill Cemetery, an interesting stroll through York's Civil War history. A tour guide brochure is available at the gift shop of the York County Heritage Trust at 250 East Market Street (the historic Lincoln Highway) in downtown York. The tour guide discusses the Rebels, as well as scores of Civil War personalities also buried in the cemetery, including several Yankees mortally wounded at Gettysburg.

BIG MOUNT, PARADISE TOWNSHIP, York County

Imagine 4,000 Confederate troops showing up at your farm! That is precisely what was experienced on the evening of June 27, 1863, by George Jacob Altland and his immediate neighbors of Big Mount, Paradise Township, York County. General Jubal Early arrived and set camp here for the night. Somewhere in the Big Mount area, a farmer shot and killed Pvt. Charles Brown of the Louisiana Tigers, who was prowling around the region looking for food or supplies. Brown's service record reads "murdered by the citizens of York County, Pa." The grave is unmarked.

MANADA GAP CEMETERY, Dauphin County, PA

About 20 miles northeast of Harrisburg's Camp Curtin lay the graves of several Confederate soldiers who were prisoners of war—likely captured at Gettysburg. They were being used as laborers at the nearby Manada

Furnace, a local industry located along Manada Creek. The Grubb family, who owned the furnace, used prisoners as woodcutters to feed the busy furnace that produced many tons of pig iron. The soldiers lived nearby in wooden shacks and died during the war, most likely from disease. The marked burial site is only the best known. Up to a dozen more prisoners are buried near the original site of the workers' shacks, the stone foundations of which can still be seen. Additional Confederates are said to be buried near the Old Hanover Cemetery only a few miles away. All died during the war before they could be released to return home.

WEST LAUREL HILL CEMETERY, Bala Cynwyd

The following Confederate veterans are interred in West Laurel Hill Cemetery:

• **Captain John P. Donaldson, Jr.,** CSA (June 13, 1838–July 22, 1901): born and raised in Philadelphia, the son of John P. and Matilda Nice Donaldson. He was a descendant of the family for which the Nicetown section of Philadelphia was named. Donaldson's grandfather, William Donaldson, was Sheriff of Philadelphia from 1808 to 1810. Donaldson enlisted with the rebels in Charlestown, Virginia (now West Virginia), and saw action in several battles, receiving wounds at Droop Mountain and Gaines Farm.

• **Private William D. Mason,** CSA (December 7, 1846–October 22, 1909): the son of James W. Mason and Martha Cooke of Clarke County, Virginia. William married Louise "Lula" Clarke of Philadelphia. He enlisted at Brandy Station at age 15 and served one year until discharged for health reasons.

• **Private Frederick L. Pitts,** CSA (October 1842–1928): born in Berlin, Worcester County, Maryland. In 1861, he joined the Maryland Infantry at Richmond and fought throughout the war. After the war, Pitts studied art at the Pennsylvania Academy of Fine Arts in Philadelphia. He later was president of the Philadelphia Sketch Club, the oldest organization of artists in the United States. His art focused on marine subjects, as in his painting *The Wharf at Kaighn's Point*.

LAUREL HILL CEMETERY, Philadelphia

The following Confederate veterans are interred in Laurel Hill Cemetery:

• **Private George Lehman Ashmead,** CSA (December 15, 1837–December 15, 1898): served in Company E, 4th Texas Infantry Regiment, Hood's Texas Brigade. He died in Germantown, Philadelphia County, Pennsylvania.

• **Assistant Surgeon Fitz Henry Babbitt, MD,** CSA (December 29, 1829–February 14, 1909): born in Natchez, Mississippi, and graduated from the medical school of the University of Pennsylvania, class of 1853. He is believed to have served as a surgeon with a Louisiana Infantry Regiment between 1861 and 1864, according to their alumni register. The 1860 and 1870 census reports list him as a physician in Red River Landing, Pointe Coupee Parish, Louisiana.

• **Major Richard V. Bonneau,** CSA (April 26, 1827–January 27, 1899): the son of William Henry Bonneau and his wife, Anna Maria Swinton. He was born in Charleston, South Carolina. Richard was appointed to the Military Academy at West Point in 1847. He graduated in June 1852 and served on the frontier with the Third Infantry. On January 10, 1859, he married Marie Louise Kiehl in Philadelphia. She was the only daughter of John Kiehl and his wife, Jane Pickering. He returned to New Mexico and then resigned his commission to join the Confederacy at the outset of the war, serving until the end. He then returned to Philadelphia, where he entered the mercantile business with his father-in-law, John Kiehl. In his later life, Maj. Bonneau became a teacher and speaker in the Church of Christ.

• **Major General Samuel Gibbs French,** CSA (November 22, 1818–April 20, 1910): born in Mullica Hill, New Jersey. He was the son of Samuel French, Jr., and Rebecca Clark. French attended the U.S. Military Academy at West Point, graduating in 1843. Some of his West Point classmates were future Union Generals Ulysses S. Grant and William B. Franklin, as well as future CSA Generals Roswell Ripley and Franklin Gardner. French served bravely in the Mexican War. His first wife was Eliza Matilda Roberts of Philadelphia, who died in 1857. His second wife was a Southern woman. French resigned his commission in 1856 to become a Southern planter. When the Civil War started, he opted for his adopted South and became a brigadier general in the Confederate Army. His service first took him to the East, where he participated in the Peninsula Campaign and operations in North Carolina. Promoted to major general in August 1862, he was assigned to command a division in the Army of the Tennessee, leading his command in the Battles of Jackson, Atlanta, and Nashville. Illness forced him to return home in December 1864, but he soon returned to service commanding forces in Mobile, Alabama, until the end of the war. French spent the next 45 years of his life as a successful planter in Florida. He wrote an autobiographical account of his war services, entitled *Two Wars*. Though buried in Pensacola, Florida, a cenotaph stands here for him in his family's plot.

• **1st Lieutenant Henry A. Parr,** CSA, (ca. 1843–August 4, 1932): a cavalryman who became involved in the Confederate Secret Service. His actual place of birth is unknown—New York City, Nashville, and Nova Scotia are all possibilities. Parr joined General John Hunt Morgan's Raiders at the outbreak of the Civil War. Sometime in 1863, he began clandestine activities for the Confederate Secret Service. Along with Lieutenant John C. Braine, he helped to seize Union steamships in retaliation for former slave Robert Small's similar taking of the Confederate steamer USS *Planter* in 1862. Between 1863 and 1865, the officers and their crews hijacked the Union steamers *Chesapeake, Roanoke,* and the schooner *St. Mary's* at sea. After the war, Parr returned from exile in Nova Scotia, where he established a career as a pharmacist. In 1878, he became the last Confederate tried for war crimes for the murder of Chesapeake engineer Owen Schaffer. Parr was able to invoke the amnesty granted Confederate soldiers by President Andrew Johnson since he was working under the command of a duly commissioned Confederate officer, Braine. In 1884, Parr earned a dental degree from the prestigious Baltimore School of Dentistry, where he later became a clinical instructor. He became an expert in crowns and bridgework, often giving clinics at national dental meetings. He also held patents in non-dental fields. Dr. Parr died in New York City.

• **Surgeon William Mason Turner,** CSA/CSN (December 15, 1835 – October 13, 1877): born in Petersburg, Virginia, he went on to graduate from Brown University in 1855 and the University of Pennsylvania Medical School in 1858. He began a medical practice in Petersburg, where he married Hannah Adelie Ford. With the outbreak of the Civil War, Turner joined the Confederate Army as a surgeon. In 1862, he resigned and was appointed an Assistant Surgeon in the Confederate Navy, where he served

William Mason Turner

aboard the ironclad CSS *Chicora*, a Confederate gunboat stationed at Charleston, South Carolina. Turner also served in the naval battalion at Drewry's Bluff, Virginia. He was captured by Union forces in April 1865 and spent the last months of the war as a prisoner. After his parole, he resumed his medical practice in Philadelphia, where he became a regular contributor of poetry, prose, and medical literature to local publications. He also authored several dime novels for the Beadle & Adams publishing house. Turner died in Philadelphia.

• **Private George L. Washington,** CSA (January 12, 1825 – February 7, 1872): born in Virginia, the great-grandnephew of President George Washington. During the Civil War, Washington enlisted in Col. John Mosby's Regiment of Partisan Rangers. On September 19, 1864, he was captured by Sheridan's forces at Winchester, Virginia. He remained a POW until paroled in 1865. Washington was married to Ann Bull Clemson, niece of the founder of Clemson University.

• **Private Phillip D. Woodhouse,** CSA: served with Company H, 16th Regiment, Virginia Infantry. His service records during the Civil War add up to an astonishing 119 pages. Private Woodhouse ended his wartime service as a hospital steward.

• **Private John Henry Zeilin,** CSA (December 25, 1834 – December 20, 1896): served in the Confederate cavalry for Georgia and was a noted chemist, pharmacist, and president of J. H. Zeilin & Company, Philadelphia. Zeilin was the son of a prominent Delaware County (PA) attorney and register of wills, John K. Zeilin. As a teenager, Zeilin began a career in business at a Philadelphia drug firm. In 1853, he went south to work for Nottingham & Fitzgerald, a drug firm in Macon, Georgia. In 1861, he and a partner bought out his employer and established the J. H. Zeilin Company in the patent drug business in Macon.

During the Civil War, Zeilin was enlisted as a private in the Georgia Cavalry and was detailed to the staff of General Howell Cobb as a dispatch rider. He later was detailed to the CSA's Medical Department and assigned to procure medical supplies. After the war, Zeilin re-established his company in Philadelphia as a major patent drug manufacturer and distributor. One of its most popular products was Simmons' Liver Regulator. He married Emmeline Cole, daughter of Judge Carelton B. and Susan Cole of Macon, Georgia. Zeilin was also the nephew of Brigadier General Jacob Zeilin, 9th Commandant of the United States Marine Corps during the Civil War. He died of a stroke at Clifton Springs, New York.

NEW BRITAIN BAPTIST CHURCHYARD, New Britain
The following Confederate veteran is interred in the New Britain Baptist Churchyard:

• **Colonel Joseph Barbiere,** CSA (November 27, 1831–October 4, 1892), was born in New York City to Joseph and Flossie Ouvre Barbiere, who were natives of Marseilles, France. Joseph's grandfathers served in the American Revolution under General Lafayette and were at the British surrender at Yorktown. In 1850, Joseph, a lawyer, editor, and state trade representative, lived in Memphis, Tennessee, with his family. Barbiere married Mary Grey Levett in 1855. In 1860, they were

Col. Joseph Barbiere

recorded as living with her parents, Joseph and Eliza Levett, in New Britain, Pennsylvania, where his occupation was listed as "Gentleman." In 1861, Barbiere returned to Memphis, where he joined the Confederate Army. He was captured in April 1862 and prisoner-exchanged in the fall of 1862. He was then promoted and became an inspector general in the Confederate Army in Alabama. In 1864, he attained the rank of colonel in an Alabama unit known as Barbiere's Reserve Cavalry. After the war, Barbiere returned to Memphis and resumed his pre-war ventures as a trade representative. His wife, Mary, died in 1867 and is buried in Memphis. In 1868, Joseph married Mary's sister, Lucy Levett. By 1880, the Barbiere family had moved to Camden, New Jersey, where he worked as an editor. Later, they lived in Doylestown, Pennsylvania, for several years and then moved to Philadelphia. Barbiere wrote a book, *Scraps from the Prison Table at Camp Chase and Johnson's Island*, about his experiences as a prisoner of war. On one trade mission to France, Joseph became acquainted with a man who was attempting to invent a device that would transmit photographs across telephone lines. One of the earliest successes was the transmission between two cities of a photograph of Joseph Barbiere. He was given the reproduced photograph and brought it back to the United States, where it was donated to the Smithsonian Institution as one of the earliest existing examples of a fax. Barbiere died at his residence in Philadelphia.

<hr />

MORRIS CEMETERY, Phoenixville

The following Confederate veteran is interred in Morris Cemetery:

• **Lieutenant Amory Coffin, Jr.**, CSA (August 9, 1841–June 5, 1916), was born in Charleston, South Carolina. Coffin was a cadet at the Citadel, class of 1861, in command of the squad, which fired the first shot of the Civil War, an alarm gun to notify the batteries around Charleston that the US Steamer *Star of the West* had been sighted and was bound for Fort Sumter. Coffin served at the Citadel throughout the war and was also an Assistant Professor of French and Drawing. Later appointed Adjutant. After the war, he joined the Phoenix Iron Company in Phoenixville. As a civil engineer with Phoenix, he designed the structural features of some of the late 19th and early 20th century's most famous buildings, including the Madison Square Garden in New York City, the Crocker Building in San Francisco, the Provident Life and Trust Company in Philadelphia, and others. Later, with noted architect George B. Post, he designed the steel structure of the New York Stock Exchange building. Coffin was elected to the American Society of Civil Engineers on March 3, 1875. He died in Scranton.

HOPE CEMETERY, Kutztown

The following Confederate veteran is interred in Hope Cemetery:

• **Colonel Thomas D. Fister,** CSN (October 25, 1838–April 21, 1915) was born in Kutztown, Pennsylvania. He graduated from the U.S. Naval Academy, class of 1859. When Louisiana seceded from the Union in January 1861, Fister was serving aboard the Revenue Marine Service Cutter *Robert McClelland*. Captain John G. Breshwood, the commander, turned his ship over to the State of Louisiana at New Orleans. A telegraphed message sent to Lieutenant S. B. Caldwell by U.S. Treasury Secretary John A. Dix ordered Caldwell to arrest Breshwood, and gave him the famous order, "If anyone attempts to haul down the American flag, shoot him on the spot." Lieutenants Caldwell and Fister did not carry out that order against their Captain. The *McClelland* was renamed the CSS *Pickens*. Breshwood, Caldwell, and Fister were dismissed from the Revenue Marine Service by order of the President and Treasury Secretary John A. Dix. Fister resigned his commission and joined the Confederate Navy. He survived the naval Battle of Fort Jackson and Fort Saint

Thomas Fister

Phillip, April 18-28, 1862, on the Mississippi River below New Orleans. His gunboat, the CSS *McCrae*, "riddled like a sieve" during the battle, transported the wounded to New Orleans under a flag of truce, then sank on April 27 at the New Orleans wharves. Fister escaped through the Union lines just after New Orleans fell to the Union Army. He made his way to Mobile, Alabama, and served on the CSS *Manassas* and CSS *Selma*. Later he commanded the naval brigade at Drewry's Bluff, Virginia, with the rank of colonel. After the war, Fister served in the Alabama legislature representing Calhoun County. He subsequently returned to Kutztown, Pennsylvania, with his wife, Julia L. Swan Fister, and family. He was a prominent citizen of Kutztown. Colonel Fister died in St. Paul, Minnesota.

ALLEGHENY CEMETERY, Lawrenceville

More than 250 Civil War soldiers and veterans are buried in the Soldiers Memorial Plot, including eight Confederates—most likely prisoners of war who did not survive their incarceration. Separated as they were in life from their white Union comrades, there are about 132 black Civil War veterans—members of the United States Colored Troops—who are buried about 30 yards away from the cluster of Union and Confederate graves.

EVERGREEN CEMETERY, Gettysburg

Two Confederates who were mortally wounded during the Battle of Gettysburg, Private Hooper Caffey, and Sergeant Matthew Goodson, were initially buried in Evergreen Cemetery. Due to public outrage, their remains were relocated to unmarked locations. The current markers are merely cenotaphs.

And what about the Confederate dead at Gettysburg?
Over 3,300 Confederate dead were buried in shallow graves and trenches at Gettysburg. Today, they are gone, having been returned to the South.

Confederate casualties at Gettysburg

Of these Confederate dead, 1,100 were buried in marked graves, and two Gettysburg residents, Dr. J.W.C. O'Neal and Mr. Samuel Weaver, recorded their locations. During the period October 27, 1863, to March 18, 1864, Weaver superintended the exhuming and removal of the Union dead to the Soldiers' National Cemetery at Gettysburg. He also, at that time, examined the graves of more than 3,000 Confederate dead. While examining the exhumed rebels, he was able to identify their remains by the burial locations, and then by the color, gray or brown, and the material (cotton) of the uniforms, the style of the shoes, and even by the undershirts, all of which were different than those of the Union soldiers. After the war, Ladies Memorial Associations contracted Weaver to remove and ship their lost soldiers south. Before the work could be started, however, Mr. Weaver died and his son, Dr. Rufus B. Weaver, took over the contract. Despite the many obstacles, including stubborn landowners, Rufus Weaver was able to complete the work.

34.

THADDEUS STEVENS

The Dictator of Congress

County: Lancaster • Town: Lancaster
Buried at Shreiner-Concord Cemetery
Mulberry and West Chester Streets

There have been many powerful congressmen who have served in the United States House of Representatives. A majority have held the title Speaker of the House. Members who have held that lofty position include Henry Clay, Champ Clark, Sam Rayburn, and Tip O'Neill. However, only one member of the House was ever called "The Dictator of Congress." His name was Thaddeus Stevens, and many historians hold the opinion that he wielded more power than any other congressman in the history of the country.

Stevens was born on April 4, 1792, in Vermont. He faced numerous hardships in his early life, including a club foot. Also, his father was an alcoholic who found it impossible to hold a steady job. It is not known what happened to the elder Stevens, but he left his wife and four sons in poverty. Stevens himself was ambitious and saw the value of education. He studied at Peacham Academy and afterward entered Dartmouth as a sophomore from where he graduated in 1814. Stevens then moved to York, Pennsylvania, where he worked as a teacher while he studied law. He was admitted to the bar and established himself first as a lawyer in Gettysburg and later in Lancaster.

Stevens would never marry, though he did have two boys who were the sons of his mixed-race housekeeper, Lydia Hamilton Smith, who lived with him, and would be considered a common-law wife by today's standards. Smith would manage Stevens's home and businesses in Lancaster for 24 years. She also served as his hostess during his days in

Thaddeus Stevens

Washington. During this time, society operated under a policy of segregation. As a result, rumors swirled about their relationship. Based on their correspondence and accounts by those who knew them, it appears that the relationship they established could best be described at the time as a respectful friendship.

Stevens was deeply interested in politics. Initially, he joined the Federalist Party. When that party faded, he joined the Anti-Masonic Party. He then became a Whig before finding his final home as a

Republican. In 1833 he was elected to the Pennsylvania State House of Representatives, where he served on and off until 1842. His record during this time reflects beliefs he would carry forward throughout his political career. He was against secret societies, he favored funding to Pennsylvania colleges, and he wanted a constitutional limit established on the state debt. His support for black citizens surfaced when he refused to sign the Pennsylvania Constitution of 1838 because it failed to allow those citizens to vote. He also championed the establishment of free public schools. Though Stevens had been elected by a constituency that favored repeal of the public education act, he fought to preserve it. He was instrumental in persuading the Pennsylvania Assembly to vote overwhelmingly in favor of keeping the new law.

Those who knew Stevens agreed that he was a man who could be counted on to employ his considerable energies toward furthering those causes in which he believed. It was his view that slave owners were attempting to gain control of the federal government to ensure that slavery would be permitted to grow. He vowed to fight to further the cause of liberty. He was first elected to Congress in 1848, and he served until 1853. In 1859 he returned to Congress as a Republican and continued to serve until his death in 1868. As a member of Congress, he supported Native Americans, Mormons, Jews, and women. However, no cause was dearer to him than that of the abolition of slavery. He was an active member of the Underground Railroad, and he assisted in helping runaway slaves make their way to Canada. A possible Underground Railroad site has been discovered under his office in Lancaster, Pennsylvania.

When the Civil War broke out, Stevens used his political skills to enhance his influence and power. He became the chairman of the Ways and Means Committee, and combining the power of this position with his oratorical skills, he soon became the leader of a group that would be known as the Radical Republicans.

Stevens was outraged in July of 1861 when Congress passed the Crittenden-Johnson Resolution, which held that the war would be won by restoring the Union while preserving slavery. Stevens worked hard for its repeal, which occurred that December. In that same month, he was calling for the emancipation of the slaves to weaken the Confederate States. In early 1862 he was calling for total war. On January 22nd he addressed the House and declared that the war would not end until, ". . . one party or the other be reduced to hopeless feebleness, and the power of further effort shall be utterly annihilated." In that same speech, he again urged the immediate emancipation of all slaves, arguing that such a move would assist in crippling the Confederate economy that relied on slave labor to raise cotton, rice, tobacco, and grain.

That January, Lincoln also acted within his cabinet. He appointed his embattled Secretary of War, Simon Cameron (*see* Chapter 2), to the post of United States Minister to Russia. Upon hearing this news, Stevens said, "Send word to the Czar to bring in his things of the night." Besides, before his departure to Russia, the House censured Cameron for adopting policies that flagrantly damaged the public service.

By the time the war was ending, Stevens was the acknowledged leader of the Radical Republicans. The elections of 1866 put this group in firm control of the Congress. Stevens became the architect of the country's policies governing the Reconstruction of the Southern states. He planned to use military power to force the South to recognize the equality of the freed slaves. Lincoln's successor, President Andrew Johnson, opposed most of Stevens's plans. Stevens was up for the fight in August of 1866 during a Congressional speech. He proclaimed:

You will remember in Egypt he sent frogs, locusts, murrain,
lice, and finally demanded the firstborn of every one of the
oppressors. Almost all these have been taken from us. We have
been oppressed with taxes and debts, and he has sent us worse
than lice and has afflicted us with Andrew Johnson.

It was Stevens who proposed the resolution for the impeachment of Johnson in 1868. Every Republican voted in favor of the measure, and Stevens made it a point to put members of both the House and Senate on notice relative to their ultimate decision on the matter. After the articles of impeachment were adopted, he said, "Let me see the recreant who would vote to let such a criminal escape. Point me to one who would dare do it, and I will show you one who would dare the infamy of posterity."

That man turned out to be a Republican Senator Edmund Ross from Kansas who found Johnson to be not guilty, and as a result, the president's impeachment failed by one slender vote. Rather than daring the infamy of posterity, Ross was hailed for his stand and vote in John F. Kennedy's *Profiles in Courage*.

While Stevens failed in his efforts to impeach the President, he was largely successful in having his policies adopted in terms of the Reconstruction of the South. In terms of historical judgment, Reconstruction is largely viewed as having failed. Historians differ as to the reasons for this outcome, and that remains a matter of controversy to this day.

Three months after the acquittal of Johnson on August 11, 1868, Thaddeus Stevens died in Washington. He was 76 years of age. His coffin

Formal notice of the impeachment of Andrew Johnson, by the House Committee, Thaddeus Stevesn and John A. Bingham, at the bar of the Senate, Washington, D.C., on February 25, 1868.

The tomb of a man that would not accept slavery in the United States.

lay in state in the Capitol Rotunda, attended by a black honor guard. His funeral in Lancaster was attended by over 20,000 people, half of which were African Americans. He decided to be buried in the Shreiner Cemetery because it would accept people without regard to race. Stevens composed the inscription on his headstone. It reads:

> I repose in this quiet and secluded spot, not from
> any natural preference for solitude, but finding other
> cemeteries limited as to race, by charter rules. I have
> chosen this that I might illustrate in my death the
> principles which I advocated through a long life,
> equality of man before his Creator.

In death, Stevens attempted to carry on the causes he worked for during his life. He left $50,000 to establish the Stevens School. The school provided refuge and education to homeless orphans. The students were admitted without regard to their race or the religion of their parents. The school is now the Thaddeus Stevens College of Technology, and its goal remains to provide the underprivileged with opportunities they would otherwise be denied.

If You Go:

We identified several sites worth visiting in Lancaster. We would urge you to review chapters 1 and 12 in this volume and *Keystone Tombstones Volume 1* (Chapter 21), which covers the careers of President James Buchanan, Major General John Fulton Reynolds, and the Pennsylvania patriot Thomas Mifflin.

35.

MEDAL OF HONOR RECIPIENTS

"A nation reveals itself not only by the men it produces but also by the men it honors, the men it remembers."

—President John F. Kennedy

Soldiers and Sailors Grove in Harrisburg (photo by Joe Farrell)

The Medal of Honor is the highest award for valor in action against an enemy force that can be bestowed upon an individual serving in the Armed Forces of the United States. The President awards the Medal of Honor in the name of Congress to a person who, while a member of the army or other service in the military of the United States, distinguishes himself or herself conspicuously by gallantry and intrepidity at the risk of his or her life above and beyond the call of duty while engaged in an action against an enemy of the United States, while engaged in an armed conflict against the opposing armed force in which the United States is not a belligerent party. The deed performed must have been one of personal bravery or self-sacrifice so conspicuous as to distinguish the individual above his comrades clearly and must have involved risk of life. Incontestable proof of the performance of the service will be exacted, and each recommendation for the award of this decoration will be considered on the standard of extraordinary merit.

In *Keystone Tombstones Volume I*, we visited and memorialized fifteen of Pennsylvania's Medal of Honor Recipients. The response from readers was extremely positive. In *Volume II*, we once again visited Medal of Honor Recipients everywhere we went and included eighteen in that volume. Along the way, we discovered that Pennsylvania honors its Medal of Honor recipients in Soldiers and Sailors Grove in Harrisburg. Located directly behind the State Capitol, the park serves as a memorial to all Pennsylvanians who have served in the U.S. armed forces. Included within the ribbon-like bands that represent various conflicts are the names of each Medal of Honor recipient for that conflict from Pennsylvania. Pennsylvania is second only to New York in the number of Medal of Honor recipients.

On the following pages are listed the Civil War Medal of Honor recipients buried in Pennsylvania.

———

• **Ammerman, Robert Wesley,** Lost Creek Presbyterian Cemetery, McAlisterville. One of four 148th Pennsylvania Infantry soldiers to be awarded the Medal of Honor, Private Ammerman was awarded his CMOH for bravery at the Battle of Spotsylvania, Virginia, on May 12, 1864. His citation read: *Capture of battle flag of 8th North Carolina (C.S.A.), being one of the foremost in the assault.*

• **Anderson, Everett W.,** Morris Cemetery, Phoenixville. One of six 15th Pennsylvania Cavalry soldiers to receive the Medal of Honor, Anderson's was awarded for bravery at Crosbys Creek, Tennessee, on January 14, 1864. His citation reads: *Captured, single-handed, Confederate Brig. Gen. Robert B. Vance during a charge upon the enemy.*

• **Baker, Charles,** Mount Moriah Cemetery, Philadelphia. A Quarter Gunner in the Union Navy onboard the USS *Metacomet*, Baker was awarded the CMOH for his bravery on August 5, 1864, in Mobile Bay, Alabama. He served as a member of the boat's crew, which went to the rescue of the Union monitor USS *Tecumseh* when a torpedo struck that vessel in passing the enemy forts. His citation reads: *Q.G. Baker braved the enemy fire, which was said by the admiral to be "one of the most galling" he had ever seen and aided in rescuing from death 10 of the crew of the* Tecumseh, *eliciting the admiration of both friend and foe.*

• **Beaumont, Eugene Beauharnais,** Holleback Cemetery, Wilkes-Barre. A major in the Cavalry Corps, Army of the Mississippi, Beaumont was awarded the Medal of Honor for action on December 17, 1864, and April 2, 1865, at Harpeth River, Tennessee, and Selma, Alabama. His citation reads: *Obtained permission from the corps commander to advance upon enemy's position with the 4th Cavalry, of which he was a lieutenant; led an attack upon a battery, dispersed the enemy, and captured the guns. At Selma, Ala., charged, at the head of his regiment, into the second and last line of the enemy's works.*

• **Betts, Charles Malone,** West Laurel Hill Cemetery, Bala Cynwyd. Betts served during the Civil War as Colonel and commander of the 15th Pennsylvania Volunteer Cavalry. He was awarded the CMOH while Lieutenant Colonel of the regiment for his bravery at Greensboro, North Carolina, on April 19, 1865. He was one of six 15th Pennsylvania Cavalry soldiers to be awarded the Medal of Honor for bravery during the Civil War, and his feat was the last action of the Civil War to merit a Medal of Honor. His citation reads: *With a force of but 75 men, while on a scouting expedition, by a judicious disposition of his men, surprised and captured an entire battalion of the enemy's cavalry.*

• **Beyer, Hillary,** Lower Providence Presbyterian Church, Eagleville. A 2nd lieutenant in the Union Army in the 90th Pennsylvania Volunteer Infantry, Beyer was awarded the Medal of Honor for action on Sept. 17, 1862, at Antietam, Maryland. His citation reads: *After his command had been forced to fall back, remained alone on the line of battle, caring for his wounded comrades and carrying one of them to a place of safety.*

• **Binder, Richard,** West Laurel Hill Cemetery, Bala Cynwyd. A sergeant in the United States Marine Corps on board the USS *Ticonderoga*, Binder was awarded the CMOH for his heroism during the Union Army-Navy assault and capture of Fort Fisher, North Carolina, on January 13–15, 1865. One of nine USS *Ticonderoga* crewmembers to be awarded the CMOH for bravery during the Civil War, his citation reads: *Despite heavy return fire by the enemy and the explosion of the 100-pound Parrott rifle which killed eight men and wounded 12 more, Sgt. Binder, as captain of a gun, performed his duties with skill and courage during the first two days of battle. As his ship again took position on the 13th, he remained steadfast as the* Ticonderoga *maintained a well-placed fire upon the batteries on shore, and thereafter, as she materially lessened the power of guns on the mound which* *had been turned upon our assaulting columns. During this action, the flag was planted on one of the strongest fortifications possessed by the rebels.*

• **Bingham, Henry Harrison,** Laurel Hill Cemetery, Philadelphia. A captain in Company G, 140th Pennsylvania Volunteer Infantry, Bingham was awarded the CMOH for his bravery at the Battle of the Wilderness, Virginia, on May 6, 1864. His citation reads: *Rallied and led into action a portion of the troops who had given away under the fierce assaults of the enemy.* He was later elected to represent Pennsylvania's 1st District in the United States House of Representatives, serving from 1879 until he died in office in 1912. Bingham County, Idaho, is named for him.

• **Blackwood, William R.D.,** Chelten Hills Cemetery, Philadelphia. Born in Ireland, Blackwood was a graduate of the University of Pennsylvania medical school. He served as Chief Surgeon for the 48th Pennsylvania Volunteer Infantry. He was awarded the CMOH for his bravery during the final Union Army assaults on Confederate positions at Petersburg, Virginia, on April 2, 1865. His grave lain unmarked from his death in 1922 until 2006. His citation reads: *Removed severely wounded officers and soldiers from the field while under a heavy fire from the enemy, exposing himself beyond the call of duty, thus furnishing an example of most distinguished gallantry.*

• **Bonnaffon, Jr., Sylvester,** Woodlands Cemetery, Philadelphia. As First Lieutenant, Company G, 99th Pennsylvania Infantry Regiment, Bonnaffon received a Medal of Honor for his actions against Confederate forces at Boydton Plank Road, Virginia, during the Siege of Petersburg on October 27, 1864. His citation for that act reads: *Checked the rout and rallied the troops of his command in the face of a terrible fire of musketry; was severely wounded.* His post-war career saw him serve as cashier of customs for the port of Philadelphia, and as Colonel of the 20th Pennsylvania National Guard regiment.

• **Boon, Hugh Patterson,** Washington Cemetery, Washington. The Captain and commander of Company B, 1st West Virginia Volunteer Cavalry, Boon was awarded the CMOH (one of fourteen 1st West Virginia Cavalry soldiers to receive the Medal of Honor) for bravery at the Battle of Sailors Creek, Virginia, on April 6, 1865. The flag bearing the colors of the 10th Georgia Infantry was captured after Captain Boon led a charge on a battalion of infantry and during which he cut down the Confederate color-bearer. His charge was unauthorized, but because of the positive results, he received accolades from his superiors for the action. His CMOH citation simply reads *Capture of flag.*

• **Brest, Lewis,** Mercer Citizens Cemetery, Mercer. A private in Company D, 57th Pennsylvania Volunteer Infantry, Brest was awarded his CMOH for action he took in brutal hand-to-hand combat at the Battle of Sailors Creek, Virginia, on April 6, 1865. Before that time, Brest had an interesting combat history. Throughout 1862 and early 1863, he fought with his company and regiment in all the battles of the Army of the Potomac, including the Peninsular Campaign, Seven Days Battle, 2nd Bull Run, Fredericksburg, and Chancellorsville. Just before the Gettysburg Campaign, he contracted a severe case of typhoid fever, which kept him out of the battle (including his regiment's futile stand on Emmitsburg Road on July 2, 1863). Returning to his unit in late 1863 after his recovery, he served with them in Ulysses S. Grant's 1864 Overland Campaign and sustained a bullet wound in his neck during the Battle of the Wilderness. He recovered quickly from that injury and was present during the Siege of Petersburg from June 1864 to April 1865. It was during the final Union push against the Army of Northern Virginia that he captured a Confederate battle flag, garnering him a CMOH. His citation reads simply: *Capture of flag.*

• **Bryer, Charles,** Limerick Church Burial Ground, Limerick. A sergeant in the Union Army in Company I, 90th Pennsylvania Volunteer Infantry, Breyer was awarded the Medal of Honor for action at Rappahannock Station, Virginia, on August 23, 1862. His citation reads: *Voluntarily and at great personal risk, Breyer picked up an unexploded shell and threw it away, thus doubtless saving the life of a comrade whose arm had been taken off by the same shell.*

• **Bronson, James H.,** Chartiers Cemetery, Carnegie. A first sergeant in the Union Army in the 5th US Colored Infantry, Bronson was awarded the Medal of Honor for action on Sept. 29, 1864, at Chapin's Farm, Virginia. His citation reads: *Took command of his company, all the officers having been killed or wounded, and gallantly led it.*

• **Brown, Charles E.,** Schuylkill Haven Union Cemetery, Schuylkill. Brown performed distinguished service at the August 19, 1864, Battle of Weldon Railroad, Virginia, and received the CMOH for his bravery. In that battle, his regiment was part of a charge that captured Confederate breastworks and sent the defending rebels retreating. First armed only with a sword, Sergeant Brown noticed Confederates with a battle flag, picked up a discarded rifle (which turned out to be empty), and captured the men and the flag, after which he planted on the breastworks. That act drew both cheers from his Union Army comrades and gunfire from the Confederates (which resulted in several men killed and several holes in Sergeant Brown's uniform). After sleeping next to the flag that night, it was sent to Washington, D.C., by General Oliver B. Wilcox, with the proper accreditation given to Sergeant Brown. His CMOH citation reads simply: *Capture of flag of 47th Virginia Infantry (C.S.A.).* The actual flag he captured can still be seen today at the Museum of the Confederacy in Richmond, Virginia.

• **Brown, Jeremiah Z.,** Squirrel Hill Cemetery, New Bethlehem. After being promoted to Captain and company commander of the 148th Pennsylvania Volunteer Infantry, Company K on July 31, 1864, Brown performed a feat of bravery on October 27, 1864, during the Siege of Petersburg, Virginia, that would see him awarded the CMOH (one of four 148th Pennsylvania Infantry soldiers to be awarded the Medal of Honor for bravery during the Civil War). In the charge, Captain Brown had men from various companies follow him as he led them under fire through first open land, then blockaded ditches that ringed fort Crater. After reaching the Fort, he was the first of his men inside, and his command captured the position, as well as several Confederate officers and men. After an hour, Captain Brown was forced to retreat and relinquish the fort while waiting for reinforcements that never came. When he asked about them to brigade commander General Nelson A. Miles, the officer who ordered the charge, he was informed that no reinforcements were planned because it was never believed that Captain Brown's men had a chance of succeeding. His CMOH citation for his acts reads: *With 100 selected volunteers, Brown assaulted and captured the works of the enemy, together with a number of officers and men.*

• **Brutsche, Henry,** Lawnview Cemetery, Rockledge. A landsman in the Union Navy, Brutsche was awarded a Medal of Honor for bravery in action aboard the USS *Tacony* on October 31, 1864. His citation reads: *Served on board the USS* Tacony *during the taking of Plymouth, NC, 31 October 1864. Carrying out his duties faithfully during the capture of Plymouth, Brutsche distinguished himself by a display of coolness when he participated in landing and spiking a 9-inch gun while under a devastating fire from enemy musketry.* Brutsche was initially interred in Monument Cemetery, Philadelphia, but when that cemetery was closed in 1956, he was re-interred in Lawnview Cemetery.

• **Caldwell, Daniel G.,** Mount Peace Cemetery, Philadelphia. On February 6, 1865, at the Battle of Hatcher's Run, Virginia, he performed an act of bravery that would garner him the CMOH. His citation reads: *In a mounted charge, Caldwell dashed into the center of the enemy's line and captured the colors of the 33rd North Carolina Infantry.*

• **Carey, James Lemuel,** Chartiers Cemetery, Carnegie. A sergeant in the Union Army in the 10th New York Cavalry, Carey was awarded the Medal of Honor for action on April 9, 1865, at Appomattox Courthouse, Virginia. His citation reads: *Daring bravery and urging the men forward in a charge.*

• **Carlisle, Casper R.,** Mount Lebanon Cemetery, Mount Lebanon. A private in the Union Army in the Independent Pennsylvania Light Artillery, Carlisle was awarded the Medal of Honor for action on July 2, 1863, at Gettysburg, Pennsylvania. His citation reads: *Saved a gun of his battery under heavy musketry fire, most of the horses being killed and the drivers wounded.*

• **Cart, Jacob,** Ashland Cemetery, Carlisle. Awarded the Medal of Honor as a private in Company A, 7th Pennsylvania Reserve Corps, for action on December 13, 1862, at Fredericksburg, Virginia, Cart's citation reads: *Capture of flag of 19th Georgia Infantry (C.S.A.), wresting it from the hands of the color bearer.*

• **Chambers, Joseph,** Oak Park Cemetery, New Castle. A private in Company F, 100th Pennsylvania Volunteer Infantry, Chambers was awarded the CMOH for his bravery in the repulse of the Confederate assault on Fort Stedman at Petersburg, Virginia, on March 25, 1865. His citation reads: *Capture of colors of 1st Virginia Infantry (C.S.A.).*

• **Clark, James G.,** Fernwood Cemetery, Lansdowne. One of four soldiers from the 88th Pennsylvania to receive the Medal of Honor, Clark's CMOH, was awarded for bravery in action on June 18, 1864, at Petersburg, Virginia. His citation reads simply: *Distinguished bravery in action; was severely wounded.*

• **Clausen, Charles H.,** Mount Peace Cemetery, Philadelphia. One of eight 61st Pennsylvania Infantry soldiers to be awarded the Civil War CMOH, he performed an act of bravery under fire at the May 12, 1864, Battle of Spotsylvania, Virginia. His citation for that act reads: *Although severely wounded, he led the regiment against the enemy, under a terrific fire, and saved a battery from capture.*

• **Clopp, John E.,** Lawnview Cemetery, Rockledge. A Private in Company F, 71st Pennsylvania Infantry, Clopp was awarded the CMOH for action on July 3, 1863, at Gettysburg, Pennsylvania. His citation reads: *Capture of flag of 9th Virginia Infantry (C.S.A.), wresting it from the color bearer.*

• **Collis, Charles Henry Tucky,** Gettysburg National Cemetery, Gettysburg. Collis was serving as Colonel of the 114th Pennsylvania Infantry at Fredericksburg, Virginia, on December 13, 1862, when he earned the Medal of Honor. His citation reads: *Gallantly led his regiment in battle at a critical moment.* He was subsequently a colonel of the 118th Pennsylvania Infantry at the Battle of Gettysburg. After the war ended, he moved to Gettysburg and established his residence there, and hence is buried in the Gettysburg National Cemetery (his grave is adorned with a monument that includes a bronze bust).

• **Conner, Richard,** North Cedar Hill Cemetery, Philadelphia. A private in Company F, 6th New Jersey Volunteer Infantry, Conner was awarded the CMOH for his bravery at the 2nd Battle of Bull Run, Virginia, on August 29, 1862. His citation reads: *The flag of his regiment having been abandoned during retreat, he voluntarily returned with a single companion under a heavy fire and secured and brought of the flag, his companion being killed.*

• **Cooke, Walter Howard,** Saint Thomas Episcopal Church Cemetery, Whitemarsh. Cooke was awarded the Medal of Honor as a captain in Company K, 4th Pennsylvania Infantry Militia for action on July 21, 1861, at Bull Run, Virginia. His citation reads: *Voluntarily served as an aide on the staff of Col. David Hunter and participated in the battle, his term of service having expired on the previous day.*

• **Corson, Joseph Kirby,** West Laurel Hill Cemetery, Bala Cynwyd. A major and assistant surgeon of the 6th Pennsylvania Reserves (35th Pennsylvania Volunteer Infantry), Corson was awarded the CMOH for his bravery at Bristoe Station, Virginia (October 14, 1863). His citation reads: *With one companion returned in the face of the enemy's heavy artillery fire and removed to a place of safety, a severely wounded soldier who had been left behind as the regiment fell back.*

• **Crawford, Alexander,** Cedar Hill Cemetery, Philadelphia. Served as a fireman in the Union Navy. His Medal of Honor citation recites the events which led to his award: *On board the USS* Wyalusing, *Crawford volunteered 25 May 1864, in a night attempt* *to destroy the rebel ram Albemarle in the Roanoke River. Taking part in a plan to explode the rebel ram Albemarle, Crawford executed his part in the plan with perfection, but upon being discovered, was forced to abandon the plan and retire, leaving no trace of the evidence. After spending two hazardous days and night without food, he gained the safety of a friendly ship and was then transferred back to the Wyalusing. Though the plan failed, his skill and courage in preventing detection were an example of unfailing devotion to duty.*

• **Cripps, Thomas,** Woodlands Cemetery, Philadelphia. A quartermaster on board the warship USS *Richmond*, Cripps—one of 31 *Richmond* crewmembers to receive the Medal of Honor—exhibited bravery during the Union Naval assault on Mobile Bay, Alabama, on August 5, 1864, which earned him a CMOH. His citation reads: *Despite damage to his ship and the loss of several men on board as enemy fire raked her decks, Cripps fought his gun with skill and courage throughout a furious 2-hour battle which resulted in the surrender of the rebel ram* Tennessee *and the damaging and destruction of batteries at Fort Morgan.*

• **Cunningham, Francis M.,** Sugar Grove Cemetery, Ohiopyle. A first sergeant in Company H, 1st West Virginia Volunteer Cavalry, Cunningham—one of fourteen 1st West Virginia Cavalry soldiers to receive the Medal of Honor—was awarded the CMOH for his bravery at the Battle of Sailors Creek, Virginia, on April 6, 1865. His citation reads *Capture of battle flag of 12th Virginia Infantry (C.S.A.) in hand-to-hand battle while wounded.*

• **Davidsizer, John A.,** First Methodist Cemetery, Lewistown. A sergeant in Company A, 1st Pennsylvania Volunteer Cavalry, Davidsizer was awarded the Medal of Honor for action on April 5, 1865, at Paine's Crossroads, Virginia. His citation reads simply: *Capture of flag.*

• **Day, Charles,** Prospect Cemetery, Mansfield. A private in Company K, 210th Pennsylvania Volunteer Infantry, Day was awarded the Medal of Honor for his bravery on February 6, 1865, at the Battle of Hatcher's Run, Virginia. His citation reads: *Seized the colors of another regiment of the brigade, the regiment having been thrown into confusion, and the color bearer killed and bore said colors throughout the remainder of the engagement.*

• **De Lacy, Patrick,** Saint Catherine's Cemetery, Moscow. A first sergeant in Company A, 143rd Pennsylvania Volunteer Infantry, De Lacy was awarded the CMOH for his bravery at the Battle of the Wilderness, Virginia, on May 6, 1864. His deed was performed on the second day of the battle and was a countercharge to a massive attack by the corps of Confederate General James Longstreet, which had rolled up the Union Army's left flank. Sergeant De Lacy was in command of his company after its officers were all incapacitated. His capture of the Confederate flag, the colors of the 1st South Carolina Infantry Regiment, demoralized the Rebel soldiers who were following it and ensured a measure of success in the 143rd Pennsylvania's attack. His citation for his acts reads: *Running ahead of the line, under a concentrated fire, he shot the color bearer of a Confederate regiment on the works, thus contributing to the success of the attack.*

• **Delavie, Hiram Adam,** Saint Peters Cemetery, Pittsburgh. A sergeant in Company I, 11th Pennsylvania Infantry (Washington Blues), Delavie was awarded the Medal of Honor for action on April 1, 1865, at Five Forks, Virginia. His citation reads simply: *Capture of flag.*

• **Denig, John Henry,** Prospect Hill Cemetery, York. A sergeant in the United States Marine Corps aboard the USS *Brooklyn*, Denig was awarded the Medal of Honor for action on Aug. 5, 1864, at Mobile Bay, Alabama. His citation reads: *On board the USS* Brooklyn *during action against rebel forts and gunboats and with the ram Tennessee, in Mobile Bay, 5 August 1864. Despite severe damage to his ship and the loss of several men on board as enemy fire raked her decks, Sgt. Denig fought his gun with skill and courage throughout the furious 2-hour battle which resulted in the surrender of the rebel ram Tennessee and in the damaging and destruction of batteries at Fort Morgan.*

• **Densmore, William,** Holy Cross Cemetery, Yeadon. A chief boatswain's mate in the Union Navy at New York, Densmore was awarded a Medal of Honor, the citation of which reads as follows: *As captain of a gun on board the USS* Richmond *during action against rebel forts and gunboats and with the ram Tennessee in Mobile Bay, 5 August 1864. Despite damage to his ship and the loss of several men on board as enemy fire raked her decks, Densmore fought his gun with skill and courage throughout a furious two-hour battle, which resulted in the surrender of the rebel ram Tennessee and in the damaging and destruction of batteries at Fort Morgan.* Densmore was initially buried in St. Joseph's Cemetery (aka Bishops Burial Ground) in Philadelphia. This cemetery was closed in 1905, and the bodies were reinterred at Holy Cross Cemetery in Yeadon, in Section 13, Ranges 11, 12, and 13 (no lists are available showing who was buried where).

• **Dougherty, Michael,** Saint Marks Roman Catholic Churchyard, Bristol. A private in the Union Army in Company B, 13th Pennsylvania Volunteer Cavalry (117th Pennsylvania Volunteers Regiment), Dougherty was awarded the Medal of Honor for action on October 12, 1863, at Jefferson, Virginia. His citation reads: *At the head of a detachment of his company, he dashed across an open field, exposed to a deadly fire from the enemy, and succeeded in dislodging them from an unoccupied house, which he and his comrades defended for several hours against repeated attacks, thus preventing the enemy from flanking the position of the Union forces.*

• **Elliott, Alexander,** Highwood Cemetery, Pittsburgh. A sergeant in Company A, 1st Pennsylvania Volunteer Cavalry, Elliott was awarded the CMOH for his bravery at Paines Crossroads, Virginia, on April 5, 1865. His citation reads simply: *Capture of flag.*

• **English, Edmund,** Old Cathedral Cemetery, Philadelphia. A 1st sergeant in Company C, 2nd New Jersey Volunteer Infantry, English was awarded the CMOH for his bravery at the Battle of the Wilderness, Virginia, on May 6, 1864. His citation reads: *During a rout and while under orders to retreat, seized the colors, rallied the men, and drove the enemy back.*

• **Evans, Thomas,** Bethel Baptist Cemetery, Ebensburg. A private in the Union Army in Company D, 54th Pennsylvania Infantry, Evans was awarded the Medal of Honor for action on June 5, 1864, at Piedmont, Virginia. His citation reads: *Capture of flag of 45th Virginia (C.S.A.).* His name is on a bronze plaque attached to a Civil War monument located in Veterans Square in the town.

• **Ewing, John C.,** Ligonier Valley Cemetery, Ligonier. A private in Company E, 211st Pennsylvania Volunteer Infantry, Ewing was awarded the CMOH for his bravery in action on April 2, 1865, during the final Union assaults on Confederate positions at Petersburg, Virginia. During the action, his regiment lost a total of 135 officers and men (who were either killed, wounded, or went missing). His citation reads simply: *Capture of flag.*

• **Fasnacht, Charles H.,** Greenwood Cemetery, Lancaster. Born Karl Heinrich Fasnacht in Lancaster County, Pennsylvania, he performed an act of bravery at the May 12, 1864, Battle of Spotsylvania that would see him awarded the CMOH. During that bloody conflict, he fought and wrenched the 2nd Louisiana's flag from its flag bearer but was soon wounded where he stood. After lying on the battlefield for several days, Fasnacht was finally recovered by the Confederates and sent to Richmond, Virginia. Before he got there, he was rescued by Union troops, and it was revealed he had hidden the captured Rebel flag in his shirt while under guard by the rebels. His citation reads: *Capture of flag of 2nd Louisiana Tigers (C.S.A.) in a hand-to-hand contest.*

• **Fisher, Joseph,** Fernwood Cemetery, Lansdowne. One of eight 61st Pennsylvania Infantry soldiers to be awarded the Civil War CMOH, Fisher earned his by exhibiting bravery during the final Union assaults on Petersburg, Virginia, on April 2, 1865. His citation reads: *Carried the colors 50 yards in advance of his regiment, and after being painfully wounded, attempted to crawl into the enemy's works in an endeavor to plant his flag thereon.*

• **Frick, Jacob G.,** Presbyterian Cemetery, Pottsville. A colonel in the Union Army in the 129th Pennsylvania Infantry, Frick, was awarded the Medal of Honor for action on December 13, 1862, at Fredericksburg, Virginia, and on May 3, 1863, at Chancellorsville, Virginia. His citation reads: *At Fredericksburg seized the colors and led the command through a terrible fire of cannon and musketry. In a hand-to-hand fight at Chancellorsville, recaptured the colors of his regiment.*

• **Furman, Chester S.,** Old Rosemont Cemetery, Bloomsburg. A corporal in Company A, 6th Pennsylvania Reserves, Furman was awarded the CMOH for his bravery during the second day of the Battle of Gettysburg, Pennsylvania (July 2, 1863). His citation reads: *Was 1 of 6 volunteers who charged upon a log house near Devil's Den, where a squad of the enemy's sharpshooters were sheltered, and compelled their surrender.*

• **Furness, Frank,** Laurel Hill Cemetery, Philadelphia. Served as Captain and commander of Company F, 6th Pennsylvania Volunteer Cavalry ("Rush's Lancers"). Furness was awarded the CMOH for his bravery at the Battle of Trevailian Station, Virginia, on June 12, 1864. His citation reads: *Voluntarily carried a box of ammunition across an open space swept by the enemy's fire to the relief of an outpost whose ammunition had become almost exhausted but was thus enabled to hold its important position.* He had been recommended for the medal after the war but refused it until later in his life. Captain Furness was better known as a significant Philadelphia architect; he designed over 400 buildings between 1870 and 1900.

• **Galloway, George Norton,** Mount Moriah Cemetery, Philadelphia. A private in Company G, 95th Pennsylvania Volunteer Infantry, Galloway was awarded the CMOH for his bravery at Alsop's Farm, Virginia, on May 8, 1864. His citation simply reads: *Voluntarily held an important position under heavy fire.*

• **Galloway, John,** Mount Moriah Cemetery, Philadelphia. A commissary sergeant of the 8th Pennsylvania Volunteer Cavalry, Galloway was awarded the CMOH for his bravery at Farmville, Virginia, on April 7, 1865. His citation reads: *His regiment being surprised and nearly overwhelmed, he dashed forward under a heavy fire, reached the right of the regiment, where the danger was greatest, rallied the men, and prevented a disaster that was imminent.*

• **Gilligan, Edward Lyons,** Oxford Cemetery, Oxford. A first sergeant in Company E, 88th Pennsylvania Infantry, Gilligan was awarded the Medal of Honor as for action on July 1, 1863, at Gettysburg, Pennsylvania. His citation reads: *Assisted in the capture of a Confederate flag by knocking down the color sergeant.*

• **Gion, Joseph,** Saint Martins Cemetery, Pittsburgh. A private in Company A, 74th New York Volunteer Infantry, Gion was awarded the CMOH for his bravery at the Battle of Chancellorsville, Virginia, on May 2, 1863. He and three other 74th New York soldiers had volunteered to perform a dangerous reconnaissance, which requested by Union General Hiram G. Berry, and was done in the night after Stonewall Jackson had crushed the Union Army of the Potomac's right flank. Without the Rebels discovering them, Gion and his three fellow soldiers (all of whom were awarded the CMOH for these acts as well) heard the accidental shooting of General Jackson by his men and were able to return with that information, as well as information about the location of the Confederate troops. When they returned to Union lines, they learned that General Berry had been mortally wounded and that one of his last requests was that four-member scouting party be rewarded. The citation on Gion's CMOH reads: *Voluntarily and under heavy fire advanced toward the enemy's lines and secured valuable information.*

• **Goodman, William Ernest,** Saint Thomas Episcopal Church Cemetery, Whitemarsh. A first lieutenant in Company D, 147th Pennsylvania Infantry, Goodman was awarded the Medal of Honor for action on May 3, 1863, at Chancellorsville,

Virginia. His citation reads: *Rescued the colors of the 107th Ohio Volunteers from the enemy.*

• **Gresser, Ignatz,** Union & West End Cemetery, Allentown. A corporal in the 128th Pennsylvania Volunteer Infantry, Company D, Gresser was awarded the CMOH for his bravery at the Battle of Antietam on September 17, 1862. That day, early in the battle, Corporal William Henry Snowden suffered a severe wound in the attack of the 128th Pennsylvania's brigade on Confederate forces in the now infamous Cornfield. After Corporal Snowden went down, Gresser, braving the murderous fire coming from the Confederate lines (the 128th Pennsylvania sustained 118 casualties that day), exposed himself to retrieve Corporal Snowden and carry him to safety (thereby making the two terms Corporal Snowden would later serve as a United States Congressman possible). Today a monument to the 128th Pennsylvania stands on Cornfield Avenue in the Antietam National Battlefield. The Allentown Soldiers and Sailors Monument, which stands in the center of the town, came about mainly through the efforts of Corporal Gresser. Gresser's actions that day resulted in an award of a CMOH, the citation for which reads simply: *While exposed to the fire of the enemy, carried from the field a wounded comrade.*

• **Harris, George W.,** Union Cemetery, Bellefonte. A private in Company B, 148th Pennsylvania Volunteer Infantry, Harris—one of four 148th Pennsylvania Infantry soldiers to be awarded the Medal of Honor was awarded his CMOH for bravery at the Battle of Spotsylvania, Virginia, on May 12, 1864. His citation reads: *Capture of flag, wresting it from the color bearer and shooting an officer who attempted to regain it.*

• **Hill, Henry,** Schuylkill Haven Union Cemetery, Schuylkill. A corporal in Company C, 50th Pennsylvania Infantry, Hill was awarded the Medal of Honor for action on May 6, 1864, during the Wilderness Campaign, Virginia. His citation reads: *This soldier, with one companion, would not retire when his regiment fell back in confusion after an unsuccessful charge, but instead advanced and continued firing upon the enemy until the regiment re-formed and regained its position.*

• **Hoffman, Thomas W.,** Pomfret Manor Cemetery, Sunbury. The Captain and commander of Company A, 208th Pennsylvania Volunteer Infantry, Hoffman was awarded the Medal of Honor for his bravery in action on April 2, 1865, at Petersburg, Virginia. His citation reads: *Prevented a retreat of his regiment during the battle.*

• **Huidekoper, Henry Shippen,** Greendale Cemetery, Meadville. The Lieutenant Colonel and commander of his unit, the 150th Pennsylvania Volunteer Infantry, Huidekoper was awarded the CMOH for his bravery on the first day of the Battle of Gettysburg (July 1, 1863). He had commanded a portion of the 150th Pennsylvania in the initial heavy fighting around McPherson's Farm northwest of the town. When the 150th's Colonel, Langhorne Wister, took over command of the brigade, Lt. Colonel Huidekoper assumed command of the regiment. He then sustained a severe arm wound that eventually cost him his arm. He continued to direct his regiment despite the wound until the loss of blood forced him to retire; his remaining in the battle proved invaluable since every officer of the regiment had been killed or wounded. His citation reads: *While engaged in repelling an attack of the enemy, he received a severe wound of the right arm, but instead of retiring, he remained at the front in command of the regiment.* After the war, he served as a major general of the Pennsylvania National Guard and was active in suppressing the 1877 Labor Riots. He also served as Postmaster of Philadelphia, Pennsylvania, from 1880 to 1885, and was responsible for increasing the standard weight for mailing a letter from a half-ounce to an ounce.

• **Hunterson, John C.**, Gloria Dei (Old Swedes) Church Burial Ground, Philadelphia. While serving in the 3rd Pennsylvania Cavalry in the Peninsular Campaign, Private Hunterson performed acts of bravery amidst an intense crossfire between the Union and Confederate lines on June 5, 1862, that would result in him being awarded the Medal of Honor. His citation reads: *While under fire, between the lines of the two armies, voluntarily gave up his horse to an engineer officer whom he was accompanying on reconnaissance and whose horse had been killed, thus enabling the officer to escape with valuable papers in his possession.*

• **Ilgenfritz, Charles Henry,** Prospect Hill Cemetery, York. A sergeant in the Union Army in the 207th Pennsylvania Infantry, Ilgenfritz was awarded the Medal of Honor for action on April 2, 1865, at Fort Sedgwick, Virginia. His citation reads: *The Color Bearer falling, pierced by seven balls, Sergeant Ilgenfritz immediately sprang forward and grasped the colors, planting them upon the enemy's forts amid a murderous fire of grape, canister, and musketry from the enemy.*

• **Johnson, Wallace W.**, West Laurel Hill Cemetery, Bala Cynwyd. A sergeant in Company G, 6th Pennsylvania Reserves (35th Pennsylvania Volunteer Infantry), Johnson was awarded the CMOH for his bravery at the Battle of Gettysburg, Pennsylvania (July 2, 1863). His citation reads: *With five other volunteers gallantly charged on a number of the enemy's sharpshooters concealed in a log house, captured them, and brought them into Union lines.*

• **Kelley, Robert Teleford,** Laurel Hill Cemetery, Philadelphia. Kelley served in the Union Navy as a master-at-arms on board the USS *Shokokon* under the alias "Robert T. Clifford." Awarded the CMOH for his bravery at an engagement at New Topsail Inlet off Wilmington, North Carolina, on August 22, 1863. Since he never asked for it to be re-issued under his real name, Seaman Kelley's official citation is still listed alphabetically under his Clifford alias. His citation reads: *Participating in a strategic plan to destroy an enemy schooner, Clifford aided in the portage of a dinghy across a narrow neck of land separating the sea from the sound. Launching the boat in the sound, the crew approached the enemy from the rear, and Clifford gallantly crept into the rebel camp and counted the men who outnumbered his party 3 to 1. Returning to his men, he ordered a charge in which the enemy was routed, leaving behind a schooner and a quantity of supplies.*

• **Kelly, Alexander,** Saint Peters Cemetery, Pittsburgh. A first sergeant in the Union Army in Company F, 6th United States Colored Infantry, Kelly was awarded the Medal of Honor for action on September 29, 1864, at Chapin's Farm, Virginia. His citation reads: *Gallantly seized the colors, which had fallen near the enemy's lines of abatis, raised them, and rallied the men at a time of confusion and in a place of the greatest danger.*

• **Landis, James Parker,** Yeagertown Lutheran Cemetery, Yeagertown. A chief bugler in the Union Army in the 1st Pennsylvania Cavalry, Landis was awarded the Medal of Honor for action on April 5, 1865, at Paines Crossroads, Virginia. His citation reads simply: *Capture of flag.*

• **Laverty, John,** Mount Moriah Cemetery, Philadelphia. One of only 24 men in United States history to be awarded the Medal of Honor twice, Laverty's first CMOH was awarded for his Civil War service, for which he enlisted as "John Lafferty" and served in the Union Navy as a fireman on board the USS *Wyalusing*. He was awarded the CMOH for his bravery on the Roanoke River, North Carolina, on May 25, 1864. His citation for that deed reads: *Served on board the U.S.S.* Wyalusing *and participated in a plan to destroy the rebel ram* Albemarle *in Roanoke River, 25 May 1864. Volunteering for the hazardous mission, Lafferty participated in the transfer of two torpedoes across an island swamp and then served as sentry to keep guard of clothes and arms left by other members of the party. After being rejoined by others of the party who had been discovered before the plan could be completed, Lafferty succeeded in returning to the mother ship after spending 24 hours of discomfort in the rain and swamp.* When he re-enlisted in the Navy in 1881 (during which he performed acts of bravery that would lead to the awarding of his second CMOH), he used the "Laverty" name, which is the one on his government-issue headstone.

• **Lear, Nicholas,** Mount Moriah Cemetery, Philadelphia. A quartermaster in the Union Navy onboard the USS *New Ironsides*, Lear was awarded the CMOH for his bravery during action in several attacks on Fort Fisher, North Carolina, on December 24-25, 1864, and on January 13-15, 1865. His citation reads *Bravery while his ship steamed in and took the lead in the ironclad division close inshore and immediately opened its starboard battery in a barrage of well-directed fire to cause several fires and explosions and dismount several guns during the first two days of fighting. Taken under fire as she steamed into position on 13 January, the* New Ironsides *fought all day and took on ammunition at night despite severe weather conditions. When the enemy came out of his bombproofs to defend the fort against the storming party, the ship's battery disabled nearly every gun on the fort facing the shore before the cease-fire order was given by the flagship.*

• **Leonard, William Edman,** Jacksonville Cemetery, Wind Ridge. A private in the Union Army in Company F, 85th Pennsylvanian Infantry, Leonard was awarded the CMOH for action on August 16, 1864, at Deep Bottom, Virginia. His citation reads: *Capture of battle flag.*

• **Lewis, Dewitt Clinton,** Oaklands Cemetery, West Chester. A captain in the Union Army in the 97th Pennsylvania Infantry, Lewis was awarded the Medal of Honor for action on June 16, 1862, at Secessionville, South Carolina. His citation reads: *While retiring with his men before a heavy fire of can1ster shot at short range, returned in the face of the enemy's fire and rescued an exhausted private of his company who but for this timely action would have lost his life by drowning in the morass through which the troops were retiring.*

• **Lilley, John,** First Methodist Cemetery, Lewistown. A private in Company F, 205th Pennsylvania Volunteer Infantry, Lilley was awarded the CMOH for his bravery in action on April 2, 1865, at Petersburg, Virginia. His citation reads: *After his regiment had begun to waiver, he rushed on alone to capture the enemy flag. He reached the works and the Confederate color bearer who, at bayonet point, he caused to surrender with several enemy soldiers. He kept his prisoners in tow when they realized he was alone as his regiment in the meantime withdrawn further to the rear.*

• **Luty, Gotlieb,** Union Dale Cemetery, Pittsburgh. A corporal in the Union Army in Company A, 74th New York Infantry, Luty was awarded the Medal of Honor for action on May 3, 1863, at Chancellorsville, Virginia. His citation reads: *Bravely advanced to the enemy's line under heavy fire and brought back valuable information.*

• **Lyons, Thomas George,** Mount Moriah Cemetery, Philadelphia. Lyons' CMOH citation reads: *Served as seaman on board the U.S.S.* Pensacola *in the attack on Forts Jackson and St. Philip, 24 April 1862. Carrying out his duties throughout the din and roar of the battle, Lyons never once erred in his brave performance. Lashed outside of that vessel, on the port-sheet chain, with the lead in hand to lead the ship past the forts, Lyons never flinched, although under a heavy fire from the forts and rebel gunboats.*

• **Marquette, Charles D.,** Fairview Cemetery, Wrightsville. A sergeant in the Union Army in Company F, 93d Pennsylvania Infantry, Marquette was awarded the Medal of Honor for action on April 2, 1865, at Petersburg, Virginia. His citation reads: *Sgt. Marquette, although wounded, was one of the first to plant colors on the enemy's works.*

• **Martin, James,** Mount Moriah Cemetery, Philadelphia. A sergeant in the U.S. Marine Corps on board the warship USS *Richmond*, Martin was one of 31 *Richmond* crewmembers to be awarded the Medal of Honor. His CMOH was awarded for bravery at Mobile Bay, Alabama, on August 5, 1864. His citation reads: *As captain of a gun during action against rebel forts and gunboats and with the ram* Tennessee *in Mobile Bay, 5 August 1864. Despite damage to his ship and the loss of several men on board as enemy fire raked her decks, Sgt. Martin fought his gun with skill and courage throughout the furious 2-hour battle which resulted in the surrender of the rebel ram* Tennessee *and in the damaging and destruction of batteries at Fort Morgan.*

• **Martin, Sylvester Hopkins,** Mount Moriah Cemetery, Philadelphia. A lieutenant in Company K, 88th Pennsylvania Volunteer Infantry, Martin was awarded the

CMOH for his bravery at the Battle of Weldon Railroad, Virginia, on August 19, 1864. His citation reads: *Gallantly made a most dangerous reconnaissance, discovering the position of the enemy and enabling the division to repulse an attack made in strong force.*

• **Matthews, John Calvin,** Homewood Cemetery, Pittsburgh. A corporal in Company A, 61st Pennsylvania Volunteer Infantry, Matthews—one of eight 61st Pennsylvania Infantry soldiers to receive the Medal of Honor—was awarded his CMOH for his bravery in the final Union assaults on Petersburg, Virginia, on April 2, 1865. His citation reads: *Voluntarily took the colors, whose bearer had been disabled, and, although himself severely wounded, carried the same until the enemy's works were taken.*

• **McAdams, Peter,** Saint John the Baptist Catholic Church Cemetery, Manayunk. A corporal in Company A, 98th Pennsylvania Infantry, McAdams was awarded the Medal of Honor for action on May 3, 1863, at Salem Heights, Virginia. His citation reads: *Went 250 yards in front of his regiment toward the position of the enemy and, under fire, brought within the lines a wounded and unconscious comrade.*

• **McKeever, Michael,** Holy Sepulchre Cemetery, Cheltenham. A private in Company K, 5th Pennsylvania Volunteer Cavalry, McKeever—born in Ireland—was awarded the CMOH for his bravery at Burnt Ordinary (now Toano), Virginia, on January 19, 1863. His citation reads: *Was one of a small scouting party that charged and routed a mounted force of the enemy six times their number. He led the charge in a most gallant and distinguished manner, going far beyond the call of duty.*

• **McKown, Nathaniel,** Sunnyside Cemetery, Tunkhannock. A sergeant in Company B, 58th Pennsylvania Infantry, McKown was awarded the Medal of Honor for action on September 29, 1864, at Chapin's Farm, Virginia. His citation reads simply: *Capture of flag.*

• **Mears, George W.,** Old Rosemont Cemetery, Bloomsburg. A sergeant in Company A, 6th Pennsylvania Reserves, Mears was awarded the CMOH for his bravery during the second day of the Battle of Gettysburg, Pennsylvania (July 2, 1863). His citation reads: *Was 1 of 6 volunteers who charged upon a log house near Devil's Den, where a squad of the enemy's sharpshooters were sheltered, and compelled their surrender.*

• **Miller, John,** Northwood Cemetery, Philadelphia. He served as a private in the Union Army in Company H, 8th New York Cavalry. Miller (real name: Henry Fey) was awarded the Medal of Honor for action on March 2, 1865, at Waynesboro, Virginia. His citation simply reads: *Capture of flag.*

• **Miller, William E.,** Gettysburg National Cemetery, Gettysburg. The Captain in command of Company H, 3rd Pennsylvania Volunteer Cavalry, Union Army, Miller exhibited bravery on the third day of the Battle of Gettysburg, Pennsylvania, July 3, 1863, that would garner him a CMOH. That day, Captain Miller—on his own and without orders—led a charge upon a Confederate East Cavalry Field position with a squad of four troopers from his company. In this attack, he cut off and dispersed the enemy to the rear of his column. For this gallantry in the face of the enemy, he was awarded the Medal of Honor. His citation reads: *Without orders, he led a charge of his squadron upon the flank of the enemy, checked his attack, and cut off and dispersed the rear of his column. After the war, he served as a member of the Pennsylvania State Senate.*

• **Monaghan, Patrick H.,** Saint Josephs Cemetery, Girardville. A corporal in Company F, 48th Pennsylvania Infantry, Monaghan was awarded the Medal of Honor for action on June 17, 1864, at Petersburg, Virginia. His citation reads: *Recapture of colors of 7th New York Heavy Artillery.*

• **Morrison, Francis,** Sugar Grove Cemetery, Ohiopyle. A private in the Union Army in Company H, 85th Pennsylvania Volunteer Infantry, Morrison was awarded the CMOH for action on June 17, 1864, at Bermuda Hundred, Virginia. His citation reads: *Voluntarily exposed himself to a heavy fire to bring off a wounded comrade.*

• **Mostoller, John William,** IOOF Cemetery, Stoystown. A private in the Union Army in Company B, 54th Pennsylvania Infantry, Mostoller was awarded the Medal of Honor for action on June 18, 1864, at Lynchburg, Virginia. His citation reads: *Voluntarily led a charge on a Confederate battery (the officers of the company being disabled) and compelled its hasty removal.*

• **Mulholland, St. Clair Augustin,** Old Cathedral Cemetery, Philadelphia. The Colonel and commander of the 116th Pennsylvania Volunteer Infantry (which was part of the famed "Irish Brigade"), Mulholland took part in the Battles of Antietam, Fredericksburg, Chancellorsville, and Gettysburg. He was awarded the CMOH for his bravery at the Battle of Chancellorsville (May 3-4, 1863), while Major of the 116th PA. His citation reads: *In command of the picket line held the enemy in check all night to cover the retreat of the Army.* His Medal was issued March 26, 1895. He is interred in an unmarked tomb that does not indicate either his status as a Brevet General or a CMOH recipient.

• **Oliver, Charles,** Richland Cemetery, Dravosburg. A sergeant in Company M, 100th Pennsylvania Infantry, Oliver was awarded the Medal of Honor for action on March 25, 1865, at Petersburg, Virginia. His citation reads: *Capture of flag of 31st Georgia Infantry (C.S.A.).*

• **Orr, Robert Levan,** Lawnview Cemetery, Rockledge. The Colonel of the 61st Pennsylvania Volunteer Infantry, Orr was one of eight 61st Pennsylvania Infantry soldiers to receive the Medal of Honor. He was awarded for bravery at Petersburg, Virginia, on April 2, 1865. His citation reads: *Carried the colors at the head of the column in the assault after two color bearers had been shot down.* Initially interred in Philadelphia's Monument Cemetery, he was reinterred in Lawnview in 1956.

• **Orth, Jacob George,** West Laurel Hill Cemetery, Bala Cynwyd. A corporal in Company D, 28th Pennsylvania Volunteer Infantry, Orth was awarded the CMOH for his bravery at the Battle of Antietam, Maryland (September 17, 1862). His citation reads: *Capture of flag of 7th South Carolina Infantry (C.S.A.), in hand-to-hand encounter,* *although he was wounded in the shoulder.* He was also wounded in the leg at the Battle of Chancellorsville, Virginia (May 3, 1863).

• **Payne, Irvin C.**, Dunmore Cemetery, Dunmore. A corporal in Company M, 2nd New York Cavalry, Payne was awarded the Medal of Honor for action on April 6, 1865, at Deatonsville (Sailor's Creek), Virginia. His citation reads: *Capture of Virginia state colors.*

• **Pearson, Alfred L.**, Allegheny Cemetery, Pittsburgh. The Colonel and commander of the 155th Pennsylvania Volunteer Infantry, Pearson rendered particularly distinguished services in the September 30, 1864, Battle of Peeble's Farm and during the 1864-1865 Petersburg Campaign in Virginia, garnering official praise from Army of the Potomac commander, George G. Meade. He was awarded the CMOH for his bravery at the Battle of Lewis's Farm, Virginia, on March 29, 1865. His citation for that action reads: *Seeing a brigade forced back by the enemy, he seized his regimental color, called on his men to follow him, and advanced upon the enemy under a severe fire. The whole brigade took up the advance, the lost ground was regained, and the enemy was repulsed.*

• **Peirsol, James Kastor**, Grove Cemetery, New Brighton. A first lieutenant in the Union Army, Peirsol was awarded the Medal of Honor as a sergeant in Company F, 13th Ohio Cavalry for action on April 5, 1865, at Paines Crossroads, Virginia. His citation reads: *Capture of flag.*

• **Pennypacker, Galusha**, Philadelphia National Cemetery, Philadelphia. On April 28, 1865, he was promoted to Brigadier General of Volunteers; one month before his 21st birthday. This made him the youngest general officer in United States Military history, a distinction he still holds. He was awarded the CMOH for bravery exhibited at Fort Fisher, N.C., on 15 January 1865. His citation reads: *Gallantly led the charge over a traverse and planted the colors of one of his regiments thereon, was severely wounded.*

• **Petty, Philip**, Daggett Cemetery, Daggett. A color sergeant in the Union Army in Company A, 136th Pennsylvania Infantry, Petty was awarded the Medal of Honor for action on December 13, 1862, at Fredericksburg, Virginia. He citation reads: *Took up the colors as they fell out of the hands of the wounded color bearer and carried them forward in the charge.*

• **Pitman, George J.**, Laurel Hill Cemetery, Philadelphia. A private in Company C, 1st New York Volunteer Cavalry (known as the "Lincoln Cavalry," the company was recruited for New York service in Philadelphia), Pitman was awarded the CMOH for his bravery at Sailors Creek, Virginia, on April 6, 1865. His citation reads simply: *Capture of flag of the Sumter Heavy Artillery (C.S.A.).*

• **Platt, George Crawford**, Holy Cross Cemetery, Yeadon. A private in the Union Army in the 6th US Cavalry, Platt was awarded the Medal of Honor for action on July 3, 1863, at Fairfield, Pennsylvania. His citation reads: *Seized the regimental flag upon the death of the standard-bearer in a hand-to-hand fight and prevented it from falling into the hands of the enemy.*

• **Preston, Noble Delance,** Chelten Hills Cemetery, Philadelphia. A native of New York, Captain Preston was awarded the CMOH for his fearless leadership during the 1864 cavalry battle at Trevillian Station, Virginia. The citation reads: *Voluntarily led a charge in which he was severely wounded.*

• **Purcell, Hiram W.,** Laurel Cemetery, White Haven. A sergeant in the Union Army in Company G, 104th Pennsylvania Volunteer Infantry, Purcell was awarded the Medal of Honor for action on May 31, 1862, at Fair Oaks, Virginia. His citation reads: *While carrying the regimental colors on the retreat, he returned to face the advancing enemy, flag in hand and saved the other color, which would otherwise have been captured.*

• **Quay, Matthew Stanley,** Beaver Cemetery and Mausoleum, Beaver. Quay—a colonel in the 134th Pennsylvania Infantry—was awarded a Medal of Honor for his actions in battle near Fredericksburg, Virginia, on December 13, 1862. His citation reads: *Although out of service, he voluntarily resumed duty on the eve of battle and took a conspicuous part in the charge on the heights.* After the war, he was elected to represent Pennsylvania in the U.S. Senate, serving from 1887 to 1899 and from 1901 to 1904. He was an immensely powerful Pennsylvania political boss, so much so that President Benjamin Harrison once dubbed him a "kingmaker." Quay ultimately died in office.

• **Rannahan, John,** Saint Martins Cemetery, New Derry. Born in County Monaghan, Ireland, Rannahan entered the United States Marine Corps in Pennsylvania. His rank was corporal. His Medal of Honor citation reads: *On board the U.S.S.* Minnesota, *in the assault on Fort Fisher, 15 January 1865. Landing on the beach with the assaulting party from his ship, Cpl. Rannahan advanced to the top of the sandhill and partly through the breach in the palisades, despite enemy fire which killed or wounded many officers and men. When more than two-thirds of the men became seized with panic and retreated on the run, he remained with the party until dark when it came safely away, bringing its wounded, its arms, and its colors.*

• **Reed, George W.,** Grandview Cemetery, Johnstown. A private in the Union Army in the 11th Pennsylvania Infantry, Reed was awarded the Medal of Honor for action on Aug. 21, 1864, at Battle of Globe Tavern near Petersburg, Virginia. His citation reads: *Capture of flag of 24th North Carolina Volunteers (CSA).*

• **Reed, William,** Riverview Cemetery, Huntingdon. A private in the Union Army in Company H, 8th Missouri Infantry, Reed was awarded the Medal of Honor for action on May 22, 1863, at Vicksburg, Mississippi. His citation reads: *Gallantry in the charge of the "volunteer storming party."*

• **Reid, Robert Alexander,** Odd Fellows Cemetery, Pottsville. A private in Company G, 48th Pennsylvania Infantry, Reid was awarded the Medal of Honor for action on June 17, 1864, at Petersburg, Virginia. His citation reads: *Capture of flag of 44th Tennessee Infantry (C.S.A.).*

• **Reigle, Daniel P.**, Mount Carmel Cemetery, Littlestown. A corporal in Company F, 87th Pennsylvania Infantry, Reigle was awarded the Medal of Honor for his action on October 19, 1864, at Cedar Creek, Virginia. His citation reads: *For gallantry while rushing forward to capture a Confederate flag at the stone fence where the enemy's last stand was made.*

• **Reisinger, James Monroe**, Greendale Cemetery, Meadville. A corporal in Company C of the 150th Pennsylvania Volunteer Infantry, Reisinger performed heroically and bravely during the fight around McPherson's Farm on the first day of the Battle of Gettysburg (July 1). Those actions would garner him a CMOH, the citation for which reads simply: *Specially brave and meritorious conduct in the face of the enemy.* When his medal was awarded to him on January 25, 1907, he was the last of the sixty-three Union soldiers and officers to be issued the Medal of Honor for bravery at Gettysburg.

• **Rhodes, Sylvester D.**, Hollenback Cemetery, Wilkes-Barre. A sergeant in Company D, 61st Pennsylvania Volunteer Infantry (one of eight soldiers from that unit to receive a Medal of Honor), he was awarded the CMOH for his bravery at Fisher's Hill, Virginia, on September 22, 1864. His citation reads: *Was on the skirmish line which drove the enemy from the first entrenchment and was the first man to enter the breastworks, capturing one of the guns and turning it upon the enemy.*

• **Rodenbough, Theophilus F.**, Easton Cemetery, Easton. A captain in the Union Army in the 2nd US Cavalry, Rodenbough was awarded the Medal of Honor for action on June 11, 1864, at Battle of Trevilian Station, Virginia. His citation reads: *Handled the regiment with great skill and valor, was severely wounded.*

• **Rohm, Ferdinand Frederick**, Westminster Presbyterian Cemetery, Mifflintown. A chief bugler in the Union Army, 16th Pennsylvania Cavalry, Rohm was awarded the Medal of Honor for action on August 25, 1864, at Ream's Station, Virginia. His citation reads: *While his regiment was retiring under fire, voluntarily remained behind to succor a wounded officer who was in great danger, secured assistance, and removed the officer to a place of safety.*

• **Rought, Stephen**, Spring Hill Cemetery, Spring Hill. A sergeant in the Union Army in Company A, 141st Pennsylvania Infantry, Rought was awarded the Medal of Honor for action on May 6, 1864, at the Wilderness Campaign, Virginia. His citation reads: *Capture of flag of the 13th North Carolina Infantry (C.S.A.).*

• **Roush, J. Levi**, Saint Patricks Cemetery, Newry. A corporal in Company D, 6th Pennsylvania Reserves (35th Pennsylvania Volunteer Infantry), Roush, and five of his fellow soldiers were awarded the CMOH for bravery on the 2nd day of the Battle of Gettysburg (July 2, 1863). His citation reads: *Was one of six volunteers who charged upon a log house near the Devil's Den, where a squad of the enemy's sharpshooters were sheltered, and compelled their surrender.*

• **Rowand, Archibald H.,** Allegheny Cemetery, Pittsburgh. A private in Company K, 1st West Virginia Volunteer Cavalry, Rowand—one of fourteen 1st West Virginia Cavalry soldiers to receive the Medal of Honor—was awarded his CMOH for bravery during the Winter of 1864-65. His citation reads: *Was 1 of 2 men who succeeded in getting through the enemy's lines with dispatches to Gen. Grant.*

• **Rutter, James May,** Hollenback Cemetery, Wilkes-Barre. A sergeant in the Union Army in Company C, 143d Pennsylvania Infantry, Rutter was awarded the Medal of Honor for action on July 1, 1863, at Gettysburg, Pennsylvania. His citation reads: *At great risk of his life went to the assistance of a wounded comrade and, while under fire, removed him to a place of safety.*

• **Schoonmaker, James Martinus,** Homewood Cemetery, Pittsburgh. The Colonel and commander of the 14th Pennsylvania Volunteer Cavalry, Schoonmaker was awarded the Medal of Honor for action on September 19, 1864, at the Third Battle of Winchester, Virginia. His citation reads: *At a critical period, gallantly led a cavalry charge against the left of the enemy's line of battle, drove the enemy out of his works, and captured many prisoners.*

• **Scott, John Wallace,** Upper Octorara Church Cemetery, Parkesburg. Scott was awarded the Medal of Honor as a captain in Company D, 157th Pennsylvania Infantry, for action on April 1, 1865, at Five Forks, Virginia. His citation reads: *Capture of the flag of the 16th South Carolina Infantry, in hand-to-hand combat.*

• **Seitzinger, James M.,** Christ Church Cemetery, Fountain Springs. A private in Company G, 116th Pennsylvania Infantry, Seitzinger was awarded the Medal of Honor for action on June 3, 1864, at Cold Harbor, Virginia. His citation reads: *When the color bearer was shot down, this soldier seized the colors and bore them gallantly in a charge against the enemy.*

• **Sellers, Alfred Jacob,** Mount Vernon Cemetery, Philadelphia. He was a brevet colonel in the Union Army. He was awarded the Medal of Honor as a major in the 90th Pennsylvania Infantry for action on July 1, 1863, at Gettysburg, Pennsylvania. His citation reads: *Voluntarily led the regiment under a withering fire to a position from which the enemy was repulsed.*

• **Shanes, John,** Lantz Cemetery, Brave. A private in the Union Army in Company K, 14th West Virginia Infantry, Shanes was awarded the Medal of Honor for action on July 20, 1864, at Carter's Farm, Virginia. His citation reads: *Charged upon a Confederate fieldpiece in advance of his comrades and by his individual exertions silenced the piece.*

• **Shiel, John,** Greenmount Cemetery, Philadelphia. He was also known as John "Shields," and was buried under the name John "Spiel." A corporal in Company E, 90th Pennsylvania Infantry, Shiel was awarded the Medal of Honor for action in December 1862 at Fredericksburg, Virginia. His citation reads: *Carried a dangerously wounded comrade into the Union lines, thereby preventing his capture by the enemy.*

• **Shutes, Henry,** Mount Moriah Cemetery, Philadelphia. The Captain of the Forecastle on board the USS *Wissahickon* in the Union Navy, Shutes was awarded the CMOH for his bravery during the Battle of New Orleans, April 24 and 25, 1862; and in the engagement at Fort McAllister, February 27, 1863. His citation reads: *Going on board the USS* Wissahickon *from the USS* Don *where his seamanlike qualities as gunner's mate were outstanding, Shutes performed his duties with skill and courage. Showing a presence of mind and prompt action when a shot from Fort McAllister penetrated the* Wissahickon *below the water line and entered the powder magazine, Shutes contributed materially to the preservation of the powder and safety of the ship.*

• **Slusher, Henry C.,** Lone Pine Cemetery, Lone Pine. A private in the Union Army in Troop F, 22d Pennsylvania Volunteer Cavalry, Slusher was awarded the Medal of Honor for action on September 11, 1863, near Moorefield, West Virginia. His citation reads: *Voluntarily crossed a branch of the Potomac River under fire to rescue a wounded comrade held prisoner by the enemy. Was wounded and taken prisoner in the attempt.*

• **Sowers, Michael,** Saint Columbkille Cemetery, Imperial. His actual name was Michael Sauers. He served as a private in the Union Army in Company L, 4th Pennsylvania Cavalry. He was awarded the Medal of Honor for action on December 1, 1864, at Stony Creek Station, Virginia. His citation reads: *His horse having been shot from under him, he voluntarily and on foot participated in the cavalry charge made upon one of the forts, conducting himself throughout with great personal bravery.*

• **Storey, John H.R.,** Laurel Hill Cemetery, Philadelphia. A sergeant in Company F, 109th Pennsylvania Infantry, Storey was awarded the CMOH for his bravery at Dallas, Georgia on May 28, 1864. His citation reads: *While bringing in a wounded comrade, under a destructive fire, he was himself wounded in the right leg, which was amputated on the same day.*

• **Taylor, Anthony,** Saint James the Less Episcopal Churchyard, Philadelphia. One of six 15th Pennsylvania Cavalry soldiers to be awarded the Medal of Honor for bravery during the Civil War, he was serving as 1st Lieutenant when he performed an act bravery at the Battle of Chickamauga, Georgia, on September 20, 1863. His citation reads: *Held out to the last with a small force against the advance of superior numbers of the enemy.*

• **Thomas, Hampton Sidney,** Lawnview Cemetery, Rockledge. A major in the 1st Pennsylvania Volunteer Cavalry, Thomas was awarded the CMOH for his bravery at Amelia Springs, Virginia, on April 5, 1865. His citation reads: *Conspicuous gallantry in the capture of a field battery and a number of battle flags and the destruction of the enemy's wagon trains. Maj. Thomas lost a leg in this action.* Initially interred in Philadelphia's Monument Cemetery, he was reinterred in Lawnview in 1956.

• **Thompson, William,** Mount Moriah Cemetery, Philadelphia. A signal quartermaster on board the USS *Mohican* in the Union Navy, Thompson was awarded the CMOH for his bravery during the action of the main squadron of ships against heavily defended Forts Beauregard and Walker on Hilton Head, South Carolina, on November 7, 1861. His medal, one of the first for a Union Naval Officer, was issued on July 10, 1863. His citation reads: *Serving as signal quartermaster, Thompson steadfastly steered the ship with a steady and bold heart under the batteries; was wounded by a piece of shell but remained at his station until he fell from loss of blood. Legs since amputated.*

• **Vanderslice, John Mitchell,** Saint James Perkiomen Church Cemetery, Evansburg. A private in Company D, 8th Pennsylvania Volunteer Cavalry, and first wounded at the June 1864 Battle of Cold Harbor, Vanderslice would go on to be awarded the CMOH for his bravery at the February 6, 1865, Battle of Hatcher's Run, Virginia. His citation reads: *Was the first man to reach the enemy's rifle-pits, which were taken in the charge.* After the war, Vanderslice was very active in Veterans' affairs; he sat in on the executive committee for the Gettysburg Battlefield Memorial Commission for seventeen years, and it was on his suggestion that states erect monuments to mark the positions on the battlefield where the individual regiments fought.

• **Vaughn, Pinkerton Ross,** Laurel Hill Cemetery, Philadelphia. A sergeant in the United States Marine Corps, Vaughn was awarded the CMOH for his bravery at Port Hudson, Mississippi, on March 14, 1863. His citation reads: *Serving on board the U.S.S.* Mississippi *during her abandonment and firing in the action with the Port Hudson batteries, 14 March 1863. During the abandonment of the* Mississippi, *which had to be grounded, Sgt. Vaughn rendered invaluable assistance to his commanding officer, remaining with the ship until all the crew had landed, and the ship had been fired to prevent its falling into enemy hands. Persistent until the last, and conspicuously cool under the heavy shellfire, Sgt. Vaughn was finally ordered to save himself as he saw fit.*

• **Veale, Moses,** West Laurel Hill Cemetery, Bala Cynwyd. A captain in Company F, 109th Pennsylvania Volunteer Infantry, Veale was wounded several times, taken prisoner at the Battle of Cedar Mountain, and was held at the infamous Libby Prison. Exchanged, he served on the staff of Union General John W. Geary during Sherman's March to the Sea. He was awarded the CMOH for his bravery at Wauhatchie, Tennessee, on October 28, 1863. His citation reads: *Gallantry in action, manifesting throughout the engagement coolness, zeal, judgment, and courage. His horse was shot out from under him, and he was hit by four enemy bullets.*

• **Walton, George Washington,** Oxford Cemetery, Oxford. A sergeant in the Union Army, Walton was awarded the Medal of Honor as a private in Company C, 97th Pennsylvania Infantry for action on August 29, 1864, at Fort Hell, Petersburg, Virginia. His citation reads: *Went outside the trenches, under heavy fire at short-range, and rescued a comrade who had been wounded and thrown out of the trench by an exploding shell.*

• **Warfel, Henry Clay,** Philipsburg Cemetery, South Philipsburg. A private in the Union Army in Company A, 1st Pennsylvania Cavalry, Warfel was awarded the Medal of Honor for action on April 5, 1865, at Paine's Crossroads, Virginia. His citation reads: *Capture of Virginia state colors.*

• **White, John Henry,** Arlington Cemetery, Drexel Hill. A private in Company A, 90th Pennsylvania Infantry, White was awarded the CMOH for action on August 23, 1862, at Rappahannock Station, Virginia. His citation reads: *At the imminent risk of his life, crawled to a nearby spring within the enemy's range and, exposed to constant fire, filled a large number of canteens, and returned in safety to the relief of his comrades who were suffering from want of water.*

• **Williams, Elwood N.,** West Laurel Hill Cemetery, Bala Cynwyd. A private in Company A, 28th Illinois Infantry, Williams was awarded the CMOH for action on April 6, 1862, at Shiloh, Tennessee. His citation reads: *A box of ammunition having been abandoned between the lines, this soldier voluntarily went forward with one companion, under a heavy fire from both armies, secured the box, and delivered it within the lines of his regiment, his companion being mortally wounded.*

• **Wilson, Francis A.,** Mount Moriah Cemetery, Philadelphia. Served in the Civil War as a corporal in Company B, 95th Pennsylvania Volunteer Infantry. He was awarded the CMOH for his bravery at Petersburg, Virginia, on April 2, 1865. His citation reads: *Was among the first to penetrate the enemy's lines and himself captured a gun of the two batteries captured.*

• **Wray, William J.,** Philadelphia Memorial Park, Frazer. First wounded at the Battle of Fredericksburg on December 13, 1862 (getting shot through the eye), Wray spent the 1862 Christmas holiday recovering but soon was back defending the Union in Company K of the 1st Veterans Reserve Corps, which was designated for wounded or invalid soldiers who wanted to fight. During the July 12, 1864, Confederate strike at Washington, D.C., Wray was stationed at Fort Stevens and was awarded the CMOH for his bravery there that day. His citation reads: *Rallied the company at a critical moment during a change of position under fire.* When Wray died in 1919, he was buried in American Mechanics Cemetery in Philadelphia. In 1951, that area was developed, and the bodies removed, at which time his body was disinterred and re-interred (along with several other Wray family members) in Philadelphia Memorial Park. Marked only with a small stone that gave just his last name, his grave went virtually unnoticed until it was rediscovered in 2002.

• **Young, Andrew J.,** Jefferson Cemetery, Jefferson. A sergeant in Company F, 1st Pennsylvania Volunteer Cavalry, Young was awarded the CMOH for his bravery at Paines Crossroads, Virginia, on April 5, 1865. His citation reads simply: *Capture of flag.*

Sources

Books & Journals:

Baker, Jean H. *Affairs of Party: The Political Culture of Northern Democrats in the Mid-Nineteenth Century*. New York: Fordham University Press, 1998.

———. *James Buchanan*. New York: Times Books, 2004.

Baker, La Fayette C. *History of the United States Secret Service*. Bowie, MD: Heritage Books, 1992.

Barbière, Joseph. *Scraps from the Prison Table, At Camp Chase and Johnson's Island*. Doylestown, PA: W.W.H. Davis, Printer, 1868.

Catton, Bruce. *Mr. Lincoln's Army: The Army of the Potomac*. New York: Doubleday and Co, 1951.

———. *Glory Road; The Bloody Route from Fredericksburg to Gettysburg*. Doubleday, 1962.

———. *A Stillness at Appomattox*. Garden City, NY: Doubleday, 1954.

Donaldson, Francis Adams, and J. Gregory Acken. *Inside the Army of the Potomac: The Civil War Experience of Captain Francis Adams Donaldson*. Mechanicsburg, PA: Stackpole Books, 1998.

Dunkelman, Mark H. *Gettysburg's Unknown Soldier: The Life, Death, and Celebrity of Amos Humiston*. Westport, CT: Praeger, 1999.

Foner, Eric. *The Fiery Trial: Abraham Lincoln and American Slavery*. New York: W.W. Norton, 2012.

Foote, Shelby. *The Civil War: A Narrative*. 2010.

Freeman, Douglas Southall. *Lee's Lieutenants: A Study in Command*. New York: C. Scribner's Sons, 1945.

Gerbner, Katharine. "'We Are Against The Traffik Of Men-Body': The Germantown Quaker Protest Of 1688 And The Origins Of American Abolitionism." *Pennsylvania History: A Journal of Mid-Atlantic Studies* 74, no. 2 (2007): 149-72.

Grant, Ulysses S. *Personal Memoirs of Ulysses S. Grant*. 1883.

Grow, Matthew J. *Liberty to the Downtrodden: Thomas L. Kane, Romantic Reformer*. New Haven: Yale University Press, 2009.

Guelzo, Allen C. *Gettysburg: The Last Invasion*. New York: Vintage Books, 2014.

Jordan, David M. *Winfield Scott Hancock: A Soldier's Life*. Bloomington, IN: Indiana University Press, 1995.

Krumwiede, John F. *Disgrace at Gettysburg: The Arrest and Court-Martial of Brigadier General Thomas A. Rowley, USA*. Jefferson, NC: McFarland & Co, 2006.

Longacre, Edward G. *General John Buford*. Cambridge, MA: Da Capo Press, 2003.

McPherson, James M. *Battle Cry of Freedom: The Civil War Era*. New York: Oxford University Press, 2003.

Miller, Francis Trevelyan, and Robert S. Lanier. *The Photographic History of the Civil War*. New York: Review of Reviews, 1911.

Miller, Jr., Arthur P. & Marjorie L. Miller. *Pennsylvania Battlefields and Military Landmarks*. Mechanicsburg, PA: Stackpole Books, 2000.

Millett, Allan R. & Peter Maslowski. *For the Common Defense: A Military History of the United States of America*. New York: The Free Press, 1984.

Naglee, Henry Morris. *The Love Life of Brigadier General Henry Naglee, Consisting of a Correspondence on Love, War, and Politics*. New York: Hilton & Company, 1867.

Nichols, Edward J., and John F. Reynolds. *Toward Gettysburg*. University Park: Pennsylvania State Univ. Press, 1958.

Potter, David Morris, and Don E. Fehrenbacher. *The Impending Crisis, 1848-1861*. New York: Harper and Row, 1977.

Sandburg, Carl. *Abraham Lincoln*. New York: Dell Pub, 1959.

Sears, Stephen W. *Chancellorsville*. New York: Mariner Books, 2014.

———. *Gettysburg*. Boston: Houghton Mifflin, 2004.

Shaara, Michael. *Killer Angels*. New York: Ballantine Books, 1996.

Silverman, Kenneth. *Lightning Man: The Accursed Life of Samuel F.B. Morse*. Cambridge: Da Capo Press, 2004.

Small, Cindy L. *The Jennie Wade Story: A True and Complete Account of the Only Civilian Killed During the Battle of Gettysburg*. Gettysburg, PA: Thomas Publications, 1991.

Smith, Timothy H. *John Burns: The Hero of Gettysburg*. Gettysburg: Thomas Publications, 2000.

(Audio Course)

Gallagher, Gary W. *The American Civil War*. Chantilly, VA: The Teaching Company, 2000.

(Films)

Gettysburg. Directed by Ronald F. Maxwell. Atlanta: Turner Pictures, 1993.

Glory. Directed by Edward Zwick. Hollywood: TriStar Pictures, 1989.

Gods and Generals. Directed by Ronald F. Maxwell. Atlanta: Turner Pictures, 2003.

The Civil War. Directed by Ken Burns. Walpole, NH: Florentine Films, 1990.

Online Resources:

Ancestry.com – Family tree information and vital records.

FamousAmericans.net – for information on many individuals.

FindaGrave.com – for burial information, vital statistics, and obituaries.

Newspapers.com – Hundreds of newspaper articles were accessed—too numerous to mention here.

TeachingAmericanHistory.com – for information on many individuals.

TheHistoryJunkie.com – for information on many individuals.

Thoughtco.com – John Burns, Civilian hero of Gettysburg.

USHistory.org – for information on many individuals.

Wikipedia.com – for general historical information.

Other Resources:

Cumberland County Historical Society – Information about Lincoln Colored Cemetery.

Index

Index

www.ingramcontent.com/pod-product-compliance
Lightning Source LLC
Chambersburg PA
CBHW021354090426
42742CB00009B/854